Tolley's
Domain Names:
A Practical Guide

Simon Halberstam
&
Joanne Brook
of

S · G · H

SPRECHER GRIER
HALBERSTAM LLP

SOLICITORS

& Jonathan D.C. Turner, Barrister

with contributions from David Perrin and Paul Westley

Tolley
LexisNexis™

Members of the LexisNexis Group worldwide

United Kingdom	LexisNexis Butterworths Tolley, a Division of Reed Elsevier (UK) Ltd, 2 Addiscombe Road, CROYDON CR9 5AF
Argentina	LexisNexis Argentina, BUENOS AIRES
Australia	LexisNexis Butterworths, CHATSWOOD, New South Wales
Austria	LexisNexis Verlag ARD Orac GmbH & Co KG, VIENNA
Canada	LexisNexis Butterworths, MARKHAM, Ontario
Chile	LexisNexis Chile Ltda, SANTIAGO DE CHILE
Czech Republic	Nakladatelství Orac sro, PRAGUE
France	Editions du Juris-Classeur SA, PARIS
Hong Kong	LexisNexis Butterworths, HONG KONG
Hungary	HVG-Orac, BUDAPEST
India	LexisNexis Butterworths, NEW DELHI
Ireland	Butterworths (Ireland) Ltd, DUBLIN
Italy	Giuffrè Editore, MILAN
Malaysia	Malayan Law Journal Sdn Bhd, KUALA LUMPUR
New Zealand	Butterworths of New Zealand, WELLINGTON
Poland	Wydawnictwo Prawnicze LexisNexis, WARSAW
Singapore	LexisNexis Butterworths, SINGAPORE
South Africa	Butterworths SA, DURBAN
Switzerland	Stämpfli Verlag AG, BERNE
USA	LexisNexis, DAYTON, Ohio

A CIP Catalogue record for this book is available from the British Library.

ISBN 0-75451-491-9

Typeset by Letterpart Ltd, Reigate, Surrey

Printed and bound in Great Britain by Hobbs the Printers Ltd, Totton, Hampshire

Visit Butterworths LexisNexis *direct* at www.butterworths.com

In memory of my parents, Alfred Halberstam and Marilyn (Wigoder) Halberstam, both lawyers, whose professional and personal standards I endeavour to follow.

Simon Halberstam

Preface

Very few areas in the legal panoply have given rise to as many disputes as that of domain names. Various factors have contributed to this state of affairs. Unlike trade marks, where the same mark can co-exist in different hands in different territories and for different areas of activity, domain names are unique and global in nature. This leaves little room for compromise when each of two or more parties considers itself entitled to the same domain name. Some speculators who latched onto the potential value of these assets very early on made substantial gains. Whilst the *BT v One in a Million* line of decisions in the UK and similar decisions elsewhere have sounded the death knell for those who tried to exploit brand owners, those speculators who were astute enough to register generic names have in certain cases legitimately continued to prosper.

The bodies charged with dispute resolution in different countries have adopted a variety of dispute resolution procedures. These procedures differ, allowing for inconsistencies in the approaches of different countries. As many of these disputes, especially those concerning the .com, .org and .net suffixes are international in nature, it is not difficult to see the scope for cross-border disputes and forum shopping. Moreover, as there is no formal doctrine of precedent, there is enormous scope for different panellists reaching different decisions when faced with similar facts. This has, indeed, led to the phenomenon of 'panellist shopping' – choosing those panellists whose past decisions seem likely to favour a particular point of view. Certain countries leave domain name disputes to the traditional law courts, which may involve judges with no particular understanding of the often subtle global and intellectual property right implications of this evolving area of the law.

Not only is this a litigious and complicated area of law, but it is also one of the fastest-evolving. The recent launch of the .info and .biz domains is destined to be followed shortly by others, including .pro and .name as well as the industry specific .aero and .museum. This ensures that, like rust, lawyers should never sleep if they wish to keep abreast. To assist in this task, we intend to use the Sprecher Grier Halberstam e-commerce website at www.weblaw.co.uk to cover the latest developments in this field.

We have tried to create a pragmatic guide for both lawyers and business people to what we consider to be the major topics in this field. We have not limited ourselves to the legal issues and have addressed technical and commercial matters such as valuation and the factors which determine how to select and register an appropriate domain name. Also included is a glossary, which should help the reader through the plethora of acronyms that inhabit the world of domain names. We are indebted to Paul Westley of Internetters and David Perrin of WJB Chiltern, and for their lucid contributions in this context.

I would also like to thank Joanne Brook, my colleague in the E-Commerce Law Group at Sprecher Grier Halberstam LLP, for her substantial contribution.

We are particularly grateful for the participation of barrister and WIPO panellist Jonathan DC Turner, who has drawn on this extensive experience in the field of domain name disputes.

Finally, a special word of thanks to Joanna Moore and her colleagues at Tolley, who understood the need for a dedicated book covering this legal minefield.

Simon Halberstam
SPRECHER GRIER HALBERSTAM LLP
June 2002

Contents

Part D: Domain Name Disputes 101

Part A: Choosing and Registering a Domain Name

A1 – Introduction

Domain names and site branding A1.1

The internet is a vast global network with millions of computers worldwide linked to it. Each computer has a unique IP address, comprising a series of four numbers (or octets), each of between one and three characters, for example 207.228.254.7. The internet uses these addresses to locate information and retrieve it from a particular website at a numbered location.

As these strings of numbers are not easy to remember, and because from a marketing perspective the numbers have no obvious association with a particular brand or the company's website, they are converted into user-friendly memorable words, phrases and names called 'domain names'. By using an addressing system whereby computers can locate one another (known as the uniform resource locator (or 'URL') addressing system) when an internet user types in a domain name, the computer is able to locate a site with a particular IP address. As the site address enables computers to locate the information, each site address is unique and each domain name must also be unique. Domain names are used for website addresses and are commonly, but not exclusively, preceded by the prefix 'www' (worldwide web) (for example www.butterworths.com). Domain names are also used for e-mail addresses (for example info@butterworths.com).

As all domain names are unique, there is tremendous pressure on domain names, with generic names and those which are obviously attractive and/or memorable being valuable intellectual property assets selling for thousands, and sometimes millions, of pounds.

The most basic way that a website is branded is by the domain name used to locate it. This is the first contact a web user will have with a site and so the branding is critical. The plethora of 'new media' agencies still ready to brand sites, even after the dot com/dot bomb downturn of the past twelve months, is illustrative of how important business considers it to get site branding right.

With the prospect of spending a large amount of money on site branding, website owners will obviously be keen to protect that brand.

Whether they do this before or after the site launch is a matter of personal choice, albeit that they should seek legal advice on the subject so that an informed choice can be made! This chapter is intended to give guidance through some of the legal issues raised when choosing a domain name. Matters relating to registration are dealt with later in this book (see A2 REGISTERING A DOMAIN NAME and A3 REGISTERING A DOMAIN NAME AS A TRADE MARK).

Some important background A1.2

At this stage, it is probably helpful to explain more fully how the various domain name registration systems work and the different types of domain name which exist.

Domain name registries A1.3

As well as monitoring the operation of gTLDs, the Internet Corporation for Assigned Names and Numbers ('ICANN') is responsible for awarding contracts to registries to operate the various gTLDs and for approving ('accrediting') registrars. Generally a single registry is responsible for a specific gTLD.

A single registry holds the primary details for each domain name such as the name servers (the computers) on which the domain name's IP address is stored, and the identity of the registrar which holds the details of the domain name's registrant (or 'owner'). In turn, these registrars provide a facility for anyone to verify the registrant and contact details (the name and address of the registrant, the name, address, telephone number, fax number and e-mail address for each of the administrative contact, billing contact and technical contact, names of the name servers holding the IP address) for domain names managed by them. This is called the WHOIS record.

Until 1999, there was a single combined registry and registrar for all gTLDs. Both functions were carried out by Network Solutions ('NSI'), based in Virginia, USA, as it had a monopoly contract awarded by the US Government. From July 1999, although the registry function for .com, .net and .org remained with NSI (later bought by and transferred to Verisign), many new registrars were appointed.

The registry does not deal directly with any customers. Registrars and their appointed resellers or partners deal directly with customers to carry out functions such as registering domain names, modifying records and transferring domain names.

Current registries are:

- for .com, .net and .org – Verisign Registry Services (formerly NSI);

- for .biz – Neulevel;

- for .info – Afilias; and

- for .name – Global Name Registry.

Only a very small proportion of companies involved with domain name registration have achieved registrar status. ICANN-accredited registrars offering public domain name registration and based in the UK are currently as follows.

Registrar	Website
BB Online UK Ltd	www.nominate.net
Direct Connection Ltd	www.dircon.net
Eastern Counties Newspaper Group Ltd	www.ecnet.co.uk
Easyspace Ltd	www.easyspace.com
Internetters Ltd	www.internetters.co.uk
Netbenefit plc	www.netbenefit.com
Total Web Solutions Ltd	www.totalregistrations.com
Virtual Internet plc	www.vi.net

Choosing a registrar   **A1.4**

It is very important to choose the company used to register domain names carefully. Prices vary, but so do levels of service. Many companies come and go in this industry. Thus a good track record and several years of trading are important credentials. Accreditation of the registrar by a neutral body like ICANN, and/or membership of a recognised scheme like the Consumers' Association's Which? Web Trader Scheme, can give you added confidence. It is all too easy for a domain name registration company to put up an impressive website when in fact it may have just started trading, have no real premises and merely be a completely automated website. Any of these factors could potentially cause problems should anything beyond simply registering the domain name need to be done. If in doubt, those wishing to register a domain name should deal with a recognised, well-established company based in the UK which can be easily contacted by telephone.

For more information on choosing a registrar see A2 REGISTERING A
DOMAIN NAME.

Costs A1.5

The cost of registering a domain name can range from as little as £20
(often when using a fully automated system) to £100 or more for a two
year registration. As a domain name is an important and valuable business
asset, choosing a registration company simply for the lowest headline
price may become a disadvantage if you ever need to contact it again in
the future. Rather than using an intermediary, it is always advisable to go
direct to one of these registrars to register a domain name and only to
register a domain name using a company you feel safe with. Watch out
for any hidden charges or other potential drawbacks. Remember how
important the domain name is likely to be to the company which owns
it.

gTLDs can be registered for periods of whole years (up to a maximum of
ten). The registration can be extended or renewed at any time up to the
ten year maximum. For example, as of 1 January 2002, a domain name
registration could be extended to expire no later than 31 December
2011. It is vital not to let a domain name lapse if it is still required.
Domains not renewed will be permanently deleted by the registrar
between 30 and 45 days after the renewal date. The deleted domain name
will subsequently be released back to the marketplace, potentially for
someone else to register.

Types of domain name A1.6

There are two main types of domain name – gTLDs and ccTLDs. There
are also third level and fourth level domains.

Global top level domains A1.7

Until 2001, there were only six gTLDs. These are:

- .com;
- .net;
- .org;
- .edu;

- .gov; and

- .mil.

Whilst .com was intended for commercial organisations or companies, .net was intended for use by companies providing network infrastructure, servers, internet service providers (ISPs) etc., and .org was intended for non-profit organisations such as charities, trade unions and political bodies, the rules for these three gTLDs have since been greatly relaxed. Now any person or organisation is able to register any of these three suffixes without restriction.

The other three original gTLDs (.edu, .gov and .mil) remain restricted and are not available for general commercial use. These gTLDs are intended for use as follows:

- .edu for US degree-awarding educational institutions;

- .gov for US Government departments; and

- .mil for the US military.

By 2000, it was clear that there were insufficient gTLDs available for the massive growth in internet use and there were calls within the internet industry and from net users to create new gTLDs. After much discussion within the industry, ICANN, the body which is ultimately responsible for the domain name system, agreed to create seven new gTLDs. These new gTLDs are:

- .biz − intended solely for business use, and not for personal use;

- .info − unrestricted use;

- .name − for personal use (domain names within this gTLD will be in the format of firstname.secondname.name, for example john.smith.name);

- .pro − for professional use, such as lawyers, accountants etc. (domain names in this format will be, for example, sgh.law.pro or johnsmith.md.pro);

- .coop − for use solely by co-operatives;

- .aero − for use solely by aviation companies; and

- .museum − for use solely by museums.

In July 2001, two of these new gTLDs (.biz and .info) were launched. There are already over 700,000 live .biz domains and over 700,000 live .info domains. These two new gTLDs have proved especially popular in the UK and Europe.

Country code domains **A1.8**

Each country has the right to issue domain names using its own two character International Standards Organisation code. In the UK, the body responsible for this function is Nominet. Nominet is a non-profit company set up by the UK internet community to manage domain names. Its membership largely comprises UK domain name registration companies and internet service providers ('ISPs').

Nominet is the registry for .uk domains, and provides a WHOIS service on its website, where it is possible to check the availability of names or the identity of the registrant.

UK domains are registered under one of a number of second level domains. The principal second level domains are:

- .co.uk – intended for use by companies;
- .org.uk – intended for use by non-profit making organisations;
- .ltd.uk – reserved for use by UK limited companies;
- .plc.uk – reserved for use by UK plcs;
- .net.uk – reserved for use by UK ISPs; and
- .me.uk – intended for personal use by individuals.

In reality, anybody is free to register any .co.uk or .org.uk domain name. The specific rules for .ltd.uk and .plc.uk domains are set out at A2.7 below. There are also special suffixes for schools (.sch.uk), universities (.ac.uk), UK central and local government (.gov.uk), the emergency services (.police.uk, .fire.uk), etc.

An important ccTLD for any organisation doing business with the USA is the newly relaunched .us country code domain. This ccTLD, although always the official USA country code, had only previously been used in third-level format, for example losangeles.ca.us (.ca.us being the state of California). These domains were very difficult to register with complicated rules, and as a result most US companies preferred to use the more simple and unfettered .com gTLD domains as their web addresses.

The US Department of Commerce relaunched the .us domain in 2002 with Neustar being the appointed registry for these domains. Only a handful of UK registrars have so far become accredited for the .us domains (as at March 2002): Internetters Limited, Net Benefit plc and Virtual Internet plc (see A1.3 above for the web addresses of these registrars).

UK companies with a *bona fide* presence in the US (see A2.10 below for a fuller explanation of the rules determining this) are entitled to register .us domains. If you trade or have a physical presence in the USA, you should strongly consider protecting your brands in this vital market. In addition, as the .us name space has been very little used in the past, there are vast numbers of highly desirable unregistered .us domains available (generic and otherwise).

Third level domains　　　　　　　　　　　　**A1.9**

A third level domain is one in respect of which the registrant for the ordinary second level domain (for example .uk.com) is offering other parties third level domains on top of the primary domain (such as gardens.uk.com). One UK company, CentralNIC (www.centralnic.com), specialises in these third level domains and has secured a number of two letter country codes in .com and .net, for example:

- .uk.com;
- .uk.net;
- .gb.com;
- .gb.net;
- .us.com;
- .eu.com; and
- .br.com.

CentralNIC have been registering these domains for some years, generally via resellers.

Another UK company, BB Online (www.bb-online.uk.co), has secured the rights to the UK second level domain (.uk.co) but on the Colombian ccTLD which is '.co'. Although these domains should function properly, they are dependent on arrangements set up with the Colombian registry. These .uk.co domains may be marketed as an alternative to .co.uk, but caution is advised as there could be confusion with the same domain under .co.uk.

Similarly, some other companies are offering third level domains under, for example:

- gbr.cc – marketed as 'British commercial company', but actually under the Cocos Islands domain;

- sco.fm – marketed as 'Scottish firm', but under the Federation of Micronesia domain;

- eng.st – marketed as 'English site', but under the Sao Tome domain; and

- co.ni – marketed as the domain for 'Northern Ireland companies', but under the Nicaragua domain.

Extreme caution is advised regarding the adoption of certain of these domains as explained in A2 REGISTERING A DOMAIN NAME.

Fourth level domains **A1.10**

In competition with the mainstream ICANN-controlled domains, a US company, New.net, is marketing supposed new domains with suffixes such as .shop, .sex, .kids and .law, and offers around 30 alternatives at the time of going to print. Whilst the domain name book.shop may appear very attractive, it is not quite what it seems. In reality, the domain name registered is book.shop.new.net, with 'shop' itself being a third level domain on new.net, and 'book' being a fourth level domain. The promoters claim to have made special technological arrangements with certain ISPs (largely in the USA), which enable a visitor's browser to automatically translate book.shop into book.shop.new.net, and transport the visitor invisibly to the correct website. This is also understood to be possible by downloading special software (a plug-in) from New.net. If you registered one of these domains, your customers would not be able to visit your website without the plug-in or special ISP arrangements unless they typed in the complete real URL, that is book.shop.new.net. It should be borne in mind that many internet users will therefore be excluded from visiting a website which uses such a domain name because they are either reluctant or unable to download the necessary plug-in.

There are also serious drawbacks currently relating to sending e-mail to such domain names, as users would need to type the full e-mail address of mail@book.shop.new.net and not simply mail@book.shop. In addition, there is likely to be confusion if ICANN were to introduce one of these suffixes, or if New.net were to offer domains on .biz.new.net or even .com.new.net, as there would then be a risk of people arriving at different websites through keying in the same URLs. It is strongly advised to avoid these domains, and to stick with conventional ICANN-approved domain suffixes.

Domain name 'ownership' A1.11

Domain names are not actually owned by the user or registrant. Instead they are effectively a licence from the appropriate registrar to use the domain name during the period paid for. Title for the domain name always belongs ultimately to the registrar. For further detail, you should consult the appropriate registrar's terms and conditions.

Note: For definitions of words with which you are not familiar, please refer to the glossary at APPENDIX 1.

A2 – Registering a Domain Name

Choosing a domain name registration company   A2.1

As mentioned in A1.4 above, it is very important to carefully select the company used to register domain names. It is all too easy for a domain name registration company to put up an impressive website in English and with slick graphics, but the company may be located offshore. It may have a seemingly efficient voicemail system which says, for example, 'all operators are currently busy handling other customer calls'. However, the reality could be that the company is run from home by a single person with a separate day job, but who uses sophisticated computer and telephone technology to make the company appear more substantial than it really is. It may have just started trading, with no real premises, a totally automated website, and no telephone number for contact, but rather just an e-mail address or a form on the website. The WHOIS record of the company's own domain name should be used to see how long it has been established, where it is located and how long its own domain name is registered for. Because gTLDs can be registered for up to ten years, you could reasonably infer that a registration company, whose own name is only registered for one or two years may not have much faith in its own viability.

Companies which have gone bust or ceased trading have on occasion left clients with domain names for which the registrar has not been paid and for which the client has consequentially had to pay twice, or the client has found that its domain name is 'locked'. By 'locked', it is meant that it is very difficult to make changes to the WHOIS record, for example changing the name servers to enable use of the domain name. The terms and conditions and any frequently asked questions ('FAQs') on the domain name registration company's website should be read carefully to see how it deals with these administrative matters. Likewise, if you cannot find any terms and conditions, or if they are minimal, this should also serve as a warning.

Costs and pricing A2.2

Good advice would be always to have made contact by phone with a real person before committing to use a particular registration company. Be cautious of the very cheap prices for domain names advertised in some internet magazines. The headline rate can often hide additional charges, which could quickly negate the apparent 'bargain'. In some cases there may be additional charges to 'release' or transfer a domain name to another domain name registration company, or extra charges for changes to name servers, etc. Reassuringly, most of the major domain name registration companies make no additional charges for these services, which tend to be associated with the apparently cheaper companies. Ideally, choose a domain name registration company which sets out clearly all current and future charges.

The cost of registering a domain name can range from as little as £20 (often when using a fully automated system) to £100 or more for a two year registration. A domain name is an important and valuable business asset. Choosing a registration company simply for the lowest headline price may become a disadvantage if you ever need to contact it again in the future but are unable to do so. As a guideline, at the time of writing Internetters Limited (www.internetters.co.uk), which is ICANN-accredited and a Which? Web Trader, will register domain names for £40, or less for two years, and also provides human telephone support; Netbenefit plc (www.netbenefit.com), also ICANN-accredited, charges from £38 to £99 for two years, dependent on the package selected. There are also many other companies offering similar services. The best advice is to shop around, and to choose a company you feel safe with. Watch out for any hidden charges or other potential drawbacks, and read the terms and conditions carefully. Remember how important your domain name is likely to be to your company.

Registering the domain name A2.3

To register a domain name, once you have selected a suitable registrar either telephone the company and order your domain name or use the form on the company's website. Most registrars should have a tool on their website for searching for available domain names. When registering you will need to provide the following details:

- domain name;

- name of registrant (or 'owner' or licensee – usually your company's legal title);

- address, telephone number and fax number;

- name of an administrative contact and his/her phone, fax and e-mail address; and

- other contacts (if different) for billing and technical matters (the latter is usually the hosting company hosting the website).

Registration itself is quite simple and should be completed within a matter of hours. The domain names should be operational and capable of working within two days.

Registering different types of domain name   A2.4

Specific information on registering different types of domain names is set out below. For additional information see A1 INTRODUCTION.

Global top level domains   A2.5

As set out in A1.5 above, gTLDs, for example .com, .net, .biz and .info, can be registered for periods of whole years (one to ten).

UK country code top level domains   A2.6

UK ccTLDs, for example .co.uk and .org.uk, can only be registered and renewed for two year periods. There are no special rules applicable to .co.uk or .org.uk domains.

.ltd.uk and .plc.uk domains   A2.7

These domains are reserved for UK limited companies and plcs. Only the exact name of the company, as recorded at Companies House, can be registered. Spaces can either be ignored or replaced by hyphens. For example, British Alarms Limited can only register either 'britishalarms. ltd.uk' or 'british-alarms.ltd.uk'. Companies cannot use abbreviations instead, for example bal.ltd, unless BAL Limited is the actual registered company name. Detailed rules for these domains can be found on Nominet's website at www.nic.uk/rules/rup1.html.

15

.me.uk domains   A2.8

.me.uk (for example johndoe.me.uk) domains are intended for personal
use and should only be registered by individuals. Further details can be
found on the Nominet website at www.nic.uk/meuk/.

US country code top level domains   A2.9

US domain names can be registered for periods of up to ten years. As .us
domains were very little used prior to their relaunch in 2002, there are
large numbers of highly desirable generic domains still available for
registration. At the time of writing there are only three UK-based
registrars able to register .us domains:

- Internetters Limited – www.internetters.co.uk;

- Netbenefit Plc – www.netbenefit.co.uk; and

- Virtual Internet Plc – www.vi.net.

The Nexus rules   A2.10

Any company seeking to register a .us domain name needs to satisfy what
are known as the Nexus rules (set out below). Most UK-based
companies would probably fall within Nexus Category 3, and, if they are
clearly trading in the USA, they should qualify.

Registrants for the .us TLD must fall into one of the following
categories.

- **Nexus Category 1:** A natural person:

  ○   who is a United States citizen;

  ○   who is a permanent resident of the United States of America
      or any of its possessions or territories; or

  ○   whose primary place of domicile is in the United States of
      America or any of its possessions.

- **Nexus Category 2:** A United States entity or organisation that is:

  ○   incorporated within one of the 50 US states, the District of
      Columbia, or any of the United States' possessions or
      territories; or

  ○   organised or otherwise constituted under the laws of a state of
      the United States of America, the District of Columbia or any

of its possessions (including a federal, state, or local government of the United States, or a political subdivision thereof, and non-commercial organisations based in the United States).

- **Nexus Category 3:** A foreign entity or organisation that has a *bona fide* presence in the United States of America or any of its possessions or territories.

Factors that should be considered in determining whether an entity or organisation has a *bona fide* presence in the United States shall include, without limitation, whether such prospective .us domain name registrant:

○ regularly performs lawful activities within the United States related to the purposes for which the entity or organisation is constituted (for example selling goods or providing services to customers, conducting regular training activities, attending conferences), provided such activities are not conducted solely or primarily to permit it to register for a .us TLD and are lawful under the laws and regulations of the United States, and satisfy policies for the .us TLD, including policies approved and/or mandated by the Department of Commerce; and

○ maintains an office or other facility in the United States for a lawful business, non-commercial, educational or governmental purpose, and not solely or primarily to permit it to register for a .us domain name.

Other country code top level domains A2.11

Major domain name registration companies like Internetters, Netbenefit and Virtual Internet generally have arrangements with various national domain registries and will be able to offer advice and registrations on other country code domains around the world, for example .fr and .de. Prices and rules vary widely.

There is a list of major ccTLDs included in APPENDIX 5.

Special country code top level domains A2.12

Some ccTLDs must be considered separately. At the time of going to print, .eu domains had not been launched. When they are, it is anticipated that most major domain name registration companies will be able to register them.

17

Special ccTLDs such as .tv and .ws are often targeted to particular areas of business as if they were a generic TLD specifically created for business. For example .co is often marketed to businesses, but it does not represent 'company'. In fact, .co is the ccTLD of Colombia. There are risks inherent in registering these types of ccTLDs, for example in Colombia the national registry is operated by the University of Colombia and there is a national debate taking place over whether a university is the best organisation to sell and operate this national asset. (See also A2.15 and A2.16 below for information on .co (Colombia) and .ni (Nicaragua).)

Some ccTLDs known to have been marketed in a possibly misleading way are set out below (this is not an exhaustive list).

ccTLD	Sometimes marketed as representing:	Actual country code for:
.am	AM radio	Armenia
.co	company	Colombia
.dj	disc jockey	Djibouti
.fm	FM radio, or firm	Federation of Micronesia
.hm	home or homepage	Heard & McDonald Islands
.la	Los Angeles	Laos
.md	Doctor (MD)	Moldova
.ni	Northern Ireland	Nicaragua
.nu	nude (sex websites)	Niue
.tm	trade mark	Turkmenistan
.to	to (travel websites)	Tonga
.tv	TV station	Tuvalu
.ws	website	Western Samoa

It should be borne in mind that if you have not heard of a particular suffix before looking into it, it is highly likely that your clients and website visitors may also not have heard of it, and you will risk them mistyping the name, for example possibly followed by .com or .co.uk, thereby going to the wrong website or having their e-mails misrouted. It is recommended that you seek advice from your domain name registration company if you are unsure. If you must have one of these domains, again ask your normal domain name registration company as they should be able to register these for you.

For reference a list of major ccTLDs appears in APPENDIX 5.

Third level domains A2.13

For an explanation of the nature of third level domains please see A1.9.

.uk.com A2.14

.uk.com domains are resold by a number of UK-based registration companies, although they may not always be actively promoting them. In view of the risk of confusion of website visitors regarding the extra fullstop ('.') in the web address, it is sometimes worth considering registering the domain name in simple .com, for example mycompanynameuk.com either instead of, or in addition, to mycompanyname.uk.com.

If you are keen to register a .uk.com domain, you should enquire of your normal domain name registration company as it should be able to register these for you.

.uk.co A2.15

As with .uk.com, many UK-based domain name registration companies do not promote these domains, especially as they are dependent on the Colombian registry. However, if you must have one of these domains, again ask your normal domain name registration company as it should be able to register these for you.

Other third level domains A2.16

As explained in A1 INTRODUCTION, it is not recommended that you use these third level domains, for example .gbr.cc, .sco.fm and .co.ni, but again ask your normal domain name registration company as it may be able to register them for you if you are set on having one.

Fourth level domains A2.17

Fourth level domains, for example .shop, .sex, .kids, .law and .ltd, are in reality www.*.shop.new.net, www.*.sex.new.net etc., and they are not recognised by ICANN. Furthermore they do not currently work for around 50 per cent of internet users. (See A1.10 for further information on fourth level domains.)

For the reasons outlined in A1 INTRODUCTION, it is strongly advised to avoid these domains, and to stick with conventional ICANN-approved domain suffixes.

Issues to consider when registering a domain name   A2.18

When registering domain names, there are a number of key issues to bear in mind. First, the domain name should be registered in either your or your company's name as the legal registrant. Otherwise, the domain name would be 'owned' by the registration company. A rare exception to this could be if you were launching a new product or company etc., and wished to keep it under wraps and not let the domain name be seen to be directly connected with your organisation at this stage. In such a case you might consider using a personal name or a 'care of' address.

Secondly, you should ensure that at least the administrative contact for the domain name is someone in your organisation. If you let the domain name registration company put itself down as administrative, billing and technical contacts, you could have problems in the future if that company were to cease trading and its e-mail addresses stopped working. In that scenario, there could be long delays trying to make any changes to your domain name record if, for example, you needed to change the website hosting company.

Thirdly, check that the domain name registration company has actually paid the registrar for the correct number of years you have paid for. This is primarily an issue with gTLDs. Some less scrupulous domain name registration companies have been known to charge a client for two to ten years registration, but have only paid the registrar for the first year. When challenged they claim that they will pay each year as it arises. This is unacceptable because if the registration company should go out of business, your domain name will be valid only until the end of the current year and you will have to pay the registrar again for the remainder of the original contract period. You can verify any of these details by checking the WHOIS record, which should show names and addresses of the registrant and all of the contacts, together with the period of pre-payment for the domain name. Carefully check all aspects of the record and ensure that your details, especially your e-mail address, are correctly spelt. Changes to the WHOIS record are often made by automated e-mail processes, and if your e-mail address is wrong it can be very difficult for you to make any changes; effectively the domain is 'locked'.

Examples of gTLD WHOIS records

A2.19

Examples of two gTLD WHOIS records are below – one with Network Solutions, the other with INWW as Registrars.

The WHOIS record below shows details of the contacts, renewal date and nameservers for the domain name 'butterworths.com'.

Registrant:

Butterworths Publishers Ltd (BUTTERWORTHS2-DOM)
35 Chancery Lane
London,
WC2A 1EL
UK

Domain Name: BUTTERWORTHS.COM

Administrative Contact, Billing Contact:

Read, Alban (AR3648) alban.read@BUTTERWORTHS.CO.UK
Butterworths Publishers Ltd
Halsbury House
35 Chancery Lane
London
WC2A 1EL
UK
+44 (0)171 400 2788 (FAX) +44 (0)171 400 4656

Technical Contact:

Corporate Suppoert (PIP-NOC) support@UK.UU.NET
UUNET UK (PIPEX)
Internet House 332 Science Park
Cambridge
Cambridgeshire
UK
+44 (0)1223 250122
Fax– +44 (0)1223 250133

Record last updated on 13–Mar–2001.

Record expires on 31–Mar–2010.

Record created on 31–Mar–1998.

Database last updated on 26–Apr–2002 01:37:00 EDT.

Domain servers in listed order:

GATEKEEPER.BUTTERWORTHS.CO.UK	194.128.172.1
NSO-B.DNS.PIPEX.NET	158.43.129.66
NS1-B.DNS.PIPEX.NET	158.43.193.66

The WHOIS record below shows details of the contacts, renewal date and nameservers for the domain name 'internetters.com'.

	WhoIs Result For internetters.com @ whois.inww.com
Domain Name	internetters.com
Creation Date	1997-07-07
Registration Date	2000-07-27
Expiry Date	2010-07-06
Organisation Name	Internetters Ltd
Organisation Address	Research House
	Fraser Road
	Greenford
	UB6 7AQ
	Middlesex
	GREAT BRITAIN (UK)
Admin Name	Paul Westley
Admin Address	Research House
	Fraser Road
	Greenford
	UB6 7AQ
	Middlesex
	GREAT BRITAIN (UK)
Admin Email	paul@internetters.co.uk
Admin Phone	44 870 160 555
Admin Fax	44 870 165 666
Tech Name	Internetters Hostmaster
Tech Address	Research House
	Fraser Road
	Greenford
	UB6 7AQ
	Middlesex
	GREAT BRITAIN (UK)
Tech Email	hostmaster@internetters.co.uk
Tech Phone	44 870 160 555
Tech Fax	44 870 165 666
Name Server	ns1.internetters.net
	ns2.internetters.net

Example of a ccTLD WHOIS record   **A2.20**

In the case of .uk domains, domain name registrations and renewals are currently only paid in two year tranches. Although Nominet's WHOIS system shows the registrant of each domain, all other details are hidden. Under current Nominet arrangements, you will receive a certificate for each domain name. This is generally sent to registrants within six months of the initial registration. Again check that all the contact details are correct and inform Nominet immediately of any errors. (Certificates are not issued for gTLDs, but the domain name registration company's invoice and a printout of the WHOIS records should act as adequate proof of 'title'.)

WHOIS query result:

Domain name: ELECTROLUX-DIRECT.CO.UK

Registered for: Electrolux Home Products

Domain registered by: INTERNETTERS

Registered on 02-May-2000.

Domain servers listed in order:

NS1.INTERNETTERS.NET   207.228.254.8
NS2.INTERNETTERS.NET   66.38.135.70

WHOIS database last updated at 09:35:01 14-Sep-2001

The NIC.UK Registration Host contains ONLY information for domains within co.uk, org.uk, net.uk, ltd.uk and plc.uk. Please use the whole server at rs.internic.net for Internet Information or the whole server at nic.ddn.mil for MILNET Information.

Unlike the gTLD domain WHOIS records (see A2.19 above), the above only shows the registrant's name, date of registration (not renewal date), name of the tag holder and name servers. It is possible that the details provided may be extended in the future.

General summary of issues to consider on selecting a domain name registration company   A2.21

With the boom in domain name registrations, many new companies entered this marketplace. However, not all companies offer the same service. Many operate only from a website and e-mail address, with no phone numbers for customers to contact. Also, quite a few domain name registration companies in the UK have ceased trading, some not having paid Nominet or other suppliers for their clients' domain names, leaving the clients to pay again. It is advised that potential registrants of domain names thoroughly vet the registration companies they intend to use. In particular, it is worth checking that a company has a trading record, offers human telephone customer support, and is accredited by external bodies, for example the Consumers' Association Which? WebTrader, ICANN, etc.

As a response to problems of customer service with some UK registration companies, Nominet are assisting with the launch of a code of practice for UK domain name registration companies. It is hoped that this will become operational during 2002, although some key areas remain outstanding, such as who will fund the costs of such a code. If it becomes active, you are advised only to deal with a company which has signed up to this code of practice. If the code is not launched, look out instead for other business and technical accreditations.

A3 – Registering a Domain Name as a Trade Mark

Historical context of trade marks A3.1

Generally speaking, a trade mark is a name used to indicate the origin or source of goods. 'Origin' in this context commonly means a particular manufacturer or supplier. Ever since the accumulation of property became acknowledged as an indicator of status and the quality and origin of goods has been deemed important, owners and manufacturers of goods have branded them with their names and marks. For over 125 years, legislation in the UK has protected such brand names against unauthorised reproduction and imitation, and trade marks and brand names are now taken for granted.

In the UK, the most recent *Trade Marks Act* was passed in 1994, just before the explosion of e-commerce; consequently the Act makes no reference to the internet or domain names. However, in spite of the fact that much trade mark legislation and case law pre-dates the rapid expansion of the internet and domain name registrations, it still has an important influence on domain name use and registrations.

What is a trade mark? A3.2

In the United Kingdom, *section 1(1)* of the *Trade Marks Act 1994* (*TMA 1994*) defines a trademark as:

> '. . . any sign capable of being represented graphically which is capable of distinguishing goods and services of one undertaking from those of other undertakings'.

The definition goes on to say that a mark may consist of:

> '. . . words (including personal names), designs, letters, numerals or the shape of goods or their packaging'.

Similar definitions exist in almost all countries which subscribe to the main international trade mark conventions.

The definition of a trade mark is important as it puts into context the relatively minor ambit of domain names. Domain names are not shapes or designs or even logos as many trade marks are. They exist to provide a memorable alternative to the long string of numbers known as a URL.

Having a trade mark registered effectively gives its owner a monopoly right to use that mark for its goods or services. In the case of words which are in common use and which are registered as trade marks, the trade mark owner will generally not be able to prevent a person from using the same word in relation to different goods and services, but will probably be able to prevent a person using that word on the same or a very similar type of goods and services. Thus, when registering an attractive domain name which indicates the nature of the website it locates or the type of goods or services offered there, it is important to also consider registering that attractive domain name as a trade mark.

National nature of trade marks   A3.3

Trade marks are registered nationally according to the class of goods and services in relation to which they will be used (see A3.4 below for an explanation of the classification system). It is crucial to understand that a registered trade mark is a national right and only offers protection against infringement in the country where it is registered.

As the protection for a registered trade mark is only national, this can create potential problems when trying to use trade mark law to protect a domain name which is in effect a global business name; at which national registry should registration of a domain name as a trade mark be sought when the domain name is used to locate a website accessible internationally on the worldwide web? The answer to this question, from a commercial perspective, is initially in the country where the website seeks to attract business and the business operates, then, or additionally, as a Community trade mark (see A3.19 below) to gain protection in all 15 European Member States, and finally in other places where the largest markets are and the website is accessed most.

The classification system   A3.4

Trade marks are classified according to the type of goods and services in relation to which the mark is used, and every mark is registered in a particular class according to those types of goods and services. The class is specified on the trade mark application form and the goods and services in relation to which the mark is used are described in the application (see A3.15 below).

There are 42 internationally recognised classes of goods and services in which trade marks can be registered (known as the 'Nice Classification'), ranging from common metals and alloys (class 6) to business management and administration (class 35). 61 countries have adopted and apply the Nice Classification for the purposes of the registration of trade marks, and national trade mark offices in more than 90 countries actually use it for trade mark classification purposes.

It is possible to register a mark in multiple classes in respect of the same goods and services, and for the same or similar marks to be registered in the same or different classes by different people in different countries. A national registration in one country will not necessarily prevent another person from registering the same or similar mark for its goods and services in a different national registry. Thus, the same mark may be registered in several countries by the same or different entities in respect of the same or different goods. As a domain name is a badge used to describe a website offering goods and services, the relevant class of trade mark registration will depend on the goods and services on the website. If the domain name is used on marketing material, for example brochures, registration should also be sought in respect of the class which corresponds to such material (usually class 16).

Differences between trade marks and domain names A3.5

To summarise the points set out at A3.4 above, the fundamental and practical differences between trade marks and domain names are as follows.

Trade marks	Domain names
Trade marks are national in scope and protection.	Domain names are global in scope and there is no protection for them *per se*.
Trade marks are not necessarily unique: the same trade mark can be registered nationally in different classes by the same or different people.	Domain names are unique.

Trade marks	Domain names
The same trade mark can be registered in different countries in the same or different classes by the same or different people.	Only one domain name can be registered for each gTLD and ccTLD.
Trade marks can be words, logos ('devices'), shapes, colours, numbers and smells.	Domain names only consist of words and numbers.

The above table shows some of the problems which arise when seeking to use national trade mark law to regulate the use of global domain names. Domain name law has sought to draw on certain themes of national trade mark laws which are not easily reconciled with the global nature of domain names. Problems arise predominantly because various intellectual property rights are claimed by different people in different countries in respect of a single global resource (a domain name). Whilst there are advantages of using trade mark law for domain names, the application of certain aspects of it has led to some perverse interpretations of trade mark legislation.

Why register a domain name as a trade mark? A3.6

The UK *TMA 1994* makes it illegal for a registered trade mark to be used by a third party without the consent of the registered trade mark owner. Similar national laws protect registered trade marks in different countries. This means that a registered trade mark is effectively a state-sanctioned monopoly right to use that word, phrase or logo. Therefore, registration of a domain name as a trade mark ensures that its owner has a right to use that name in the country in which it is registered, and that competitors cannot use the same or a similar domain name to describe their goods or services in cyberspace or otherwise. Until such time as the domain name is registered as a trade mark, it will only be protected by common law rights and not statutory rights under *TMA 1994*.

There are three situations where a domain name may be at risk if it has not been registered as a trade mark.

- A competitor or cybersquatter registers a site with a common misspelling of the domain name. Traffic is diverted from the website as a result.

- A 'sucks' site is established (see D4 THE ICANN DISPUTE RESOLUTION POLICIES (UDRP AND STOP)) and goodwill in the products, services, brand and/or domain name is diminished.

- A third party complains to the ISP that it has a prior right to the domain name based on its intellectual property rights. Use of the domain name is suspended or withdrawn and the owner has to prove its rights at common law.

In the first two scenarios the domain name owner would probably find it had a remedy, as cybersquatting and passing off have been given short shrift by the law. As regards third parties who claim a prior right to use the domain name (as in the third scenario), the courts have decided each case on its merits. Broadly speaking, in cases where domain names have been registered 'in bad faith' the courts have found for the applicant, but in cases of 'innocent use', that is where the registrant did not know of the other party's rights or had a legitimate right to use the domain name itself, they have ordered the status quo to remain. The second scenario is likely to be bad for business, as is the third scenario (if substantiated) as it could result in the website going down, being closed or being relocated to another domain name.

As a domain name serves the same branding purpose as a traditional trade mark, and registration of a trade mark grants a monopoly right to use that mark, it is sensible to register a distinctive and unique domain name as a trade mark. A domain name which is also a registered trade mark is a very attractive and valuable right to add to an intellectual property portfolio.

Unregistered trade marks A3.7

UK trade mark law recognises both registered trade marks (those which have been through formal registration procedures at a national trade marks registry) and unregistered trade marks (those which have not undergone formal registration). Unregistered trade marks are deemed to be marks which are commonly used by a manufacturer, producer or supplier of products to brand particular goods or services. They are not registered at the Trade Marks Registry and instead the owner relies on goodwill and reputation in relation to the particular goods or services in question to protect the mark against infringement.

UK trade mark law also recognises 'famous name' marks, which are those that are so famous and have such a well-known reputation that people would instantly recognise goods and services branded with that mark as originating from a particular source (see also B2 DOMAIN NAME TRANSFERS).

Matters to consider before registering a domain name as a trade mark   A3.8

There are a number of important issues to be considered before registering a domain name as a trade mark, and these are set out at A3.9–A3.13 below.

The domain name   A3.9

As considered at A3.2 above, the wide definition of a trade mark means that it is possible to register logos, shapes, colours and even smells as a trade mark. Clearly, a domain name can only consist of words and numbers and for this reason it is most common to register a domain name as a word-only trade mark.

If a considerable amount of branding and marketing is intended to be undertaken, it may be desirable to register a word and a logo (known as a 'word and device' mark) or a series of marks, which contain the same essential elements and only differ on matters of a non-distinctive character, for example font. An application for a series of marks may cover hyphenations, underscores or plural variations of a domain name. It is advisable to take specialist legal advice on whether the series of marks proposed to be registered is actually registrable as a series under *TMA 1994*.

Trade mark searches   A3.10

Before applying for the registration of a domain name as a trade mark, it is advisable to find out whether any other business is using the same or a similar name. This can prevent trade mark objections being received later in the application process and the risk of the domain name owner being accused of 'passing off'. It can also assist the domain name owner to choose a distinctive name which is different from those used by other persons. This can be done informally by checking the trade press, searching directories such as Yellow Pages and looking on the internet.

Alternatively, a more formal search of the Trade Marks Registry database can be undertaken. This can be done online at www.patent.gov.uk/tm/

dbase/index.htm. Before doing so the acceptable use policy (at www.patent.gov.uk/tm/dbase/useof.htm) and disclaimer (at www. patent.gov.uk/disclaimer.htm) should be referred to. The online search only provides results for a specific enquiry so it is important to undertake a thorough search of all variations and similar names. Searching in this way does not provide any interpretation of results so, even where this type of search has been made, it is advisable to get specialist professional advice on the results before making an application. Asking a professional to undertake the search helps to ensure that the parameters searched are correct and that the results of the search are correctly interpreted.

In addition, it is possible to undertake a formal search by submitting a form to the Trade Marks Registry, requesting that it conducts a search and supplies results on paper. The Trade Marks Registry makes a small charge for its Search and Advisory Service; details of the service and current charges can be found at www.patent.gov.uk/tm/sas/index.htm. An advisory service is also offered by the Trade Marks Registry, giving guidance on whether a mark is likely to be accepted for registration. Details of this service are available at the website cited above.

European and worldwide trade mark searches   **A3.11**

It is possible to undertake a European trade mark search. The Community Trade Marks Registry databases can be searched online at www.oami.eu.int/search/trademark/la/en_tm_search.cfm. Again, when searching online, it is important that all variations of the domain name and similar names (including slight variations in spelling and punctuation) are investigated to get a picture of identical or similar marks registered. The online search provides results to specific enquiries and there is no interpretation of the search results.

It is also possible to instruct a trade mark agent or solicitor to undertake a Community Trade Mark search, but this can be expensive. The cost varies, but tends to be around £2,500 plus VAT. As there is no standardisation of search results between European Member States' trade mark registries, however, it is generally worthwhile to instruct a trade mark attorney or a solicitor to undertake the search and provide an analysis of the results.

A further possible search is a worldwide identical search (known sometimes as a 'WIS' search), which reveals identical marks registered elsewhere. However, because it only indicates trade marks identical to the one searched, the results should be treated with caution. For example, a WIS search will not reveal a hyphenated version of the domain name which is registered as a trade mark if only the non-hyphenated version is inspected. Moreover, if no identical marks are revealed by the search, this does not necessarily mean that the mark would be accepted for registration at each national trade mark registry or that no other rights owner would object to its registration.

Problems revealed by the search A3.12

If the search reveals that the same or a similar mark is already registered, there are ways of dealing with these prior registrations, but methods for doing so can be highly technical and are outside the scope of this book. In the event that a search reveals potentially conflicting marks, specialist professional advice should be sought on those results and on ways of overcoming likely objections to registration.

Changing a domain name after application for a trade mark A3.13

If a domain name owner decides to change the domain name once it has applied for a related trade mark registration, it will probably find that it has to submit an entirely separate application. For this reason, it is advisable to finalise the domain name before seeking to register it as a trade mark.

UK trade mark application procedure A3.14

The procedure for registering a domain name as a trade mark is straightforward, but does differ slightly between each national registry. The following is a summary of the UK registration procedure. The Community Trade Mark registration procedure is dealt with at A3.19–A3.23 below.

Broadly, the UK Trade Mark Registry application and registration procedure is as follows:

- application (see A3.15 below);
- examination (see A3.16 below);
- publication (see A3.17 below); and
- registration (see A3.18 below).

Application A3.15

A trade mark is applied for by completing and submitting an application form to the Trade Marks Registry for registration of a domain name as a trade mark. Generally speaking, it is only necessary to register a domain name as a word-only trade mark. In fact, registration of a logo comprising the words of the domain name will not necessarily grant protection for the domain name alone. Since 1999, the UK Trade Marks Registry has refused to register the top level or country code part of a domain name and the words 'web', 'net' or 'e' for internet and electronic goods and services. Similar prohibitions are registry practice in many countries. The Trade Marks Registry guide to the registration of domain names is available online at www.patent.gov.uk/tm/notices/regular/domain.htm.

The TM3 application form can be downloaded from the Trade Marks Registry website at www.patent.gov.uk/tm/forms/tm3.pdf, but it is not currently possible to apply for registration online. The Trade Marks Registry guidance booklet 'Applying to Register a Trade Mark' is also available online at www.patent.gov.uk/tm/info/applying.pdf.

A clean and legible copy of the mark applied for must be attached to the application form, and the class and specification of the goods and services in relation to which the mark is used (classified according to the Nice Classification – see A3.4 above) must be given. The idea is to register a domain name for the type of goods and services available on the website it refers to. For example, a domain name for a recruitment website would be registered in class 35 (advisory services relating to personnel recruitment) and a travel website may be registered in class 39 (agency services for arranging travel). If the travel agent also wanted to register the domain name for its travel brochures then it might also be possible to register it in class 16 (printed material). In this way, the goods and services which may be branded and protected with the mark are extended.

The application form must be accompanied by the relevant application fee. The fee for filing a trade mark application in the UK is currently £200 for the first class of registration and £50 for each additional class in which the mark is to be registered. A fee sheet must be completed and attached and the requisite fee paid for the application.

Examination A3.16

The mark applied for is examined by the Trade Marks Registry to ensure that it fulfils the criteria of a trade mark as set out in *TMA 1994*, the

Trade Marks Rules 2000 (SI 2000/136) and practice guidelines. The Trade Marks Registry considers whether the mark:

- is a sign represented graphically;

- is capable of distinguishing one person's goods from another's;

- is not generic, descriptive, deceptive or contrary to public policy (for example because it is obscene); and

- does not conflict with:

  ○ an earlier trade mark registration,

  ○ an earlier mark which is not registered but is well-known, or

  ○ an earlier copyright or design.

The question of whether a mark is represented 'graphically' is usually easy to establish and difficulties only tend to arise for shape and smell marks. For the second part of the test, 'capable of distinguishing', the Trade Marks Registry examiner will consider whether there are other similar marks already registered. If so, the mark may not function to distinguish one person's goods and services from another's. Seeking specialist advice on the registrability of the domain name as a trade mark before making an application will help to establish whether the mark will be registrable *per se*, and undertaking a search will indicate whether there are identical or similar marks which may be obstacles to registration.

In the third stage, the examiner will look at a number of reference sources to establish that the mark is capable of being registered, including the Oxford English Dictionary for existing words, the London telephone directory for names (and other foreign city telephone directories as appropriate), various place name directories, the internet and even trade journals.

Generally speaking, a made-up word will be most likely to pass this part of the examination stage (for example 'nokia'). Words which are not usually associated with the goods or services for which they are to be registered for, such as 'orange' for mobile telephones, are also more likely to be registered than ones which are indicative of the goods or services that they are used for.

If the examiner refuses the application on the grounds that it fails one or more of the four tests above, this is not fatal to the application as it is possible to submit constructive arguments and further evidence to the Trade Marks Registry in support of the application. In the case of words deemed non-distinctive, the applicant might claim that the name has become distinctive through its use to identify its goods. If the examiner objects on grounds that the mark is similar to one already registered then it may be possible to submit evidence of the applicant's use of the domain name, or evidence that the registered mark has not been used in the last five years. There is no general rule about the type of arguments and evidence which need to be submitted and much will depend on the nature of objection raised by the Trade Mark Registry. For this reason, it is important to take legal advice if objections to the application are received.

Publication   A3.17

Once the mark has been examined and accepted for publication, the applicant will be notified by the Trade Marks Registry of the date of publication. The mark is published in the Trade Marks Journal which lists applications according to the Nice Classification (see A3.4 above). For a period of three months from the date of publication, any third party may object to registration of the mark.

Any objection received must state the grounds for the opposition. It is usually third parties who object because they own a mark which is the same or similar to the mark applied for. The costs of filing an objection are small but it is usually expensive to prosecute or defend such an objection. It is sometimes possible to overcome objections by negotiating with the third party a limitation of the goods and or services in relation to which the mark will be used. It is also possible to overcome objections by providing evidence of use and dissimilarity. Undertaking a search minimises the risk of filing an application for a mark which is already registered, and means that if the domain name owner does decide to use a domain name which is similar to a mark already on the register, it will be forewarned that objections may arise and can take steps to prevent them being made. In any event, if a third party opposes registration, it is wise to seek specialist legal advice on the matter as soon as possible.

Registration   A3.18

If no objections are received or if they are overcome, the mark will be registered. In the UK, unlike many other countries, there is no further fee to pay upon registration of the mark. A trade mark must be renewed periodically (every ten years in the UK), but this does mean that provided renewals are undertaken, it is technically possible to sustain the monopoly right to use the mark in perpetuity.

Once the domain name is registered as a trade mark, it should be demonstrated that it is a registered trade mark by using the ® symbol or some other designation on it, such as inverted commas surrounding the name or italics to indicate that the word is not used as a description or a generic term, but is a registered trade mark. Reference to the fact that the domain name is a registered trade mark should be made on the website (in the copyright disclaimer and the site use terms) and in all marketing material. If this is not done, there is a risk that the Trade Marks Registrar or a third party may seek to have the mark removed from the register for non-use or generic use.

There is also a risk of losing the registration of the domain name as a trade mark if the domain name owner acquiesces in the use of the domain name by a third party without its consent. This applies to near-cybersquatting, that is using a very similar domain name to the domain name owner's, alternative TLD or ccTLD versions of the domain name, typosquatting and sucks sites (see A3.6 above and D4 THE ICANN DISPUTE RESOLUTION POLICIES (UDRP AND STOP)). For this reason, it is essential to monitor the use of the name by competitors and those in similar industries.

Community trade marks   A3.19

Since 1996, it has been possible to file an application for registration of a Community trade mark ('CTM') in all EU Member States by simply making one application to a central registry, the Office for the Harmonisation of the Internal Market ('OHIM') in Alicante. By seeking to register a domain name as a CTM and making a single application to the OHIM, a monopoly right to use the domain name in all 15 EU Member States can potentially be secured. As a CTM is treated as a single trade mark throughout the EU, there is an all or nothing principle with regard to applications. This means that if the application fails in one Member State (for whatever reason), it will not be registered in any. A CTM registration is a separate right to a national registration; it is possible to hold both national trade mark registrations in individual EU Member States and a CTM covering all Member States.

The procedure (see A3.20–A3.23 below) is, broadly speaking, the same as that in the UK (see A3.14–A3.18 above) with the main difference being that at the examination stage, the OHIM will not refuse an application on the basis of prior registrations. The CTM system relies on a third party to file an objection to an application for registration if it believes that it has a prior right to a mark.

The advantage of a CTM registration is obviously that one application potentially secures registration in all Member States. The disadvantages are that it invariably takes longer than registering a mark locally, costs more and increases the possibility of objections from third parties because registration of the mark is sought in more countries.

Community trade mark applications A3.20

There are certain provisions about who may apply to register a CTM and what can be registered as one. For these reasons, it is sensible to seek specialist legal advice on these matters before filing a CTM application so as to avoid unnecessary expense being incurred in filing an application which is unlikely to succeed.

CTM applications are made by completing and submitting an application form to the OHIM for registration of a mark as a trade mark. The form can be downloaded from the OHIM website (www.oami.eu.int/en/ marque/pdf/demande.pdf), but it is not currently possible to apply online. As with UK trade mark procedure, a copy of the mark must be included and the class(es) of registration specified (see A3.15 above). CTMs are also classified according to the Nice Classification (see A3.4 above).

The application form is similar to the UK form. The fee for filing the application is currently €975 for registration in up to three classes and €200 for each additional class thereafter. It should be borne in mind that in addition to the application fee for a CTM, a registration fee must also be paid once the mark is ready for registration (see A3.23 below).

Additionally, the applicant must specify a first and second language for correspondence relating to the application. If the applicant is represented by a professional person, an authorisation form must be signed by the applicant and submitted to the OHIM, demonstrating that the applicant is represented by a solicitor or trade mark attorney and that he or she is instructed to act by the applicant.

Examination of a Community trade mark application A3.21

The application is examined to ensure that it meets the requirements for registration of a CTM. Searches of national trade mark registries and the CTM register are undertaken, and the results of these are supplied to the applicant. These search results are sent to the applicant without any interpretation as to likely conflict or opposition. As such, it is advisable to seek guidance on any search results received so that preparation can be made for possible objections which may be raised during the publication stage.

Publication of mark in the Community Trade Mark Journal A3.22

Once the mark has been examined, and no sooner than one month after the Community and national searches are sent to the applicant by the OHIM, the mark will be published in the CTM Journal. The mark is published for three months and during this time, third parties have the right to object to the application.

Generally speaking, objections will be received if the domain name is similar or identical to another person's existing registered or unregistered trade mark. If searches and adequate market research have been undertaken to brand the site with a unique domain name, the risk of objections being raised is reduced. The full objection procedure is outside the scope of this book, and if an objection to the CTM application is received, expert legal advice should be taken on the subject.

Registration of a Community trade mark A3.23

If no objections are received or if they are overcome, the mark will be registered. In order to have a CTM registered is necessary to pay a registration fee. The registration fee is currently €1,100 and is payable on registration of a mark in up to three classes. A fee of €200 is payable for each additional class thereafter. Due to a backlog in applications, even if no objections to the registration are received, it can take up to 18 months to register a CTM. During this time, the domain name will only be protected by common law rights and not statutory rights.

International trade mark registration and priority periods A3.24

There is no system whereby a single application can be made for registration of a domain name as a trade mark in every single country in the world. The closest to this is a system which covers more than 40 countries, known as the 'Madrid Agreement'. Under the Madrid Agreement, an initial registration is made in an applicant's home country and then, by way of a central processing system, applications are made in each additional country which subscribes to the Madrid Agreement.

Application and filing fees are charged by each country where registration of the mark is applied for.

This can be a time-consuming and expensive process but affords a mark the best potential for global protection. As a domain name is a global resource, registration in multiple countries should always be considered and specific advice should be sought on the possibility of protecting a domain name in this way.

Practical advice on registering a domain name as a trade mark   A3.25

- Carry out market research to establish whether a domain name is distinctive, and make sure that it is done in all the countries in which it is hoped to do business.

- Choose a domain name which is registrable as a trade mark. Remember that words in common parlance, which are purely descriptive or which are not distinctive are not always capable of registration.

- Whilst short, easily-remembered three-letter domain names are very attractive and valuable, they probably will not be registrable as trade marks and may be more expensive to protect against infringement as a result. For information on registration of short words and letters see the Trade Marks Registry Work Manual at www.patent.gov.uk/tm/reference/workman/chapt6/sec3(11).pdf.

- Always undertake a search before filing a trade mark application to establish whether any identical or similar marks are registered. If similar marks are registered, this is not necessarily fatal to an application, but specific advice should be sought on search results revealing prior registrations.

- Finalise the name before seeking to register it (and any variants) as a trade mark. If the domain name is altered, a new trade mark registration will probably have to be applied for.

- Get advice on the classes of registration in which it is appropriate to register the domain name before applying for registration as it is not possible to change the specification once an application has been made.

- Get advice on writing the specification to ensure that it is not so restrictive or generic that it may be challenged in future.

- Decide where the domain name is going to be registered as a trade mark. The key issue is to register the mark in all countries at which the website is targeted. Remember that trade marks are national registrations which generally afford protection against infringement only in the country in which they are registered.

- Consider taking specific advice on who will be the registered owner of the trade mark from a territorial and a tax perspective.

- Register trade marks in additional countries as the area of operation expands but get advice on the possibility of extending the first registration.

Part B: Sale and Transfer of a Domain Name

B1 – Buying a Domain Name

Purchasing a domain name already owned by another   B1.1

Domain names are like any other property, and if the domain name you would like to use for your company is already 'owned' by someone else it may be possible to purchase the domain name, with or without the associated website (if any).

Examples of this might be where:

- a shrewd investor may have registered a good generic domain name some years earlier;

- the current registrant may no longer be trading or need the domain name; or

- you may place a higher value on a domain name than the current registrant.

If, when checking domain name availability by searching on a website such as www.crsnic.net or www.nic.uk, you find your choice is not available, it does not necessarily mean it cannot be purchased.

Global top level domains   B1.2

For gTLDs, it is best to look at the WHOIS record for the contact details of the current registrant or 'owner'. It is then a good idea to check if a website exists for the domain name. Just type in 'www.' followed by the domain name and see if you get to a live website. If you get an 'Error' message, the domain name is probably not currently in use, although this result could also apply if there were a problem with the web server. Even if there is a website, it does not necessarily prevent a purchase. The current registrant may still be prepared to entertain an offer, although if a major corporation is using the domain name it will probably be unwilling to relinquish it. However, tentative contact could always be made with the administrative contact to see if it might be prepared to consider the possibility of sale of the domain name.

UK country code top level domains B1.3

For UK ccTLDs the registrant's contact details are not revealed in the WHOIS record. If there is no website, contact the tag holder (the registration company currently managing the domain) and ask it to pass on a message, or send your own e-mail to speculative e-mail addresses, such as info@, webmaster@, sales@ plus the domain name.

Auction websites B1.4

Another way to find a registered domain name available for sale is to browse the domain name auction websites, such as www.afternic.com or www.greatdomains.com, or even general auction sites, such as www.qxl.com or www.ebay.com. Some of these may offer 'escrow' services to provide for the safe exchange of funds between the parties buying and selling domain names (see B1.5 below).

Escrow services B1.5

There are also a number of web-based escrow services which can safely handle the transfer and payment for a domain name. The best-known of these is the California-based company www.escrow.com. The buyer or seller logs onto the website and logs the transaction. The escrow.com system then e-mails the other party to advise it of the registered transaction. The second party then logs on and accepts or modifies the transaction details. Once both parties have agreed, the buyer makes the payment by cheque, credit card or wire transfer to escrow.com. When this has cleared, the seller then initiates the domain name transfer. After the transfer has been confirmed, the payment is remitted to the seller. Charges are based on the value of the transaction and vary from 0.85 per cent to 3 per cent. It is highly recommended to seek professional legal advice regarding a sale contract and/or payment arrangements.

See B2.33 for a model sale contract.

Using a domain name registration company **B1.6**

Some of the major domain name registration companies may also be willing to make contact with the current registrant for a domain name you desire and to negotiate on your behalf.

See also B2 DOMAIN NAME TRANSFERS.

B2 – Domain Name Transfers

Transfer of ownership B2.1

Domain names, particularly top level domain names, can be very valuable assets. To the best of the authors' knowledge, the record price paid to date is US$7.5 million for the transfer of business.com.

There are various reasons why the registered owner of a domain name might wish to transfer it. Amongst the most common are the need to give effect to a corporate group restructuring, and the inclusion of the domain name in an asset transfer in the context of a merger or takeover.

In the case of a generic domain name, or where the rights of the owner to a branded domain name are secure, the owner is generally at liberty to sell the domain name for whatever price it can entice a purchaser to pay. The ability of the owner of a domain name to sell it, however, may be hampered or even precluded by various circumstances – for example, where the owner's legal entitlement to the domain name is established to be inferior to the rights of a third party (see A3 REGISTERING A DOMAIN NAME AS A TRADE MARK and D1 INTRODUCTION TO DOMAIN NAME DISPUTES).

More notably, the sale may be barred if the owner is adjudged to be 'cybersquatting' – referring to the practice of procuring a domain name containing the name or trade mark of an individual or entity for resale to that third party, which is usually considered to be abusive and in bad faith. Circumstances may arise where the owner of a domain name containing a famous name is not in fact a cybersquatter. For example, an owner may have registered a name before that name became famous in relation to a third party, or even before that third party existed. In cases such as these, a passive rather than a pro-active stance is generally to be advised and the domain name owner should wait for an approach by, and purchase offer from, the owner of the famous name. Nevertheless, any attempt to derive consideration in excess of the 'documented out-of-pocket costs directly related to the domain name' (that is, the cost of registration of the name and associated costs) may, chronology permitting, be taken as evidence of the 'registration and use of a domain name in bad faith' (section 4(b)(i) of the ICANN UDRP – see APPENDIX 2).

In this context, even a legitimate owner must be careful not to be led by an apparently interested purchaser into a position where bad faith can be established (see section 4(b) of the ICANN UDRP).

Considered below are the procedural rules of Network Solutions ('NSI') and Nominet (see B2.3–B2.8 and B2.9–B2.12 respectively), two of the principal registries which regulate domain name transfers. The commercial agreements which parties should enter into to regulate the legal and commercial aspects of such transfers are also considered (see B2.13–B2.27 below).

Note: It should be noted that in the course of this chapter, the terms 'domain name owner', 'registered owner', 'transferor', 'seller' and 'vendor' are used interchangeably, as are the terms 'transferee', 'buyer' and 'purchaser'.

Domain name transfer rules B2.2

The procedures involved in giving effect to a transfer will be dependent on the rules of the registry at which the domain name in question is registered. In this chapter, consideration is limited to the rules of NSI (for .com, .org and .net) and of Nominet (for .co.uk, .org.uk, .ltd.uk, .plc.uk, .net.uk and .sch.uk.).

It should, however, be mentioned that other second level domains also exist in the UK, namely .ac.uk for academic establishments, .gov.uk for government bodies, .nhs.uk for National Health Service organisations, .police.uk for police forces and .mod.uk for Ministry of Defence establishments. None of these five is administered by Nominet and each is restricted to a particular type of entity. Thus, transfer is generally not an issue which arises. However, for further information on the respective administering bodies and governing rules see (as a starting point) the Nominet website at www.nominet.org.uk/news/guides/reg4.html.

Network Solutions B2.3

A transfer of a domain name registered at NSI requires the completion of two forms:

- the Service Agreement, which can be found online at www.netsol.com/en_US/legal/service-agreement.jhtml; and

- the Registrant Name Change Agreement ('RNCA'), which can be found online at www.netsol.com/en_US/makechanges/rnca/expedited-instructions.html.

Service Agreement **B2.4**

The Service Agreement must be completed by the transferee and is extensive, comprising NSI's general terms and conditions of service. The conditions would appear to apply equally to each new registrant, whether the original owner of the domain name or a transferee. As far as transfers are concerned, the most important provisions are contained in section 23, which is self-explanatory and reproduced below.

> '**23. TRANSFER AND ASSIGNMENT**. You may transfer your domain name registration to a third party of your choice, subject to the procedures and conditions found at: http://www.networksolutions.com/en_US/makechanges/rnca/agreement.html, incorporated herein by reference. Your rights under this Agreement are not assignable and any attempt by your creditors to obtain an interest in your rights under this Agreement, whether by attachment, levy, garnishment or otherwise, renders this Agreement voidable at our option.'

Other provisions in the Service Agreement of particular interest in the context of a transfer are set out below.

- No transfer to another domain name registrar may take place within the first 60 days of registration.

- The standard duration for the initial term is two years.

- The registration may be renewed perpetually but only for one year at a time, and each renewal is subject to the payment of renewal fees.

- If the transferee acts via an ISP or other agent, it is bound by the terms as a principal.

Registrant Name Change Agreement **B2.5**

Each party will have to sign the RNCA through an individual with apparent authority to bind it. In addition, the registered owner of the domain name will have to do so in the presence of a notary public.

Completion of the RNCA   B2.6

Besides the domain name, the registered owner must insert the following details:

- the name of the transferor – this must be identical to the name which appears on the WHOIS directory on the NSI website at www.netsol.com;

- its full address with an explanation if this is not the same as the registered address; and

- the legal form of the transferor, such as corporation, partnership, limited partnership, sole proprietorship etc.

For its part, the transferee will have to complete the sections of the RNCA which cover:

- its name – this will need to be consistent with the name which appears on the submitted registration agreement (see A2 REGISTERING A DOMAIN NAME);

- its address; and

- the unique tracking number which is issued to the transferee by NSI on submission of the Service Agreement.

RNCA terms and conditions   B2.7

As explained below (see B2.13–B2.27), the RNCA really only has two primary objectives: to effect the transfer and to protect NSI. The terms and conditions are very brief. A summary of the principal provisions follows.

- NSI is discharged from all obligations and liability in respect of the domain name.

- NSI need make no refund of the original application and any other fees which it has received.

- The completion of the RNCA does not of itself operate to assign any of the domain name holder's rights.

- NSI is authorised to dissociate the domain name from the host servers. (With this in mind, the transferor, where it is not transferring content of the associated website to the transferee, must ensure that content is transferred prior to such severance.)

- The transfer only becomes effective upon NSI's transmission of an acknowledgement to the transferee that the domain name has been registered in its name. (Thus the transferee should be cautious about incurring marketing or other costs based on its new URL until such time as it has the acknowledgement to hand.)

Costs and duration   **B2.8**

At the time of writing, the NSI charges levied in respect of a domain name transfer are, as with a new registration, US$35 for the application if made via a host ISP or US$40 if the applicant does it directly. Those charges apply to a registration lasting for one year. For a two-year registration the fees are simply doubled. In either case, renewal fees will become due at the expiry of the period.

If the parties can live with the normal timescale (three to six weeks) for NSI to effect the transfer, there is no specific transfer fee. However, an expedited service, the Priority Registrant Name Change Service, is available at a cost of US$199, which provides for the processing of the transfer within two business days of receipt of complete and correct information by NSI.

Nominet   **B2.9**

In the context of transfer, .plc.uk, .ltd.uk and .sch.uk are limited in their scope, as the former two may only be owned by companies which have the relevant company name registered at Companies House, and the latter is limited to schools. They will not be considered further.

Whereas .co.uk and .org.uk domain names are freely transferable, the rules for .net.uk are more restrictive. In the case of transfers of .net.uk, the principal rules are that:

● the transferee must be an ISP;

● the domain name must be the same as, or a reasonable variant of, the transferee's name;

● the transferee must not use the domain for any service they provide on behalf of any other entity, for example the domain name may not appear in customer e-mail addresses or URLs; and

● the transferee must be either:

    ○ listed under the *Companies Act 1985* or under the *Companies (Northern Ireland) Order 1986 (SI 1986/1032)*,

    ○   a UK government department, local government body, or associated government-funded organisation,

    ○   a recognised UK academic institution, or

    ○   a UK-registered charity.

The procedure for transfer is somewhat simpler than that of NSI. The standard transfer form is to be found on the reverse of the registration certificate or can simply be obtained from Nominet by faxing them on 01865 332 295. The form must be signed by an authorised representative of each party and submitted together with a letter of confirmation signed, in each case, by the same authorised representative and, in each case, on the party's official letterhead. Each of the letters should reiterate the party's acknowledgement of adherence to Nominet's Terms and Conditions. It should be noted that the same person may not sign on behalf of both parties.

Each party agrees to be bound by Nominet's then current Terms and Conditions which are to be found at www.nominet.org.uk/terms.html.

In relation to transfer, the most important provision of the Terms and Conditions is Clause 1.7 which specifies that Nominet will:

> '. . . transfer your Domain Name and update the Register accordingly on receipt of correctly completed transfer documentation and relevant transfer fee applicable at the time of transfer'.

Nominet does, however, reserve the right to reject an application. This applies equally to a transfer, although the most frequent cause for exercise of this power seems to be where the application information provided is inaccurate.

Costs   B2.10

Nominet's Terms and Conditions provide in Clause 2.1 that the applicant (or the transferee, as the case may be) will:

> '. . . ensure that we [Nominet] receive the registration of renewal fee within one month after the issue of our invoice'.

At the time of writing, the fees are £80 for a direct application or £5 to an ISP, who is not obliged to pass any of this saving on to a client. In each case the fee covers a two-year period, subsequent to which renewal fees are payable.

Unlike the NSI procedure, the transferee gets the benefit of any unexpired part of the period for which the transferor has paid the appropriate fee. However, in Clause 1.7 of the Terms and Conditions, there is provision for payment of 'the transfer fee applicable at the time of the transfer'. This evidently allows Nominet the option to change its present policy on this matter and any parties contemplating a transfer should check the position when such transfer is under consideration.

Liquidation, administration, receivership and dissolution **B2.11**

Where a company is in liquidation, it is, as one would expect, the liquidator who has power to transfer the domain name. If the company is in administration or receivership, the first port of call will be the administrator or receiver to determine who has authority to effect the transfer. If the company has already been dissolved, the would-be transferee should contact the office of the Treasury Solicitor. In each of these cases, a fee will generally be negotiated for the transfer; in this context see B2.13–B2.27 below.

Duration **B2.12**

Nominet does not have any official parameters indicating how long a transfer might take. However, at the time of writing, four weeks would seem to be the average (assuming all the paperwork is in order).

Commercial arrangements relating to the transfer of domain names **B2.13**

The rules of bodies such as NSI and Nominet seek primarily to establish the procedure according to which transfer is to be effected and to protect the interests of the registry. The registry's transfer rules will, typically, not seek to give commercial protection or advantage to either the buyer or seller by addressing the myriad legal and commercial issues which will affect the parties. It is therefore essential for them to enter into an agreement which regulates these issues in the same way as they would for the transfer of almost any other commercial asset. The principal contents of such agreements are considered at B2.14–B2.27 below. It is, however, anticipated that the reader already has a detailed knowledge of commercial contract law and thus the review below is generally limited to provisions of particular significance in the domain name context.

(Model transfer agreements for both vendor and purchaser are included at B2.33 and B2.34 at the end of this chapter.)

Transfer and payment B2.14

On the one hand, the vendor will not want to transfer the domain name until such time as it has received payment or is convinced that it will do so. There is the possibility that the buyer may either not have the funds or may not pay up despite being able to do so.

On the other hand, the buyer (or transferee) will not want to part with its money until the domain name has been transferred to it or until it is sure that this will happen. The vendor's title to the domain name may, unbeknown to the proposed transferee, be in dispute, or the transferee may have agreed simultaneously to sell the domain name to different prospective purchasers.

The situation is complicated by the fact that the parties are both dependent on the administration and rules of a third party, the relevant domain name registrar, who may object to the proposed transfer because it infringes its rules (for example, Nominet will not allow the transfer of a .ltd.uk domain name to a partnership). Even if the registrar has no problem with the transfer, the parties must reckon on days and often weeks of delay before the transfer application is processed and the register amended.

The parties can deal with this dilemma in various ways – some possibilities are indicated at B2.15–B2.17 below.

Share of financial risk B2.15

In this scenario, the transferee might agree to pay a certain percentage of the agreed consideration on execution of the agreement and the balance after the transfer can be confirmed on the relevant WHOIS or other register maintained by the registrar in question. The transferee thus takes the risk that the transfer may not happen and that it may not recover whatever it pays in advance. The vendor is open to the possibility that the transferee may not pay the balance after the transfer is complete. Various provisions in the agreement, covering issues such as reimbursement, may reduce but not eliminate the risks.

If this plan is adopted, the vendor should consider interest provisions to cover late payment and even a provision making the time of payment of essence in the contract.

Escrow **B2.16**

In this model, after execution of the contract the purchaser might deposit the consideration monies in an escrow account held by a third party, often that of the vendor's solicitor. The monies are only to be released if and when the publicly available records accessible through the relevant WHOIS-type database show that the transfer has been effected.

Stakeholder **B2.17**

In this scheme, the purchase price is typically paid to the purchaser's solicitor who holds the funds to the vendor's order pending proof of completion of the transfer at the registry.

Vendor covenants and warranties **B2.18**

Set out at B2.19–B2.23 below are some of the principal provisions that the transferee should insist upon in this context.

Unfettered title **B2.19**

The vendor should warrant that:

- it is the sole beneficial and registered owner of the domain name;

- it has not entered into any other contract or commitment which is, or may at any time in the future, become binding upon it to sell, transfer, assign, license, or in any other way dispose of, or encumber, the domain name;

- its title is good and marketable; and

- it is entitled to sell and transfer the domain name to the purchaser free of any licence, lien, charge or encumbrance.

Non-use **B2.20**

The vendor should be obliged to give a covenant that it will cease and not recommence any use of the domain name. Additionally, no further use of associated e-mail addresses should be made.

Associated trade marks B2.21

The vendor must certify that it holds no registered or unregistered trade marks which might dilute the value of the domain name to the transferee. If there are any similar or identical trade marks, a separate sale agreement will be needed and the sale will need to be recorded at the Trade Marks Registry.

Intellectual property rights B2.22

This will comprise a warranty from the vendor that the use of the domain name does not and has not infringed the intellectual property rights of any third party, and that no third party has infringed or is infringing any of the vendor's rights in the domain name.

Further assurance B2.23

As with other commercial arrangements relating to the transfer of assets, the vendor should be obliged, at its own expense, to do all such acts and execute all such documents as may be necessary to perfect the transferee's title to the domain name.

Purchaser warranties and indemnities B2.24

Set out at B2.25–B2.27 below are some of the principal provisions that the well-informed vendor would wish to have incorporated into the agreement.

Good faith B2.25

The vendor will want to be sure that the transferee is acquiring the domain name for its own use and is not acting as a 'man of straw' for a third party whose acquisition of the domain name may be undesirable or to whom the value of the domain name would be considerably greater than the monies being offered.

Furthermore, the vendor will want to be sure that it is not being set up for a 'cybersquatting' claim whereby the apparently willing transferee may simply be trying to elicit expressions of willingness to sell from the vendor in order to try to establish that the vendor held the name in bad faith.

In this context, a provision along the following lines may be appropriate.

'The purchaser warrants to the vendor that it is purchasing [specify the domain name] in good faith for its own legitimate and lawful use and that the offer to purchase and the actual purchase of the domain name has not been undertaken for the purposes of pursuing any claim for cybersquatting or anything similar against the vendor at any time now or in the future.'

General indemnity   B2.26

The transferee may wish to acquire the domain name for a whole host of different reasons. It is possible that a third party will consider itself prejudiced and its trade mark or other rights somehow infringed by the transfer. To cover itself against any such claim, the vendor would be well advised to insist upon the inclusion of a general indemnity from the transferee to cover any claim made against the vendor, and any damage or loss suffered by the vendor as a direct or indirect result of the transfer.

Entire agreement   B2.27

This clause, which sets out the constituent parts of the agreement between the parties relating to the transfer of the domain name, should not only refer to the written agreement itself but also to any parts of the procedure or rules of the governing registry which are relevant to the transaction. For example, the RNCA in the case of NSI transfers (see B2.5–B2.7 above), or the transfer form (see B2.9 above) in the case of transfers of domain names registered by Nominet.

Transfer of registrar   B2.28

The first part of this chapter has focused on the transfer of a domain name from the existing owner to a new owner. Another form of domain name transfer occurs in relation to the registrar who administers the domain name. There may be a whole host of reasons why a domain name owner wishes to change registrars.

The most worrying cause for such transfers is the fact that certain registrars may not have appropriate security in place to prevent hackers from gaining access to the domain name servers and redirecting internet traffic, sending unaware visitors to fraudulent sites. Indeed, at the time of writing, certain computer experts claim to have discovered a flaw in software known as Berkeley Internet Name Domain ('BIND') which operates domain name servers which could facilitate such 'hijacking'.

Other reasons why a domain name owner might wish to change registrars include the following:

- another registrar may levy lower renewal charges;

- a different registrar may have what the owner considers to be a more favourable dispute resolution policy;

- the existing registrar may go out of business (a high profile example of this would be 'Justnames' which folded leaving customers having to pay certain fees again);

- the owner may select a new host for its website and that host may insist on administering the website; or

- the existing registrar may simply be inefficient.

The UK and US positions in this matter will now be considered. In effect, this means first considering the positions relating to domain names handled by Nominet (see B2.29–B2.31 below) and then regarding those handled by NSI (see B2.32 below).

United Kingdom B2.29

Nominet is the only accredited registrar in the United Kingdom. Many of its members are 'tag holders'. This means that Nominet allocates a 'tag' to them, enabling them to process domain name applications through Nominet's automated registration system ('the Automaton'). A domain name owner may wish to change the administration of its domain name:

- from an ISP which does not hold a tag to one which does; or

- from one ISP tag holder to another; or

- from an ISP tag holder to an ISP which is not a tag holder.

In any event, the domain name owner should verify whether the incumbent ISP could impose a penalty on such transfer.

Nominet will not act to transfer a domain name if it is precluded from doing so by reason of the contractual terms in force between the owner and the current ISP. In determining whether it can act, Nominet will give the ISP at least two working days in which to justify a refusal to transfer.

Moving to a Nominet tag holder   **B2.30**

Generally, it is merely necessary for the domain name owner to ask its ISP to transfer the domain name over to the tag of a different ISP. However, if the ISP refuses to do so, the owner will need to provide the Nominet Customer Support Department with the following.

- A signed request to transfer the domain name(s) to the new ISP. This should be done using the owner's letterhead and should set out full details of the problems the owner is having. This request should be on the letterhead of the domain name registrant. If the owner is a company, the letterhead must comply with the provisions of the *Companies Act 1985* – even if it is not, must clearly specify the identity of the owner(s).

- A copy of the request for transfer made to the existing ISP.

Moving to a non-tag holder   **B2.31**

The following are required:

- a request to Nominet on the owner's letterhead reciting that the new ISP is not a tag holder and specifying:

  - the domain name(s) in question,

  - details of the new ISP, and

  - details of the new host machines; and

- notification to the current ISP of the desire to transfer the domain name to a non-tag holder.

The domain name will then be moved onto a neutral Nominet tag, and be dealt with in the same way as a direct registration, including payment of the applicable charges.

United States   **B2.32**

There are over 100 registrars who have been accredited by ICANN to administer .com, .org and .net domain names. Some of the better known ones are NSI, Melbourne IT and Register.com.

Each ICANN registrar must have signed up to the NSI-Registrar License and Agreement (available at www.icann.org/nsi/nsi-rla-04nov99. htm). In relation to registrar transfer requests, this agreement specifies that each registrar must agree to implement transfers of second level domain ('SLD') registrations from one registrar to another pursuant to the Policy on Transfer of Sponsorship of Registrations Between Registrars.

The policy specifies the provisions that must be incorporated by each registrar into its official procedures and applied to transfer requests. The main provisions are that:

- no transfer is permitted within 60 days of the initial registration;

- the new registrar must obtain express authorisation from an individual with apparent authority to bind the transferor and must retain a record of this;

- where the ownership of the domain name is changing at the same time, the new registrar will also obtain appropriate authorisation of such transfer, whether that be a court order, decision of a dispute resolution body or an agreement between the parties; and

- the new registrar will submit a 'transfer command' so that the registry database can be amended to reflect the change of registrar.

The transfer request may be denied for various reasons – for example, the pending bankruptcy of the SLD holder or a dispute over the identity of the SLD holder.

Each registrar will have its own form of change of registrar agreement. NSI's Change of Registrar Agreement can be found at www.networksolutions.com/en_US/legal/cra-agreement.jhtml.

Model Transfer Agreement – Vendor   **B2.33**

Agreement for Sale of Domain Name

THIS AGREEMENT made this [   ] day of [   ] 2002

PARTIES

1.   VENDOR of [   ] (hereinafter called 'the Vendor')

2.   PURCHASER of [   ] (hereinafter called 'the Purchaser')

NOW IT IS AGREED as follows:

1.   Definitions and construction

1.1   In this Agreement the following expressions shall apply (save where the context otherwise requires).

     1.1.1   **'The Domain Name'** means all the Vendor's rights, title and interests in the domain name associated with the universal resource locator [*insert domain name*] on the internet.

     1.1.2   **'The Purchase Price'** means the consideration set out in clause 4.

     1.1.3   **'The Registry'** means the appropriate domain name registry which officially records the ownership and transfer of universal resource locators with the same top level domain, generic top level domain or country domain as the Domain Name.

     1.1.4   **'The Vendor's Solicitor'** means [*insert solicitor's name/address*].

1.2   The clause headings and any other headings are inserted for convenience only and shall not affect the construction of this Agreement.

1.3   If any of the parties hereto consist of two or more persons, their obligations hereunder shall be joint and several.

1.4   References in this Agreement to any party shall include its respective heirs, successors in title, permitted assigns and personal representatives and this Agreement shall be binding upon and inure to the benefit of the parties and their respective successors.

1.5   In this Agreement the singular includes the plural and vice versa and any gender includes any other gender and the neuter.

1.6   Reference to any statute, statutory provision, byelaw, Statutory Instrument or the like includes a reference to such provision as from time to time amended, extended or re-enacted.

1.7   References to clauses, paragraphs or a schedule are references to those clauses, paragraphs and the schedule in or annexes to this Agreement. This Agreement shall be read with the Schedule to it which shall be deemed incorporated into it.

2.   Recitals

2.1   The Vendor is the registered owner of the Domain Name as shown in the 'WHOIS' report attached as the Schedule to this Agreement.

2.2   The Vendor wishes to sell the Domain Name to the Purchaser for the Purchase Price upon the terms set out in this Agreement.

3.   Sale and purchase of domain name

3.1   The Vendor shall sell and the Purchaser shall purchase the Domain Name subject to the terms of this Agreement.

3.2   Upon execution of this Agreement each party shall fax to the other its signed counterpart hereof and each hereby undertakes to send the original of this Agreement to the other by first-class airmail. The parties acknowledge that this Agreement shall not become binding upon them until such time as each party has confirmed to the other by e-mail that it is in receipt of the signed fax copy of this Agreement from the other party which e-mail shall not be unreasonably withheld or delayed. For the purposes of this clause faxes and e-mails shall be sent to the following addresses:

Purchaser: fax: [*insert fax number*] e-mail: [*insert email address*]

Vendor: fax: [*insert fax number*] e-mail: [*insert email address*]

3.3   Upon receipt of a fax copy of the Purchaser's signed counterpart of this Agreement, the Vendor shall file a request for transfer of the Domain Name to the Purchaser with the Registry and shall immediately thereafter transmit or send by fax a copy of the said request to the Purchaser.

4. Purchase price

4.1   The Purchase Price (exclusive of Value Added Tax) to be paid by the Purchaser for the Domain Name shall be the sum of £[*insert full price to be paid*].

4.2   The Purchase Price shall be paid as follows:★

[4.2.1   50% on execution of this Agreement; and

4.2.2   50% within seven working days of the Assignment of the Domain Name being recorded at the Registry.]

[4.2.3   The Purchase Price shall be paid to the Vendor's Solicitor, who shall act as stakeholder and who shall hold the funds to the Vendor's order pending notification in writing that the Assignment has been recorded as set out in clause 4.2.4.

4.2.4   Upon receipt of a fax copy of the Vendors' counterpart of this Agreement as referred to in clause 3.2, the Purchaser shall deposit the Purchase Price into an escrow account held with the Vendor's Solicitors.

4.2.5   Within three working days of the publicly available records accessible through the 'WHOIS' database maintained by Internet Names WorldWide found at URL www.internetnamesww.com and/or the 'WHOIS' database maintained by Network Solutions, Inc. found at URL www.networksolutions.com stating that the Purchaser is the registrant of the Domain Name, the Purchaser shall instruct its aforementioned solicitors to send the Purchase Price to such bank as is nominated by the Vendor by electronic funds transfer.]

4.3   The Vendor shall acknowledge receipt of the Purchase Price and this acknowledgement shall be a full release of the Vendor from all of its obligations hereunder.

4.4   If the Purchaser fails to pay any sum due under this Agreement when it is expressed to be due, the Vendor shall be entitled to charge interest on a daily basis on all overdue amounts and on outstanding interest from the date of such failure until payment (both before and after judgment) at an annual rate 4% above the Base Rate for the time being in force of Barclays Bank plc.

4.5   For the purposes of this Agreement, time of payment shall be of the essence.

⋆ Use either clauses 4.2.1 and 4.2.2 **or** clauses 4.2.3, 4.2.4 and 4.2.5 and delete the clauses which do not apply.

5. Covenants of vendor

The Vendor covenants and undertakes to the Purchaser that it will cease and shall not recommence any and all use of the Domain Name including any use of the Domain Name as a trade mark or trade name whether registered or applied for or otherwise.⋆

⋆If the Domain Name is also a trade mark which you own, you will need a separate agreement to sell the trade mark to the Purchaser and the sale will need to be recorded at the Trade Marks Registry. If you do not wish to sell your registered trade mark, please ask your solicitor for specific advice on the legal issues which will arise.

6. Vendor's warranties⋆

6.1   The Vendor warrants to the Purchaser that there is no contract or commitment which is or may at any time in the future become binding upon it to sell, transfer, assign, license or in any other way dispose of or encumber the Domain Name other than pursuant to the provisions of this Agreement.

⋆These are standard warranties and may not apply to your particular transaction. You should review the warranties and delete any that you are not certain you can give. Please contact your solicitor if you require advice.

7. Vendor's limitation and exclusion of liability

7.1   The Vendor shall not be liable to the Purchaser for any direct, indirect or consequential loss, including without limitation any loss suffered as a result of ownership of the Domain Name by the Vendor where such loss arises from or in connection with the ownership of a trade mark (whether registered or unregistered) or any famous name or prior right which is identical to or substantially the same as the Domain Name.

7.2   The Vendor shall not be liable to the Purchaser or to any third party who owns a trade mark (whether registered or unregistered), prior right or famous name in respect of the sale of the Domain Name.

7.3   No matter how many claims are made and whatever the basis of such claims, the Vendor's maximum aggregate liability to the Purchaser under or in connection with this Agreement in respect of any direct loss (or any other loss to the extent that such loss is not excluded by clauses 7.1–7.2 above or otherwise), whether such claim arises in contract or in tort, shall not exceed twice the Purchase Price.

7.4   None of the clauses herein shall apply so as to restrict liability for death or personal injury resulting from the negligence of the Vendor, its employees or its appointed agents.

8. Purchaser's warranty and indemnity

8.1   The Purchaser warrants to the Vendor that it is purchasing the Domain Name in good faith for its own legitimate and lawful use and that the offer to purchase and the actual purchase of the Domain Name has not been undertaken for the purposes of pursuing any claim for cybersquatting (or similar) against the Vendor at any time now or in the future.

8.2   Without prejudice to the foregoing, the Purchaser hereby indemnifies and shall keep indemnified the Vendor from and against all costs, claims, demands, actions, losses (including loss of profit), liabilities, penalties and expenses sustained by the Vendor directly or indirectly (including any damages arising from any claim against it for assignment of the Domain Name to the Purchaser by the Vendor and in respect of any breach by the Purchaser of the above clause 8.1).

9. Entire agreement

This Agreement constitutes the entire agreement between the parties hereto relating to the purchase and sale of the Domain Name and supersedes all prior negotiations and agreements, whether written, oral, implied or collateral between the Vendor and the Purchaser. Nothing in this clause shall relieve either party of liability for fraudulent misrepresentations and neither party shall be entitled to any remedy for either negligent or innocent misrepresentation except to the extent (if any) that a court or arbitrator may allow reliance on the same as being fair and reasonable.

10. Amendments and waiver

10.1   No modification of or amendment to this Agreement shall be valid or binding unless set forth in writing and duly executed by both the parties hereto.

10.2   No waiver of any breach of any term or provision of this Agreement shall be effective or binding unless made in writing and signed by the party purporting to grant the waiver and unless otherwise provided, shall be limited to the specific breach waived.

11. Governing law

This Agreement shall be governed by and construed in accordance with the laws of England and Wales and the parties agree to submit to the exclusive jurisdiction of the English courts.

IN WITNESS WHEREOF the parties have signed this Agreement on the date hereof

SIGNED for and on behalf of:★

VENDOR by: [   ]

Director: [   ]

SIGNED for and on behalf of:★

PURCHASER by: [   ]

Director: [   ]

★*If the Purchaser is not a company, this clause should simply read 'SIGNED by:' and 'By:' and 'Director' should be deleted.*

Schedule

'WHOIS' report

[Insert relevant 'WHOIS' report]

Agreement for the Sale of a Domain Name

THIS AGREEMENT made this [   ] day of [   ] 2002

PARTIES

1.   VENDOR of [   ] (hereinafter called 'the Vendor')

2.   PURCHASER of [   ] (hereinafter called 'the Purchaser')

NOW IT IS AGREED as follows:

1.   Definitions and construction

1.1   In this Agreement the following expressions shall apply (save where the context otherwise requires).

1.1.1   **'The Domain Name'** means all the Vendor's rights, title and interests in the domain name associated with the universal resource locator [*insert domain name*] on the internet.

1.1.2   **'The Purchase Price'** means the consideration calculated in accordance with clause 4.

1.1.3   **'The Purchaser's Solicitor'** means [*insert solicitor's name/address*].

1.1.4   **'The Registry'** means the appropriate domain name registry which officially records the ownership and transfer of universal resource locators with the same top level domain, generic top level domain or country domain as the Domain Name.

1.2   The clause headings and any other headings are inserted for convenience only and shall not affect the construction of this Agreement.

1.3   If any of the parties hereto consist of two or more persons, their obligations hereunder shall be joint and several.

1.4   References in this Agreement to any party shall include its respective heirs, successors in title, permitted assigns and personal representatives and this Agreement shall be binding upon and inure to the benefit of the parties and their respective successors.

1.5   In this Agreement the singular includes the plural and vice versa and any gender includes any other gender and the neuter.

1.6   Reference to any statute, statutory provision, byelaw, Statutory Instrument or the like includes a reference to such provision as from time to time amended, extended or re-enacted.

1.7   References to clauses, paragraphs or a schedule are references to those clauses, paragraphs and the schedule in or annexes to this Agreement. This Agreement shall be read with the Schedule to it which shall be deemed incorporated into it.

2.   Recitals

2.1   The Vendor is the registered owner of the Domain Name as shown in the 'WHOIS' report attached as the Schedule to this Agreement.

2.2   The Purchaser, relying on the representations, warranties and undertakings by the Vendor herein contained, shall purchase the Domain Name according to the terms of this Agreement.

3.   Sale and purchase of domain name

3.1   The Vendor shall sell and the Purchaser shall purchase the Domain Name subject to the terms of this Agreement.

3.2   Upon execution of this Agreement, each party shall fax to the other its signed counterpart hereof and each hereby undertakes to send the original of this Agreement to the other by first-class airmail. The parties acknowledge that this Agreement shall not become binding upon them until such time as each party has confirmed to the other by e-mail that it is in receipt of the signed fax copy of this Agreement which e-mail shall not be unreasonably withheld or delayed. For the purposes of this clause faxes and e-mails shall be sent to the following addresses:

Purchaser: fax: [*insert fax number*] e-mail: [*insert email address*]

Vendor: fax: [*insert fax number*] e-mail: [*insert email address*]

3.3   Upon receipt of a fax copy of the Purchaser's signed counterpart of this Agreement, the Vendor shall file a request for transfer of the Domain Name to the Purchaser with the Registry and shall immediately thereafter transmit or send by fax a copy of the said request to the Purchaser.

4. Purchase price

4.1 The Purchase Price (exclusive of Value Added Tax) to be paid by the Purchaser for the Domain Name shall be the sum of £[*insert full price to be paid*].

4.2 The Purchase Price shall be paid as follows:*

[4.2.1 50% on execution of this Agreement; and

4.2.2 50% within seven working days of the Assignment of the Domain Name being recorded at the Registry.]

[4.2.3 The Purchase Price shall be paid to the Purchaser's Solicitor, who shall act as stakeholder and who shall hold the funds to the Vendor's order pending notification in writing that the Assignment has been recorded as set out in clause 4.2.4.

4.2.4 Upon receipt of a fax copy of the Vendors' counterpart of this Agreement as referred to in clause 3.2, the Purchaser shall deposit the Purchase Price into an escrow account held with the Purchaser's Solicitor.

4.2.5 Within three working days of the publicly available records accessible through the 'WHOIS' database maintained by Internet Names WorldWide found at URL www.internetnamesww.com and/or the 'WHOIS' database maintained by Network Solutions, Inc. found at URL www.networksolutions.com stating that the Purchaser is the registrant of the Domain Name, the Purchaser shall instruct its aforementioned solicitors to send the Purchase Price to such bank as is nominated by the Vendor by electronic funds transfer.]

*Use either clauses 4.2.1 and 4.2.2 **or** clauses 4.2.3, 4.2.4 and 4.2.5 and delete the clauses which do not apply.

5. Covenants of vendor

The Vendor covenants with the Purchaser as follows:

5.1   that it has the right to sell and transfer all rights, title and interests in and to the Domain Name on the terms set out in this Agreement; and

5.2   that it will at its own cost and expense, do and execute (or procure to be done and executed by any other necessary party) all such acts and documents which may be necessary to confirm the title of the Purchaser to the Domain Name as the Purchaser may from time to time require in order to vest the Domain Name in the Purchaser or as may be necessary to give full effect to this Agreement.

6.   Vendor's warranties

The Vendor warrants to the Purchaser that:

6.1   there is no contract, commitment, option or any other right of any person binding upon, or which at any time in the future may become binding upon it to sell, transfer, assign, license or in any other way dispose of or encumber the Domain Name other than pursuant to the provisions of this Agreement;

6.2   the use of the Domain Name by the Vendor does not and has not infringed or violated the intellectual property rights of any third party and no third party has infringed or is infringing or otherwise violating any of the Vendor's rights in the Domain Name;

6.3   it is the sole beneficial and registered owner of the Domain Name with good and marketable title thereto, free and clear of any licence, lien, charge or encumbrance and that it has the right to sell, transfer, and convey the Domain Name to the Purchaser.

7.   Amendments and waiver

7.1   No modification of or amendment to this Agreement shall be valid or binding unless set forth in writing and duly executed by both the parties hereto.

7.2   No waiver of any breach of any term or provision of this Agreement shall be effective or binding unless made in writing and signed by the party purporting to grant the waiver and unless otherwise provided, shall be limited to the specific breach waived.

8. Governing law

This Agreement shall be governed by and construed in accordance with the laws of England and Wales and the parties agree to submit to the exclusive jurisdiction of the English courts.

IN WITNESS WHEREOF the parties have signed this Agreement on the date hereof

SIGNED for and on behalf of:★

VENDOR by: [   ]

Director: [   ]

SIGNED for and on behalf of:★

PURCHASER by: [   ]

Director: [   ]

★*If the Purchaser is not a company, this clause should simply read 'SIGNED by:' and 'By:' and 'Director' should be deleted.*

Schedule

'WHOIS' report

[Insert relevant 'WHOIS' report]

B3 – Valuation of a Domain Name

Introduction   B3.1

It is an unenviable task to put into writing thoughts on the valuation of domain names. The internet is still a very recent business medium and techniques for integrating it into modern commercial practice are constantly changing. The consideration of value and the application of appropriate valuation techniques must follow what is happening in the commercial marketplace. With a marketplace that is constantly changing, both the considerations and the applicable techniques will change with it.

This chapter endeavours to provide a framework to assist in the consideration of value. It cannot be exhaustive but the intention is to set out some of the salient factors on which a valuation can be based.

Before considering how a valuation should be conducted, it is necessary to consider what is to be valued. The character and nature of domain names can vary widely. To explain by way of analogy, it could be considered that a domain name is a pot of paint which is intended to be placed on the canvas of the owner's choosing. How the paint is applied to the canvas is up to the artist. The canvas and the colour are a given, but the nature and skill of the artist is more important. Consider the difference in the value of paintings. There is a world of difference between the poster paint daubings of a five-year-old child and, say, something by Picasso. They may have used the same materials and the same medium but the results would be valued in different ways: the daubings of a child by reference to the joy it gives his parents; the Picasso primarily by the price that a collector would be prepared to pay for ownership at auction.

What is value?   B3.2

Before undertaking any sort of valuation it is important to understand what is meant by value. Value means different things to different people and ranges from monetary value to aesthetics. The scope of this chapter extends solely to the former. One of the best definitions the author has come across in respect of monetary value states that:

'Value is an amount expressible in terms of a single lump sum of money considered as payable or expended at a particular point in time in exchange for property, that is, the right to receive future benefits beginning at that particular time point.'

Henry Babcock PhD, FASA, Appraisal Principles and Procedures
(1994, 5th edition)

The above definition deals succinctly with the essential points in considering monetary value:

(i) value must be expressed as a single sum and not in terms of a contingent 'deal' or 'earn-out';

(ii) value is measured at a precise point in time;

(iii) value is considered by looking at the future benefits of ownership; and

(iv) value must attach to property.

Of these the first and the third are often misunderstood.

The first premise above reveals that value is effectively the cash that someone will pay, today, for an asset. Looking at actual sales of established domain names, it tends to be seen that either the asset is sold as part of a batch, or the sale contains some contingent element or is deferred. Neither of these can be related directly to a value. In order to extract the value from such a deal it is necessary to look at all deferrals, contingencies and other assets. For example, if a domain name is sold to a named company for £20,000 with £10,000 payable now and £10,000 payable in a year, then the value of the asset is not £20,000 but a figure which takes into account the delay in receiving the £10,000 and the risk that the paying company may be unable or unwilling to meet the second instalment. If the domain name also includes the computer code and data, then the proceeds need to be allocated between the various elements.

Turning to the third premise above, it is fundamentally incorrect to say that any form of value is based on the past performance of an asset, and thus the only benefits that an owner has from an asset are future benefits. Looking at historical data can be a useful tool when estimating future benefits, but to assume there is a direct correlation between historical data and value is misguided. Many 'valuations' look at averages of historical results and performance or set up complicated models to describe history, but it must be remembered that all of these techniques are trying to estimate future benefits and nothing more.

Types of value B3.3

Differing circumstances can require that the valuer make particular assumptions about the asset he is valuing. In some cases, this can lead to the valuer making widely different valuations for the same asset on the same day.

Values for tax purposes B3.4

Different taxes in different countries give directions and guidance on the assumptions and considerations that must be used in any valuation. As values are typically required in circumstances not connected to a comparable market transaction and broad consistencies must be maintained, fiscal authorities have specified, with case law providing clarification, how a valuation must take place.

It is not within the scope of this book to consider the valuation requirements of all jurisdictions, but a summary of the more common valuation requirements for UK tax purposes is set out below.

In essence, the value required is in most cases an 'open market value'. Statute does not provide a definition of the meaning of 'open market', except that it must be assumed that in the market there is available, to any prospective purchaser of the asset, the information which a prudent prospective purchaser might reasonably require if he were proposing to purchase from a willing vendor by private treaty and at arm's length.

There is no further statutory guidance on what this open market sale means. However, following the main principles established by various decided court cases, the interpretation must assume that:

- the market is a totally unrestricted one, open to all potential purchasers;

- open market value is the highest price an asset might reasonably be expected to fetch if sold in that market; and

- the sale is between hypothetical anonymous parties and the only identifiable characteristic of the vendor is that he owns the asset in question.

This is, therefore, an objective basis of valuation, which entails a depersonalised approach. This means that we cannot necessarily endow a hypothetical purchaser and vendor with the actual characteristics of the parties involved. This element has a substantial effect where partial ownership is involved.

Fair market values   **B3.5**

Valuations of this type typically are used for balance sheet purposes or commercial concerns. On occasion, this may also be the basis used for litigation purposes.

Fair market value is typically defined as the price at which one might expect the asset to be transferred between a willing seller and a willing buyer with both acting in their economic self-interest and with both being fully acquainted of the facts regarding the asset.

Fair market value could typically be thought of as representing a reasonable commercial price.

Fair values   **B3.6**

Typically this value would be used in disputes or litigation where other extraneous considerations impact on the value.

Fair value is similar to fair market value with the distinction that the price is deemed to be that which is fair between the actual parties concerned.

As a hypothetical example, XYZ Ltd is the owner of a series of domain names related to a particular service it operates. ABC Ltd owns the last domain name that could be considered relevant to XYZ Ltd. There is no dispute that ABC Ltd can continue ownership if it wishes. On the assumption that ABC Ltd does not use the name and derives no benefit from it, a fair market value of the name might be nominal, say £200. However, if the valuer were asked to comment on the fair value, he would have to take into account both what ABC Ltd could use it for and the benefit it may bring to XYZ Ltd. If it was thought that XYZ Ltd would get 'value' of £10,000 from the name then a fair value would be higher than £200.

Categorisation of domain names B3.7

The human mind finds it easier to compartmentalise and categorise objects into classes and in valuation it is no different. In view of the vastly different types and purposes of domain names and consequently the widespread of future benefits that will flow from their ownership, set out below at B3.8–B3.14 are a number of categories where similar sets of future benefits will flow. This is not intended to be exhaustive nor is it likely that any given domain name will fit into only one category.

Shop front domain B3.8

A 'shop front' domain typically relates to a website that provides e-commerce facilities for the owner. It can range from an 'outlet' domain which can be thought of as providing another outlet for an existing product or services (such as www.tesco.com) or it can be a 'principal outlet' domain where it is the main outlet for goods and services (for example www.iwantoneofthose.com). Both of these extremes use the domain to provide access to the products and services with little or no additional human input. They badge the entire retail process from advertising and demonstration through to payment and organisation of delivery.

Referrer domain B3.9

The term 'referrer domain' relates to a domain which is designed to direct business towards a particular entity but is not attached to a website which has any significant degree of e-commerce capability behind it. The majority of small businesses use this type of domain. This type of domain and the website behind it can be thought of as a commission-only salesman. Interest in the products and services is generated by the domain and website but everything from that point on is dealt with in a traditional manner.

Protection domain B3.10

A 'protection' domain is a domain name which is held merely to stop its use by another party for commercial or other reasons. The intention may be to use it for business activities in the future but in the meantime it is on hold. Typically this will be found where an entity has a trade mark or brand in a particular market but that asset is not sufficient to warrant much more of a presence other than, perhaps, the redirection of hits on the domain name to another site. A name such as www.chicken.com might be an example.

Sponsored domain **B3.11**

A 'sponsored' domain is a domain which fronts a website which in itself looks to achieve value by providing links and advertising to other domains or organisations. A typical example would be a site which offers book reviews and recommendations and which attracts sponsorship from publishers and obtains commission from referrals on to the likes of www.amazon.com.

Trawling domain **B3.12**

A 'trawling' domain is a domain which has a name related to a generic product or service. Searches for products and services will pick up these domains and the domain is used to redirect hits to another website of an entity which offers the goods or service in question. This differs from a 'referrer' domain in that the reason for the hit is the domain name itself rather than the entity behind the domain. Examples of this might be www.legaladvice.com or www.bankruptcy.com.

Affinity domain **B3.13**

An 'affinity' domain is used to front items of interest to a particular user base. There is often no immediate intention for a commercial return to be earned but the interaction between the users offers the opportunity for commerce.

At one extreme, an affinity domain can front a website with the possibility of huge benefits, such as www.friendsreunited.com. At the other it may just be a collection of acquaintances who have a common interest.

Vanity domain **B3.14**

A 'vanity' domain is the easiest to define. It is a domain name which has no commercial merit in its own right, but may have a value depending on the perceived improvement in status through its ownership. It may front a website which gives details of an individual or a website which just makes a statement. An example of the former would be www.joannebrook.co.uk whilst the latter might be www.purple.com.

Methodology   B3.15

Valuation methodology in every case follows the premise that we are looking at the future benefits accruing through ownership of the asset. Different methodologies are used where there are different costs and benefits associated with the domain. In some cases, the future benefits cannot be easily quantified as they are based entirely on what is done with the domain and what is attached to it in the future. In these cases, estimates can be based upon various techniques which, whilst they are, in the end, estimating the value of the future benefits, do so without any direct examination of those benefits.

All methodologies come down to one or more of three basic approaches: income, cost and market. Each of these is described below (see B3.16–B3.18).

Income   B3.16

Income methodologies look in some way at the enduring stream of benefits which flow to the owner of an asset. Different approaches can be used based upon the flow of cash, the recognition of profit, the alleviation of expenses or the lessening of business risk. All of these functions happen over time, and as a result the effect of time and risks both inside and outside of the model are taken into account. There are many different approaches that can be taken in various cases and for various purposes but, in some form or another, these approaches follow the mathematical model:

$$Value = \left[\sum_{1}^{n} \left(\frac{Benefit}{(1 + Discount\ Rate)^n} \right) \right] + \frac{\left(\frac{Final\ Annual\ Benefit}{n} \right)}{(1 + Discount\ Rate)}$$

Where:

- *Benefit* is the net benefit experienced in any period.

- *n* is the number of periods being considered.

- *Final Annual Benefit* is the benefit in the last period of detailed assessment.

- *Discount Rate* is the rate required to reflect risk and return during a period dependent upon the nature of the benefit.

Typically, the assessment is undertaken by projecting the benefits for a future period during which they are easier to ascertain and then arriving at a capitalised value of any enduring income stream discounting that back to the current time to reflect delay and risk.

This method is described in its simplest form, and at its most straightforward may amount to no more than predicting the current period's benefits and capitalising them using the discount rate. This is a model used in many uncomplicated cases. At the other extreme, each of the elements that make up cost and benefit in the future life of the domain name may be assigned their own risk profile. A 'value' is arrived at on the above basis which is used in aggregate to arrive at the total value of the asset.

All techniques which involve discounting future benefits in the form of ongoing benefit streams need careful consideration as there are many occasions where such methods produce anomalous or inexplicable results. Typically, this kind of method is fairly reliable when dealing with long-term benefits without extreme levels of risk. Any scenario which pushes the reliable boundaries can cause difficulties. This is most easily explained by way of example.

Example

It has been agreed that a domain name will be sold for £25,000 in a week's time providing that the current owner can remove a particular obstacle to sale. It costs nothing to remove that obstacle but the removal only has a 50 per cent chance of success. What is the value today?

Common sense suggests that the value of the domain name today is something slightly under £12,500. There is a 50 per cent chance of getting £25,000 in a week and a week's delay to be taken into account. If we assume that the cost of money is 5 per cent per annum and that there are no other risks involved, then the value of the domain name is approximately £12,488 or as near £12,500 as really makes no odds.

If we accept that value and then try to work out what annual discount rate is required to arrive at the same figure we get 450,359,861,387,773,000 per cent. Clearly utilising an enduring benefit model where relatively few benefits in a short space of time are anticipated is not workable. The closer the models get to the ideal position of smooth benefit streams over long periods the more accurate the methods are.

Hybrid methodologies based on probability scenarios tend to be used for many domain names. These look at a given set of scenarios, each of which is given a probability. The scenarios are valued as appropriate with the assumptions made in each scenario as a given. The values thrown up in each case are then multiplied by the probability of their occurrence. The aggregate of the value of these scenarios is the value of the asset.

Cost **B3.17**

The principle behind using cost as a measure of value is the broad assumption that something is worth what you've paid for it. If it were not then you would not have paid that amount for it.

This assumption can be used sensibly in the valuation of a number of different assets, but its use in domain name valuations should be countenanced only with extreme caution. With the exception of non-trading domain names, there is usually a better measure of the future benefits and thus the value.

Numerous examples of how to use 'cost' approaches to valuation can be seen in the dotcom problems of the past few years. The general principle used by many investors has been that by ploughing large quantities of money into the establishment of a website they must be creating something of value. In truth, all they were creating in some cases was the 'something' and providing temporary employment.

Market **B3.18**

This principally looks at value by reference to sales of similar assets. In many cases, this can sensibly be used, but any domain name that looks as though it should have significant value usually does so because of its uniqueness which, by definition, cannot be compared to any other. At the lower end of the valuation spectrum, and particularly in cases of vanity domains (see B3.14 above), it may be that value can be looked at by reference to the price that market is charging to allocate those domains. If that price fluctuates wildly in the future then this will have an effect on values of these domains.

Examples of contributions to value   B3.19

Set out at B3.20–B3.25 below are a number of hypothetical (at the time of writing) examples of how valuations in their simplest form might be conducted for each type of domain name. The methods used have been pared down to their essential core to illustrate the thinking behind them rather than being complete. In each case there are numerous additional elements which would need to be added in to arrive at a full valuation, but the intention is to illustrate principles rather than provide blueprints.

Sponsored domain   B3.20

The domain name www.ireallylikegardengnomes.com was set up at a cost of £20 by Mr. Sadd. Mr. Sadd's hobby is the collection of gnomes; he has travelled extensively throughout the UK visiting various gnome displays and has detailed all of these reviews on the site with maps and admission prices. He has also undertaken a review of various gnome manufacturers and maintains links through his website to these and the gnome displays. As a thank you, each of the manufacturers gives Mr Sadd five per cent commission on any sales that come through people referred from his site, and two of his favourite gnome displays allow him free access.

Future benefits:

- Mr Sadd makes about £50 a month in commission from gnome sales; and

- Mr Sadd would normally pay £5 a month to get into his favourite gnome displays.

Future costs:

- it takes Mr Sadd an hour a week to update his website and he would otherwise be working in a fast food chain earning £5 an hour; and

- it costs Mr Sadd £20 a year to have his site hosted.

A value might be considered as follows.

	£	
Annual Benefits	660	
Less		
Direct Costs	20	
Opportunity Costs	260	
Net Benefit Per Annum	380	
Required Return		25%
Total Value	1,520	

Shop front domain   B3.21

Mr Strange has registered the domain name www. strangethingstodowithstring.com. Behind that domain, he has a website selling all sorts of string-based products, from string itself through to string holders and winders, and more esoteric goods including care kits for your favourite bits of string. He sources all of these goods from an external wholesaler. His website includes full online purchasing facilities, and orders are directly processed and sent to a fulfilment house. Other than updating the website for new items as they arrive and collecting the cash rolling into his bank account, all that Mr Strange has to do is to pay for maintenance of the domain name and his e-commerce solutions.

Mr Strange estimates that it cost him around £5,000 to set up his website and, including the cost of his e-commerce solutions, it costs him £100 a month to run. He makes regular profits of £500 a month and has to spend an hour a week on maintenance. He has another job which pays him £10 an hour. He believes this to be a true reflection of the value to him of that hour.

In this case a value might be considered as follows,

	£	
Annual Benefits	6,000	
Less		
Direct Costs	1,200	
Opportunity Costs	480	
Net Benefit Per Annum	4,320	
Required Return		25%
Total Value	17,280	

However, this is not the value of the domain name, but rather the value of the domain name and the attached website. This figure will be apportioned between the two. If, for instance, it was believed that half of the benefits flowed because of the name and the fact that it was now bookmarked by many repeat customers, then the value of the domain name itself might be £8,640.

Referrer domain   B3.22

David Trugg Ltd is a UK company which has a large sales force travelling the UK selling branded Truggs, an essential part in any widget-making machine. The company has set up the domain www.brandedtruggs.co. uk, which contains details of their product, a price list and the telephone number of its mail order department. Trugg salesmen make 30 per cent commission on the sale of Truggs and these have a retail price of £100. In order not to annoy and demotivate the salesmen, the mail order price of Truggs is also £100. The company estimates that it needs an extra member of staff in the mail order department to deal with these enquiries at an annual cost, including overheads of £20,000 a year. It also sells 100 of these a month through referrals from the domain.

The company might consider the value of the domain as follows.

	£	
Hence	120,000	
Sales Commission Saved (30%)	36,000	
Less		
Direct Costs	20,000	
Net Benefit	16,000	
Required Return		25%
Total Value	64,000	

The required return in this case may in some circumstances relate to the required rate of return on an investment in the company rather than the risk associated with the domain itself. As an example, if David Trugg Ltd were up for sale and the sale were proceeding on the basis of a capitalisation multiple of 10 on the pre-tax profit this year, then crudely the domain could be responsible for adding £160,000 to the sale proceeds.

Protection domain   B3.23

Protection domains are extremely difficult to value as rather than bringing a benefit they prevent someone else obtaining a benefit. At the lowest extreme these may have a value little more than the costs of registration, but at the other extreme they may have a significant value by increasing the barrier to entry of a major competitor into the market.

Looking back at the Trugg example (see B2.22 above) and making the unlikely assumption that there is no reason why another manufacturer could not register the domain www.brandedtruggs.com, then clearly having that name would be of benefit to David Trugg Ltd. The competitor actually sells virtually identical Truggs which differ from those made by David Trugg Ltd only by colour. They are cheaper at £90 but make the same profit of £20 per Trugg as the first company, and if many of its customers found this alternative supply then it would lose some. The competitor bizarrely has no other way of making inroads into David Trugg Ltd's marketplace.

If it were estimated that David Trugg Ltd would lose ten per cent of the sales it made to any customer who found the competitor, and the statistics on www.brandedtruggs.com show that 30 of David Trugg Ltd's customers each year who account for the sale of 100 Truggs per annum (the same 30 strangely enough) accidentally look at this other site first, then we might value that name as follows.

	£	
Sales Not Lost	1,000	
Therefore		
Profit Not Lost	200	
Required Return		25%
Total Value	800	

Vanity domain B3.24

Typically a vanity domain has no value other than the cost of registering the name. However, it is worth considering circumstances in which such a name may have a value.

Take the previous example of www.joannebrook.co.uk, and assume that attached to this domain name was a website which detailed all of the bizarre and exciting social activities of the individual named. Accordingly, by word of mouth, larger numbers of individuals bookmark the domain name and see it as a place in which to look for the latest 'happening' events in the London area. Within about a year the traffic is such that it attracts the attention of events organisers in London. Such an events organiser would be prepared to pay for the domain name on the grounds that they have a captive audience who have a well-known disposition towards events in the capital. They would be prepared to make an offer based upon the proportion of the additional profit they thought they could generate from the exploitation of the bookmarking individuals.

Affinity domain   **B3.25**

At one extreme, an affinity domain could be valued in the same way as a vanity domain; at the other extreme it could be valued in a similar way to one of the other classifications of domain, depending upon the commercial and monetary return experienced by the owners of the domain.

Note: Astute readers might notice that, coincidentally, in all of the valuation examples a required rate of return of 25% is suggested. Any similarity between this required rate of return and any actual required rate of return on a given domain name is purely coincidental.

Examples of domain names sold   **B3.26**

As you would expect, the open market is typically reticent about revealing the prices at which many deals take place. However, a limited part of the sale to take place, being mainly those of sponsored or trawling domain names, is open to inspection as domain names are subject to auctions. Six domain names are set out below, alongside the current best evidence of the prices that they have fetched.

Name	Estimated Price	Type
taste.co.uk	£110,000	shop front/trawling
internetters.co.uk	$70,000	sponsored/trawling
architecture.com	$190,000	trawling
joannebrook.co.uk	£10	vanity
happybirthday.com	$55,000	sponsored/trawling
fruits.com	$160,000	trawling

Conclusion   **B3.27**

The valuation of domain names in isolation is a tricky matter. This chapter has covered the general principles behind valuations and the considerations one would need to take on board before undertaking a valuation. Typically, every valuation is unique and is made up of a number of elements. The temptation is to build up complicated models which describe the behaviour and considerations of each domain, and whilst this is an essential part of the valuation process, it cannot be over-emphasised that the overriding principle of looking at the benefits flowing to the owner must always be uppermost in the valuer's mind.

Part C: Changing Domain Name Registration Information

C1 – Changing Domain Name Registration Information

Introduction   C1.1

The procedure for changing domain name registration information differs according to whether the domain name is a gTLD or a .uk ccTLD (see C1.2–C1.16 below).

Global top level domains   C1.2

For gTLDs, such as:

- .com;
- .net;
- .org;
- .biz;
- .info; and
- .name,

the procedures for changing the contact details and name servers depend upon which registrar has management of the domain name. If it is unknown with which registrar the domain name is registered, it can be checked on the Verisign Registry website at www.crsnic.net. An example of such a check is set out at C1.3 below.

Example of Verisign registrar check   C1.3

Whois Server Version 1.3

Domain names in the .com, .net and .org domains can now be registered with many different competing registrars. Go to http://www.internic.net for detailed information.

Domain Name: NOMINET.NET

Registrar: Network Solutions, Inc.

Whois Server: whois.networksolutions.com

Referral URL: http://www.networksolutions.com

Name Server: NS1.INSNET.NET

Name Server: NS0.INSNET.NET

Name Server: NS0.NOMINET.ORG.UK

Updated Date: 13-jun-2001

This shows that the domain name 'nominet.net' is registered with Network Solutions as the registrar.

Registrars   C1.4

Details of the procedures under some of the main registrars are set out at C1.5–C1.9 below.

Network Solutions/Verisign   C1.5

If the registrar is Network Solutions/Verisign ('NSI'), control of the domain name lies with the recorded administrative contact and/or the technical contact. It is best practice for domain name registration companies to list the client as the administrative contact, and generally the website hosting company would be the technical contact. However, in some cases, all of the contacts may be the domain registration company. This information is visible by doing a WHOIS check on the domain name record. Either the administrative contact or the technical contact is empowered to change any aspect of the domain name record (apart from the legal registrant or 'owner' of the domain name). Details of the record which can be changed are:

- the address of the registrant;

- the names, addresses, telephone numbers and e-mail addresses of the administrative, billing and technical contacts; and

- the names and IP addresses of the name servers, which determine where the domain name is pointed to.

Security C1.6

There are three levels of security possible to protect the domain name from unauthorised changes. The lowest level (and the default) is 'Mail-From'. This system enables anyone, not necessarily one of the named contacts, to initiate a change to the record. An e-mail is then sent to the e-mail addresses recorded for the administrative contact and the technical contact seeking confirmation of the requested changes. Whichever of these two contacts replies first, whether they are agreeing to or declining the modification, determines whether the request is accepted or rejected. However, there is a potential major flaw in this system. If an unscrupulous person were to initiate a change, it might be possible for him to 'spoof' the e-mail response, as if it had come from one of the two named contacts, and thereby gain control of a domain name. There have been many instances of this and it could take lengthy and expensive court action to recover a name which has been 'hijacked' in this way. In the meantime, your domain name could have been 'pointing' to another website, for example an 'adult' site, or may not resolve to any active site.

More security is possible using one of the other two systems, 'Crypt-PW' or 'Pretty Good Privacy' ('PGP'). Crypt-PW requires a specified password to be entered for any domain name changes, and PGP requires a previously-advised digital signature to be used for any changes. Any contact registered with NSI can have any domain names managed by it protected by either of these systems by applying through the NSI website (www.networksolutions.com).

Critical to maintain administrative contact data C1.7

A key issue concerning the management of a NSI domain name is to ensure that the administrative and technical contacts' details are kept up-to-date. If either of the two e-mail addresses is no longer current, the confirmation e-mails will be sent to the wrong address or 'bounce'. In a worst case scenario, both may bounce, and it then becomes very difficult to manage the domain name record. NSI do provide some mechanisms to update the records, requiring faxes on letterheads and manual intervention by its staff. However, this is not easy and can be time-consuming as NSI is based in the USA and getting through by telephone to anyone who can assist with the process can be difficult. It is far easier to ensure that the administrative and technical contact records are always well-maintained.

A word of warning – some domain name registration companies use their own details for all contacts. This can cause problems if they cease to trade, or wish to try and block any changes to the records. The first situation, ceasing to trade, means that any confirmation e-mails will bounce and the domain name record is effectively 'locked'. The only solution is then to get NSI manually to update the record, with the associated difficulties explained above. The second scenario, blocking any changes, can enable such a company to prevent a move of website hosting provider for whatever reason – financial, legal, a misunderstanding or malice.

Good advice is always to insist that valid, current contact details of someone in your own organisation are used for the administrative contact for all of your domain names.

Internet Names Worldwide   **C1.8**

Internet Names Worldwide ('INWW') was one of the first batch of new registrars set up when NSI lost its monopoly on the registration of .com, .net, and .org domain names in July 1999. Originally based in Melbourne, Australia, INWW now also has offices in Virginia, USA, and works through a number of channel partners in the UK, including Internetters (www.internetters.co.uk), Net Benefit (www.netbenefit. com) and Virtual Internet (www.vi.net). INWW uses a different security system for domain name management called a 'registry key'. This is an alphanumeric password, generally of eight characters, which can be supplied to the client by the domain name registration company. The registry key enables the client, or any other authorised person, such as a website designer, to access the domain name record and change the address of the registrant, and the contacts and name servers details, all in real time.

As with any password, the registry key should be carefully protected to prevent unauthorised access. If there is reason to believe that the security could have been compromised, a new registry key can be issued.

Other registrars   **C1.9**

There are over 150 registrars in total, each with different systems, but most employ some form of user name and password access to the records. As many of these systems are automated, it is essential to retain details of the user names or passwords, as it may be difficult to contact the registrar to obtain them if they are mislaid.

It is recommended that you acquaint yourself with whichever system applies to the registrar that you or your domain name registration company have used, and that you ensure that you have the ability to make changes to your domain name records easily and effectively. If you are uneasy with the current system, you may wish to change registrar (see below for how to do this).

Changing registrar C1.10

Once 60 days have elapsed from the initial registration of your domain name, and provided that there are no existing disputes, for example unpaid bills or a challenge to the domain name by another party under the disputes policy etc., you can apply to change registrar. This may be for various reasons: operational reasons on the advice of your domain name registration or website hosting company, lower charges, better security and so on. Procedures vary so it is best to check with the domain name registration company or the registrar to determine how to proceed. This is relatively easy and can be done at any time from 60 days after the initial registration of the domain name. The cost of the process varies, but you would usually expect to retain the existing portion of the unexpired registration period already paid for, and to have at least one year added to it.

It is again important to ensure that you still retain the ability to change the records after the change of registrar.

Change of registrant C1.11

Changing the legal registrant or 'owner' of a domain name is an important modification, as it changes 'title' to the domain name. This may be required if:

- you have purchased the domain name from another party;

- the name of your company has changed; or

- the name originally used was incorrect (perhaps the domain name registration company or the website designer registered the domain name in its own name rather than yours).

Procedures vary between registrars, but it is likely that firm evidence will be required to substantiate the change, for example a formal letter on the original company's letterhead, a contract or similar document.

Network Solutions   C1.12

If the domain name was registered with NSI, a registrant name change agreement form can be downloaded from its website (www. networksolutions.com). This needs to be signed in the presence of a notary public and then sent to NSI in the USA. The change can take several weeks, but it is possible to reduce this to a few days, on payment of an 'express' fee of $199 (at the time of writing). This timescale and/or cost can sometimes mean that it is cheaper and more efficient to move from NSI to an alternative registrar and then change the registrant. In cases of uncertainty, this should be checked with the domain name registration company.

Internet Names Worldwide   C1.13

INWW empowers certain of its channel partners to initiate a change of registrant, again subject to the production of suitable evidence. The cost varies. For example, Internetters charges £25 and the process can be completed within a couple of days. There is a safeguard included for the original registrant by means of an e-mail being sent to the current administrative contact advising it of the change and inviting it to reply if it wishes to challenge it.

Other registrars   C1.14

Again with other registrars, there may be slightly different procedures in place. Check with your domain name registration company or the registrar itself.

Note: For further information on changing registrar see B2 DOMAIN NAME TRANSFERS.

Deleting a domain name   C1.15

Deleting a domain name is possible, but it is not very straightforward and in general it is probably better to leave a domain name in existence and merely point it to the new website. Generally, the view taken by registrars is that if a domain name has been prepaid for a number of years it is better to let it lapse on expiry, and then to release it back to the marketplace.

There are only a few situations where the deletion of a domain name is required. An example could be where unauthorised use has been made of a company's trade mark or service mark as part of a domain name. This could be achieved by a UDRP ruling, court action or mutual agreement. However, deletion of a domain name does not prevent a new party from then registering it. It might be better to transfer the domain name to the trade mark holder – by agreement, purchase, UDRP etc. – and then maintain the domain name, if only to prevent further abuses by new registrants.

If a domain name needs to be deleted because it is incorrect, for example if the registrant or registration company made a spelling error, or if it is simply surplus to requirements, this may be possible without charge if requested very quickly after registration, perhaps within 24 to 48 hours. By way of example, Internetters would accept the cancellation or deletion of a new domain name within those timescales without charge. After that time, the registration company itself would have irrevocably incurred charges, and even if the registrant wished to cancel it would be unlikely to receive a refund. All this would depend on the terms and conditions applicable to the registration.

.uk domains   C1.16

Generally, Nominet prefers not to register domain names directly for customers. Instead, it has appointed over 2,000 members as 'tag holders', giving them direct access to Nominet's registration systems to register domain names and update the domain name records. A list of such tag holders can be found on Nominet's website at www.nic.uk/ref/taglist. html.

Tag holders are responsible for updating any information about a domain name. Details of the record which can be changed are:

- the address of the registrant;

- the names, addresses, telephone numbers and e-mail addresses of the administrative, billing and technical contacts; and

- the names and IP addresses of the name servers, which determine where the domain name is pointed to.

In addition, the tag holder can transfer (or 'release') the tag for any domain name to another active tag holder.

To find the tag holder for any specific domain name, go to the WHOIS record and check the 'Domain registered by' line. The tag is often just the company's name, but it can sometimes be more cryptic. Further information can be found by referring to Nominet's tag holder list.

Example of a .uk domain name WHOIS record C1.17

WHOIS query result:

Domain name: ELECTROLUX-DIRECT.CO.UK

Registered for: Electrolux Home Products

Domain registered by: INTERNETTERS

Registered on 02-May-2000.

Domain servers listed in order:

NS1.INTERNETTERS.NET   207.228.254.8

NS2.INTERNETTERS.NET   66.38.135.70

WHOIS database last updated at 09:35:01 14-Sep-2001

The NIC.UK Registration Host contains ONLY information for domains within co.uk, org.uk, net.uk, ltd.uk and plc.uk. Please use the whole server at rs.internic.net for Internet Information or the whole server at nic.ddn.mil for MILNET Information.

Individual tag holders will have different procedures for handling updates or modifications to the domain record, but generally, in order to protect the client from an unauthorised person requesting changes to the domain name, it will require firm evidence in writing (by letter or fax) or by confirmed e-mail to support any changes. It may be a useful check on the procedures of any domain name registration company to ensure that it confirms who you are and requires some proof of authority before accepting verbal changes.

Generally when changing website hosting companies, at least the name servers would need to be changed to those of the new hosting company. However, many hosting companies prefer greater control, and would ask for the domain name tag to be released to them. Once authorised (usually in writing by fax on letterhead), either of these changes can be made in a few minutes by the ceding tag holder and will generally not incur any charges. In some cases though, the ceding ISP or tag holder may impose a 'release charge'. You should check the terms and conditions of your registration company to confirm if this is valid, as it has been known for some registration companies to levy such 'release charges' even though this may not be mentioned in their terms and conditions or frequently asked questions.

The tag holder is also responsible for billing you for any renewals of the domain name, which can currently only be done in two-year periods. Tag holders' charges for renewal vary greatly. It is advisable to check the renewal charges of the company you are using, or are transferring to.

Change of registrant C1.18

Changing the legal registrant or 'owner' of a domain name is an important modification, as it changes 'title' to the domain name. This may be required if:

- you have purchased the domain name from another party;

- the name of your company has changed; or

- the name originally used was incorrect (perhaps the domain name registration company or the website designer registered the domain name in its name rather than yours).

The procedure to change the registrant for a UK domain requires both parties to complete and sign the reverse of the domain name certificate. If the certificate cannot be found, a domain name transfer form can be requested by the current legal registrant who should fax a letter to Nominet on 01865 332295. The completed and signed certificate or domain name transfer form is then sent to Nominet, together with signed letters by each party on their respective letterheads, confirming the transfer and accepting Nominet's terms and conditions. Full details of this process can be found on Nominet's website at www.nominet.net/howto/transfer.html.

Deleting a domain name C1.19

To delete a .uk domain name, it is necessary to 'surrender' it. This is achieved by completing and signing the appropriate section on the back of the certificate. If the certificate has not yet been received from Nominet, the registrant can contact Nominet to request surrender documents. The certificate or surrender document is then sent to Nominet for processing. If the domain name has only just been registered (generally within 30 days) it may be possible for the tag holder to delete the domain name. If in doubt, check with your registration company. Once deleted, the domain name can then be released back to the marketplace, for someone else to register in due course.

Part D: Domain Name Disputes

D1 – Introduction to Domain Name Disputes

How domain name disputes arise   D1.1

Domain names are in most cases allocated on a first-come, first-served basis, without investigation of the registrant's entitlement to the name. It is therefore possible to register a domain name which is considered by another party to infringe its rights, resulting in a dispute.

The circumstances of such disputes vary enormously.

- Some cases concern blatant cybersquatting, where a person registers a domain name incorporating the name of a well-known company and tries to sell it for a substantial sum of money to that company, as in the *One in a Million* case (*British Telecommunications v One in a Million*).

- In other cases, two or more parties have independent, legitimate rights, such as where an American company, which sold tennis racquets under the name Prince, and an English company, which supplied software under the name Prince, disputed the domain name Prince.com, without any intervention from the pop star known as Prince (*Prince v Prince Sports Group*).

- In a third type of case, a domain name incorporating a well-known brand is registered without the consent of the brand owner, but the registrant claims that he should be permitted to use it, for example to express criticism or appreciation of the complainant ('grudge' or 'fan' sites), or in a way which does not relate to the complainant.

  An example of this last category might be the *fcuk.com* case (*French Connection v Sutton*), where this domain name was registered shortly after the clothes retailer French Connection instituted a controversial advertising campaign featuring 'fcuk', which was said to refer to 'French Connection UK'. However, the registrant, an e-mail consultant, showed that 'fcuk' was often used on the internet as an alternative to 'f★★★', and said that he registered it because it would enhance his 'street cred' in the internet community. French Connection's application for summary judgment was dismissed.

Note: References to published reports and other details of cases mentioned in chapters D1 to D5 can be found in the Tables of Cases towards the end of the book. Many of these decisions have been posted on the internet by, for example, ICANN (see www.icann.org for decisions on gTLD names under the UDRP), the WIPO Arbitration and Mediation Center (see www.arbiter.wipo.int for WIPO decisions on gTLD and ccTLD names) and Nominet (see www.nic.uk for decisions on .uk names). For other useful sites, see the links page at www.jonathanturner.com.

Procedural abnormalities   **D1.2**

In most cases it is clear that one party registered the domain name before the other party, and the question is simply whether the first-come, first-served allocation should be displaced on the ground that the complainant's rights should prevail. Occasionally, however, an issue arises as to which party should have been allocated the domain name in the first place, usually where there has been some abnormality in the procedure.

In this type of case, it may be necessary to consider whether the procedure followed when allocating the domain name was contrary to the terms and conditions of the registrar or registry. If so, the aggrieved party may be able to bring a claim against the registrar or registry for breach of contract, or possibly against the rival registrant for inducing a breach of contract. However, in the *Pitman* case (*Pitman v Nominet*), the domain name 'Pitman.co.uk' was allocated first to Pitman Publishing and then by mistake to Pitman Training. The English High Court held that Pitman Training had no valid claim against Pitman Publishing for insisting on the reallocation of the domain name, although Pitman Training may have had a claim against the registry.

It may also be possible to argue that a domain name registry is a public body subject to administrative law requirements, including, for example, the requirement to:

- act fairly;

- give both parties an opportunity to make representations; and

- take into account relevant considerations and avoid irrelevant ones.

This may be the case even if the registry is not a formal government organisation. Thus it was held in the *Datafin* case that decisions of the UK Takeover Panel, which is responsible for regulating the conduct of takeovers of UK public companies, have been held to be subject to judicial review under UK law (*R v Panel on Takeovers and Mergers, ex parte Datafin*), even though this body and its rules are constituted by agreement between institutions and associations in the City of London rather than government decision or legislation.

Cases of abnormal procedure are rare and turn on particular, atypical facts. Chapters D1–D5 will therefore focus on the much more common case where a regular, first-come, first-served registration is challenged by another party claiming rights in relation to the domain name.

National and EU laws governing domain names

D1.3

Rights in relation to names are conferred by national and EU laws on registered trade marks and unfair competition. To secure protection under a registered trade mark law, a name must be registered at a trade mark office. This requires an application, which will often be examined to determine whether the name is sufficiently distinctive to be protected as a trade mark, and whether it conflicts with earlier registrations or applications. By contrast, unfair competition laws can protect names which have not been registered, particularly if they have a reputation, and the rights thus conferred are sometimes described as 'unregistered trade mark rights'. In the UK, the relevant type of unfair competition is normally called 'passing off', and in the US, the term 'palming off' is often used.

Trade mark and unfair competition laws

D1.4

Trade mark and unfair competition laws are mostly organised on national lines, with each country having its own law applying to activities within its jurisdiction and each providing for the registration of trade marks at its national trade mark office, or, in some countries, regional or local offices. The different national laws are generally similar, but by no means identical, and a registration of a trade mark in one country does not, in general, confer rights in another country.

However, there has been a considerable degree of harmonisation of the registered trade mark laws within the EU. The national trade mark systems of the member states have been retained, but the main substantive provisions of the national laws are required to conform to *EC Directive 89/104/EC* (*First Council Directive on the approximation of trade mark laws in the Member States*). The national laws continue to be implemented by the national trade mark offices and national courts, but issues on the interpretation of the Directive are referred to the European Court of Justice ('ECJ').

In addition, Community trade marks, effective throughout the EU, can now be obtained by application to the Community Trade Mark Office, formally called the Office for Harmonisation in the Internal Market. These trade marks are governed by *EC Regulation 40/94/EC (Regulation on the Community Trade Mark)*, whose main substantive provisions are the same as those of *EC Directive 89/104/EC*. They are enforced by proceedings in national courts, but again issues on the interpretation of the Regulation are referred to the ECJ.

By contrast, there has been no EU legislation harmonising the national laws of the member states on unfair competition, although unjustified or disproportionate barriers to trade between member states of the Community are prohibited under *Articles 28* (formerly *Art 30*) and *49* (formerly *Art 59*) of the *Treaty of Rome*.

In the United States, rights in names can be protected under the federal law of registered trade marks and under both federal and state laws on unfair competition.

Protection by other laws   **D1.5**

Names may occasionally be protected by laws other than those governing registered trade marks and unfair competition in the nature of passing off. For example, a confidential plan to develop a new business under a particular name may be protected by the law on trade secrets. This may be illustrated by the *De-riskit.com* case, where the registrant got the idea of establishing a consultancy under this name, specialising in the mitigation of risks in the implementation of computer systems, from confidential discussions about its possible participation in the complainant's proposed business in the same field under the name 'Deriskit.com'. However, laws on trade secrets will not protect a name when it is no longer confidential.

Names may also be protected by special laws such as *section 12* of the *German Civil Code* which gives individuals and entities exclusive rights in their own names. The rights of the cities of Heidelberg and Celle under this provision were held to be infringed by the registration of *Heidelberg.de* and *Celle.de*, although contrary decisions were given in relation to *Kerpen.de*, *Hürth.de* and *Pulheim.de*. The significance of this law was emphasised by the *Winter* case, where the scion of a German dynasty of vintners, the fifth J.C. Winter in eight generations, objected to the use of his name by the respondent, which had bought the assets of the family business including the registered mark 'J.C. Winter gegr. 1838'. The objection was upheld by the German Supreme Court.

In the USA, the *Anti-cybersquatting Consumer Protection Act 1999* (*ACPA 1999*) specifically prohibits the registration of a domain name which is identical or confusingly similar to the name of a living person with the specific intent to profit by selling the domain name.

On the other hand, names are usually regarded as too insubstantial to qualify for copyright protection (*Exxon Corp v Exxon Insurance Consultants International*; *Francis Day Hunter v Twentieth Century Fox*).

Internet dispute resolution policies D1.6

Trade mark and unfair competition laws have been developed to resolve disputes relating to the use of names in conventional commerce. They are not ideally suited to resolving all types of domain name disputes for a number of reasons.

- In many countries, legal proceedings are expensive and slow. While the cost and delays of legal proceedings are unsatisfactory even in relation to conventional commerce, they have been particularly problematic in the context of the rapid development of the internet.

- In conventional commerce, the same or similar names can often be used and/or registered concurrently by different persons without conflict. By contrast, domain names are unique, so that the registration of a given domain name by one party makes it unavailable for use by another without the co-operation of the registrant.

- Laws and courts are generally organised along national lines, whereas the internet is international. Any domain name is accessible throughout the world and its use can readily affect the business of a company operating in other countries. However, it may be difficult and expensive for a complainant to pursue a legal claim against a registrant in another country, or even impossible if the complainant does not have rights in the country where the domain name is being used.

  In the *Crateandbarrel* case (*Euromarket Designs v Peters*), the English High Court rejected the suggestion that a shop in Ireland which established a website for its business should be regarded as 'putting a tentacle onto the user's screen', and thus using the domain name in the UK where the complainant had trade mark rights. The judge preferred the analogy that the website was like a shop window in Dublin, and the internet like a super-telescope enabling it to be seen from the Welsh hills, without any infringement being carried out by the website owner in the UK.

These difficulties have led to the development by internet authorities of DRPs to provide a more appropriate and cost-effective means of resolving domain name disputes. These policies specify in what circumstances a complaint will be regarded as justified and provide that, if it is justified, the domain name may be transferred to the complainant or revoked. They also lay down procedures under which complaints are to be determined in accordance with the applicable policy by impartial 'panels' or 'experts'.

Strictly speaking, the legal basis of DRPs is contractual. A person applying for a domain name is required to accept the applicable policy and submit to the procedure in the event of a complaint, while a complainant who wishes to invoke the procedure is also required to accept the policy and submit to the procedure. Although separate contracts are made between the respondent and the registrar and between the complainant and the service provider, it is thought that a contract between the parties to accept the policy and procedure, of the kind recognised by the House of Lords in *Clarke v Dunraven*, is also created. However, effectively DRPs constitute separate legal systems for determining domain name disputes.

ICANN UDRP D1.7

The most significant DRP is the Uniform Domain Name Dispute Resolution Policy ('UDRP') adopted by ICANN in October 1999. The policy was then applied to all names, whenever they were registered, in the existing .com, .net and .org. gTLDs, and has since been or will be extended to the new .aero, .biz, .coop, .info, .museum, .name and .pro gTLDs. (The UDRP is discussed in detail in D4 THE ICANN DISPUTE RESOLUTION POLICIES (UDRP AND STOP), and the policy and rules are reproduced in APPENDIX 2. Full information is available on the ICANN website at www.icann.org and the WIPO website at http://arbiter.wipo. int/domains/index.html.)

The UDRP has also been applied to the following ccTLDs.

.ag (Antigua & Barbuda)	.na (Namibia)
.as (American Samoa)	.nu (Niue)
.bs (Bahamas)	.pa (Panama)
.bz (Belize)	.ph (Philippines)
.cc (Cocos Islands)	.pn (Pitcairn Island)
.cy (Cyprus)	.ro (Romania)
.ec (Ecuador)	.tt (Trinidad and Tobago)
.fj (Fiji)	.tv (Tuvalu)
.gt (Guatemala)	.ve (Venezuela)
.la (Laos)	.ws (Western Samoa)

DRPs based on the UDRP have been adopted for the .ca (Canada), .mx (Mexico), .sg (Singapore) and .us (USA) ccTLDs.

Nominet DRP   D1.8

A DRP similar to the UDRP but with some significant differences was adopted in late 2001 by Nominet for the .uk ccTLD. (The Nominet DRP is discussed in detail in D5 THE NOMINET DISPUTE RESOLUTION SERVICE POLICY below, and the policy and procedure are reproduced in APPENDIX 4. Full information is available on the Nominet website at www.nic.uk.)

Supplementary DRPs for new gTLDs   D1.9

In addition to the UDRP, the new gTLDs also have or will have supplementary DRPs governing disputes in the start-up period or concerning the qualifications for registration in restricted domains:

● The .biz gTLD has a start-up trademark opposition policy ('STOP') under which complainants who filed intellectual property claims during the pre-registration period can object to the registration of domain names on essentially the same basis as under the UDRP. STOP is discussed further in D4 ICANN DISPUTE RESOLUTION POLICIES (UDRP AND STOP). The .biz gTLD also has a restrictions dispute resolution policy ('RDRP') for disputes concerning violations of the restrictions applicable to .biz registrations.

● The .info gTLD has a sunrise challenge policy ('SCP') under which registrations in the sunrise period (reserved to owners of identical trade marks) could be challenged on the basis of lack of the required qualifications for sunrise registration. The period for filing ordinary challenges under the SCP expired on 26 December 2001, but 'challenges of last resort' can still be filed by the Registry.

- The .name gTLD has an eligibility requirements dispute resolution policy ('ERDRP') for disputes concerning compliance with the applicable registration restrictions.

- It is intended that the .aero, .coop and .museum gTLDs will have a charter eligibility dispute resolution policy ('CEDRP') for disputes concerning eligibility requirements.

- It is intended that the .pro gTLD will have a SCP, but details have not yet been announced at the time of writing.

Other dispute resolution policies D1.10

A list of major ccTLDs and the applicable dispute resolution arrangements is contained in APPENDIX 5.

Which procedure? D1.11

A person wishing to complain about a domain name registration often has a choice between:

- proceedings under national or EU law in an appropriate court; and

- proceedings under an applicable DRP determined by a panel or expert appointed by or on behalf of the relevant internet authority.

However, a decision to proceed under the DRP does not rule out court proceedings pending or after the DRP determination. In particular, if a complaint under the DRP is rejected, the complainant may still bring proceedings for trade mark infringement or unfair competition in the courts. If, on the other hand, the complaint is upheld, the domain name holder is allowed a short period to submit the dispute to a court before the decision to transfer or revoke the domain name is put into effect (ICANN UDRP, clause 4(k); Nominet DRSP, clause 9(d); Nominet DRS procedure, clause 17(c)). Furthermore, a complainant is required by the UDRP rules to submit to the jurisdiction of either the principal office of the registrar or of the address for the respondent recorded in the registrar's WHOIS database (Rules for UDRP policy, para 1).

A US federal appeal court has confirmed in the *Corinthians.com* case (*Sallen v Corinthians*) that the US federal courts have jurisdiction under

ACPA 1999 to override a decision under the UDRP in favour of the complainant. A US federal district court has also held that a decision of an ICANN panel is not entitled to the 'significant deference' accorded to arbitral awards under the *Federal Arbitration Act 1925*.

It is thought that a court would have to determine a challenge to a decision under a DRP on the basis of the DRP being a contract binding on the parties. However, in doing so, it would have to resolve issues of law incorporated into the DRP, such as whether the complainant had the trade mark rights which it invoked, and whether the registrant had a right or legitimate interest in the domain name, as well as issues of fact, such as whether the domain name was confusingly similar to the complainant's mark, and whether it was registered and used in bad faith. The complainant could presumably counterclaim for trade mark infringement or unfair competition, and could prevail on this basis even if the court finds that the complaint was not justified under the UDRP (for example if the domain name was not registered and used in bad faith, but did infringe the complainant's trade mark rights).

Although it is sometimes possible for a domain name holder to take the initiative by commencing court proceedings for unjustified threats of proceedings (as in the *Prince.com* case (see D1.1 above)), or for a declaration that it is entitled to use the domain name (as in *Bancroft & Masters v Augusta National*), it is normally the complainant who starts, and therefore chooses, the initial procedure. DRP procedures are usually much cheaper than court proceedings, but the complainant has to show 'bad faith' (under the UDRP) or 'abuse' (under the Nominet DRP), which are not normally required for an infringement under national laws. In addition, DRP procedures only apply to domain names, and damages and costs are not awarded.

 A complainant is likely to prefer the DRP route (if it is available for the relevant domain):

- in cases of clear abuse;

- if the complainant does not have a presence in the domain name holder's country and so would find it more difficult to institute court proceedings;

- if the legal system of the domain name holder's country is considered unsatisfactory and it is not possible or practicable to bring proceedings in another country;

- if the domain name holder can be said to be misusing the domain name but not actually infringing any trade mark right of the complainant under conventional law;

111

- if there might be a serious challenge to the validity of the complainant's trade marks in legal proceedings; or

- if the complaint can be based on the violation of a registration restriction of the relevant domain.

Conversely, court proceedings may be preferable to a complainant if:

- there is no satisfactory DRP for the domain;

- it is difficult to show 'bad faith' or 'abuse' on the part of the respondent;

- the dispute is not limited to the domain name;

- an immediate injunction is required (a DRP complaint will normally take some three months to reach a conclusion, although transfer by the registrant is prohibited while the proceeding is pending);

- there is a reasonable prospect of recovering costs or damages through court proceedings; or

- criminal penalties or punitive damages are available and desired by the complainant.

A complainant can bring proceedings both in court and under a DRP. However, this can backfire, as in the *euro2000.com* case, where rejection of an application for an interim injunction in a French court led to rejection of a concurrent complaint under the UDRP which would otherwise have succeeded.

D2 – Registered Trade Mark Laws

Applicable laws   D2.1

As noted above (see D1.4), registered trade mark laws are organised on essentially national lines. In general, a valid registration of a trade mark in a particular country entitles the owner to object to the use of an identical or confusingly similar name in the course of trade *in that country*, subject to the conditions laid down by the national law. However, the internet is international. Any internet website can be accessed by any connected computer anywhere in the world, regardless of where it is hosted. So where is a domain name 'used' for the purposes of registered trade mark laws?

Websites   D2.2

In the case of a genuine commercial website, the position may depend on whether the website is merely a passive advertisement of a business or whether it is actively used to accept orders or supply the product. If the website is merely passive, the domain name is probably only used in the place where the business is trading. Thus, in the *Crateandbarrel* case (*Euromarket Designs v Peters*) (see D1.6 above), the passive use of a website advertising a shop in Dublin did not constitute use of the domain name in the UK, even though the website was accessible from the UK.

By contrast, where the website is actively used to trade, the domain name is used wherever there are customers who order or receive the products through it. Thus in the US case of *Playboy Enterprises v Chuckleberry Publishing* an injunction restraining the distribution or sale of a magazine called *Playmen* was held to be infringed by the availability of a web edition to subscribers in the US, although it was noted that the subscription of an Italian customer who subsequently moved to the US could be maintained. A similar conclusion would probably be reached in a similar case under the EU regime.

Where there is evidence of the misuse of domain names, courts are ready to infer that the registrant is threatening to exploit or damage the complainant's goodwill and hence that there is a threat to infringe in any country where the complainant has rights. Thus arguments that the respondent had done nothing in the jurisdiction were rejected in the US case *Panavision v Toeppen*, as were arguments that the respondents had not committed any infringing act in the English case *British Telecommunications v One in a Million*. A different result might have been reached in the *Crateandbarrel* case if the court had accepted the complainant's contention that the registrant had chosen this name to take advantage of the complainant's reputation and proposed expansion into Europe.

E-mail   D2.3

It is currently unclear whether or in what circumstances sending an e-mail would be regarded as a use of the sender's or recipient's domain name for the purposes of trade mark law.

In an old English case (*Reuter v Mulhens*), the German proprietor of the '4711' perfume brand wrote to an English company complaining that it was supplying perfume marked '4711' to another company which resold it in Somalia, infringing the German company's Somalian trade mark rights. The German company sent this letter using its letterhead and envelope which bore the mark '4711'. The Court of Appeal held that the letter infringed the UK registered trade mark '4711' which had been expropriated as enemy property during the war and sold to another party.

On this basis, the use of an e-mail address merely for correspondence could infringe trade mark law if it were confusingly similar to a registered trade mark of another party in the country of the sender or of the recipient. However, the *4711* case was decided under the old English law prior to the EU harmonising legislation (see D1.4 above), and it is not clear whether the same approach would now be followed.

By contrast, in a US case, *Hearst v Goldberger*, it was held that the sending of e-mails to people in New York using the disputed domain name as the return address did not constitute a sufficient wrongful act to found jurisdiction in New York.

In general, it seems unlikely that an e-mail would infringe on the ground that it was transmitted via a country in which the complainant had rights, if there was no infringement in the country of origin or receipt. Such a finding in relation to a transmission within the EU would appear to be contrary to the EU rules on free trade between member states (see *Commission v France (Case C-23/99)*) and EU *Electronic Commerce Directive (2000/31/EC)*.

The following parts of this chapter will focus on the main points of the harmonised laws of the EU and the EU member states relevant to domain names, with some references to particular features of the laws of some other countries. Registered trade mark laws are a complicated subject, and the following treatment should be regarded as a summary rather than a comprehensive treatment of the position in the EU.

Jurisdiction D2.4

Jurisdiction is not the same as applicable law. It is possible for a national court to have jurisdiction over and determine a case even though the law of another country applies. However, the jurisdiction in relation to trade marks is affected by the applicable law.

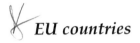

EU countries D2.5

Proceedings for infringement of Community trade marks must be brought in the respondent's home country, if this is in the EU; if not, they must be brought in the complainant's home country, if this is in the EU; and if neither the complainant nor the respondent is in the EU, the proceedings must be brought in Spain (the country where the Community trade mark office, OHIM, is located).

Proceedings for the infringement of a national trade mark in the EU can be brought against an EU respondent in his home state (*EC Regulation on jurisdiction and the recognition and enforcement of judgments in civil and commercial matters No 44/2001, Art 2*), or in the state where the infringement takes place (*Regulation 44/2001, Art 5(3)*). However, if the claim is concerned with the validity of the registered mark, the proceedings must be brought in the state where it is registered (*Regulation 44/2001, Art 22(4), 25*) (which must also be where it is infringed). It is not clear how this requirement applies where the claim is for infringement, but it is likely that the defence will challenge validity. A case raising this point in relation to patents was referred to the European Court of Justice (ECJ), but was settled before the ECJ gave a ruling (*Fort Dodge v Akzo Nobel*). However, the considerations could be different in trade mark cases, where it may be less obvious that validity will be a major issue than it normally is in a patent case.

Where concurrent proceedings are brought between the same parties in respect of the same cause of action in the courts of different EU countries, the court or courts other than the one seized first must decline jurisdiction (*Regulation 44/2001, Art 27*). Where concurrent proceedings are brought in respect of related causes of action, the courts other than the one seized first may stay the proceedings or decline jurisdiction (*Regulation 44/2001, Art 28*).

Where the respondent is not in an EU state, jurisdiction in EU countries in relation to proceedings for infringement of national trade mark laws depends on national procedural rules. Under UK rules, it appears that proceedings for infringement of a national mark can only be brought against a non-EU respondent in a UK court if there is infringement in the UK. On the other hand, in the *Prince.com* case (*Prince v Prince Sports Group*), a UK domain name holder was threatened by a US complainant with infringement proceedings in terms which did not specify where they would be brought. The UK company was held to be entitled to bring a claim in the English courts for unjustified threats. It was then able to invoke the judgment of the English court to persuade Network Solutions to cease the suspension of the domain name under the dispute policy in force prior to the UDRP.

USA   D2.6

In the USA there are separate jurisdictional rules for each state and these are subject to the limitations imposed by federal law. The most commonly used test requires that the respondent has purposefully availed itself of the privilege of conducting activities in the relevant state, thus invoking the benefits and protections of its laws. In addition, the claim must arise out of or result from the respondent's activities in relation to that state, and the exercise of jurisdiction must be reasonable (*International Shoe v Washington; Hanson v Denckla*).

In relation to websites, the US courts have distinguished between:

- websites through which products are sold or supplied (the jurisdiction being wherever there are customers, as in the case of *Zippo Manufacturing v Zippo Dot Com*);

- passive websites which merely advertise a business (the jurisdiction only being where the business is operating, for example in the cases of *Cybersell v Cybersell* and *Ben Susan v King (Blue Note Jazz Club)*); and

- interactive websites which collect information from interested consumers but do not accept orders or supply products (here all factors are to be taken into consideration; see, for example, *Maritz v Cybergold*).

It is taken that cybersquatters avail themselves of the jurisdiction of the party whom they have targeted (as, for example, in *Panavision v Toeppen*). Conversely, when the sponsor of the 'Masters' golf tournament, a corporation in Georgia, complained to the Virginia-based Network Solutions about the registration of *Masters.com* by a Californian company, it was held that the Californian courts had jurisdiction over a claim brought by the domain name holder for a declaration of non-infringement, since by complaining the golf sponsor had expressly aimed at the Californian company.

The *Anti-cybersquatting Consumer Protection Act 1999* (*ACPA 1999*) gave US trade mark owners an additional right to bring an action for forfeiture, cancellation or transfer of an infringing domain name against the registrar in the state where the registrar is located.

Infringement   D2.7

As noted at D1.4 above, trade mark law within the EU is largely harmonised. The EU identifies three categories of infringement, which are discussed at D2.8–D2.12 below.

Basic test for infringement   D2.8

Subject to various defences, a validly registered trade mark is infringed in the EU by the use of a name in the course of trade if:

(a)   the name is *identical* to the registered mark and is used for *identical* goods or services to those for which the mark is registered – there is no need to show a likelihood of confusion if there is identity of mark and identity of goods or services (*Directive on the approximation of trade mark laws in the Member States (89/104/EC), Art 5 (1)(a); EC Regulation on the Community Trade Mark No 40/94, Art 9(a); Trade Marks Act 1994 (TMA 1994), s 10(1)*);

(b)   the name is *identical* to the registered mark and is used for *similar* goods or services, or *similar* to the registered mark and used for *identical* or *similar* goods or services, and as a result there is a likelihood of confusion (*Directive 89/104/EC, Art 5(1)(b); Regulation 40/94, Art 9(b); TMA 1994, s 10(2)*); or

(c)   the name is *identical* or *similar* to the registered mark; it is used for goods or services which are not similar to those for which the mark is registered; the mark has a reputation; and the use of the name is without due cause and takes unfair advantage of, or is detrimental to, the distinctive character or repute of the trade mark (*Directive 89/104/EC, Art 5(2); Regulation 40/94, Art. 9(c), TMA 1994, s 10(3)*).

Identical mark/identical goods or services D2.9

If (*a*) at D2.8 above applies, that is the name is identical to the registered mark and it is used in relation to goods or services which are identical to the goods or services for which the mark is registered, there is no need to show confusion to establish infringement.

An important question is whether a domain name is identical to a mark if it includes the mark along with some addition. For example, is 'Nokia.net' or 'Nokiagirls.net' identical to the trade mark 'Nokia' for this purpose?

This question is the subject of a pending case before the ECJ (*LTJ Diffusion v SADAS*). Advocate-General Jacobs has recently given his opinion in this case that a name is only identical to a mark if it is the same without any addition, omission or modification other than those which are either minute or wholly insignificant. The Advocate General's opinion is influential but not binding on the court. If the ECJ comes to the same conclusion, 'Nokia.net' might be regarded as being identical to 'Nokia', but 'Nokiagirls.net' probably would not.

Identical or similar mark/identical or similar goods or services (but not both identical mark and identical goods or services) D2.10

The second category of infringement, (*b*) at D2.8 above, requires a 'genuine and properly substantiated likelihood of confusion' on the part of the average consumer (*Marca Mode v Adidas*), in the sense that he is liable to believe that goods or services in relation to which the name is used are supplied by or under the control of the owner of the mark or an undertaking which is economically linked to it (*Sabel v Puma; Lloyd Schuhfabrik Meyer v Klijsen Handel; IHT Internationale Heiztechnik v Ideal Standard; Bayerische Motorenwerke v Deenik*).

The average consumer is deemed to be reasonably well-informed, observant and circumspect, but may have imperfect recollection of the mark, and his attention is likely to vary according to the type of product (*Lloyd Schuhfabrik Meyer v Klijsen Handel; Gut Springenheide and Tusky*).

The assessment of the likelihood of confusion must take into account all relevant factors. A lesser degree of similarity between the goods or services may be offset by a greater degree of similarity between the marks, and vice versa. The more distinctive the earlier mark (whether due to its nature or its recognition on the market), the greater will be the likelihood of confusion (*Canon*; *Lloyd Schuhfabrik Meyer v Klijsen Handel*).

An important question which has not been resolved is whether temporary or 'initial interest' confusion is sufficient to infringe under the EU regime. For example, a person may access a website because the domain name incorporates a well-known brand, although it is immediately clear when he sees the page that it is not a website of the proprietor of the brand. The website operator may benefit from the initial 'confusion'; for example, the website may market a cheaper alternative to the well-known brand.

Differing conclusions as to whether initial interest confusion is actionable have been reached in a number of American cases relating to domain names and metatags. (Claims of infringement succeeded in *The New York Society of Certified Public Accountants v Eric Louis Associates*; *Brookfield Communications v West Coast Entertainment*; *SNA v Paul Array*; *Paccar v Telescan Technologies*; *Chatam International v Bodum*. Claims failed in *Playboy Enterprises v Netscape Communications*; *Hasbro v Clue Computing*; *Marianne Bihari v Ross*; *Northland Insurance Companies v Blaylock*; *Strick v Strickland*). These cases suggest that initial interest confusion is more likely to be actionable where the respondent is a rival trader seeking to use the trade mark owner's reputation to attract users to its site.

In the UK, the use of the complainant's marks in metatags was held to constitute trade mark infringement and passing off in the *Roadtech* case (*Roadtech Computer Systems Ltd v Mandata*), but liability was not seriously disputed and the decision was by a Master (procedural judge), so it would not normally be regarded as authoritative. It has also been held by the Court of Appeal of Northern Ireland that BP's trade mark for the green livery of its petrol stations was infringed by a petrol station of a similar colour, because motorists might make preparations to turn off into it in the belief that it was a BP station, even though they would realise that it was not BP before they filled their tanks (*BP Amoco v John Kelly*).

By contrast, it was held by the Privy Council in an appeal from the Australian High Court that there was no unfair competition where a new entrant adopted a style for drinks cans similar to that of the brand leader, and a number of consumers took them to the supermarket check-out before they realised that they were not those of the brand leader (*Cadbury Schweppes v Pub Squash*). In other words, 'initial interest confusion' was held not to be actionable in that case, even though the respondent was a rival trader taking advantage of the complainant's reputation.

UK passing off law is considered to be the same as that of Australia, and the Privy Council comprises mainly the same judges as the House of Lords (the highest UK court), so this ruling can also be regarded as authoritative for the purposes of UK passing off law. However, the interpretation of the phrase 'likelihood of confusion' in EU *Directive 89/104* and *Regulation 40/94* is ultimately a matter for the ECJ, and it remains to be seen how it will be approached in relation to this issue.

Identical or similar mark/reputation/unfair advantage or detriment to reputation   D2.11

The third category of infringement, (c) at D2.8 above, is of considerable importance where domain names are alleged to have been registered to take unfair advantage of the reputation of famous trade marks, but are not used in relation to goods or services similar to those for which the complainant's mark is registered. For example, infringement in this category was found in the *One in a Million* case (*British Telecommunications v One in a Million*).

However, the scope of this category is far from clear. It has been held that there can be infringement on this basis even if there is no likelihood of confusion (*Premier Brands v Typhoon Europe*), but it appears that there must be some possibility of association by the relevant public between the use of the name and the mark (*Daimler Chrysler v Alavi*). The corresponding objection to registration was considered well-founded in relation to an application to register 'Visa' for condoms (*Sheimer*), but dismissed in relation to the mark 'Eveready', also for condoms (*Oasis*).

There is also a question of whether there can be infringement under this third category if the alleged infringing sign is used in relation to goods or services which are similar to those for which the mark is registered. This could be important where a similar sign is said to take unfair advantage of the mark but does not cause confusion (for example, use in metatags). On a literal reading of the legislation, the third category does not apply if the goods or services are similar, but this produces the anomaly that more extensive rights are granted in relation to different goods or services than in relation to similar ones. The judgment of the ECJ in *Sabel v Puma* appears to support the view that the third category applies whether the goods or services are similar or not. This issue is also the subject of a case pending in the ECJ (*Zino Davidoff v M&S Toiletries*).

It should also be noted that category (*c*) applies in relation to Community trade marks and the trade marks of a number of Member States including the UK. However it is optional in the Directive and has not been implemented in relation to national trade marks in all Member States.

Use in the course of trade D2.12

In relation to all three categories of infringement, a name must be used in the course of trade in order to infringe. Thus a cybersquatter may seek to avoid liability by not using the domain name in question. However, in such a case, the courts may well infer that the registrant is threatening to use the domain name or to sell it to someone who would use it, and that this justifies an order to deliver the domain name up to the complainant. For example, in the *One in a Million* case (*British Telecommunications v One in a Million*), the registrant of burgerking.co.uk wrote to Burger King stating:

> 'In answer to your question regarding as to what we would do with the name should you decide not to purchase it – the domain name would be available for sale to any other interested party.'

It was held that the registrant was threatening to sell this and other domain names to someone who would use them to deceive.

An important unresolved question is whether it is 'use in the course of trade' to use a sign identical or similar to a registered mark to describe the goods or services, rather than to identify who produced them, for example if 'Arsenalfc.co.uk' is used for a clearly unofficial website supplying information or advertising souvenirs relating to the football club. This issue is the subject of two pending cases in the ECJ (*Arsenal v Reed*; *Holterhoff v Freiesleben*). Advocate-General Jacobs has given his opinion in the *Holterhoff* case, stating that descriptive use does not necessarily constitute use in the course of trade, but it remains to be seen whether this will be accepted by the court.

Defences to infringement D2.13

Even if one or more of the three categories set out at D2.8 above applies, there are various defences which may avoid infringement. In particular, a registered trade mark is not infringed by the use:

● by a person of his own name or address;

- of indications concerning the kind, quality, quantity, intended purpose, value, geographical origin, time of production or other characteristics of goods or services; or

- of a trade mark where it is necessary to indicate the intended purpose of a product or service, in particular, as accessories or spare parts (*Directive 89/104/EC, Art 6; Regulation 40/94, Art 12; TMA 1994, s 11(2)*).

In each of these cases, the defence only applies where the use is 'in accordance with honest practices in industrial or commercial matters'. This excludes, for example, use which is unnecessarily misleading (see *Volvo v Heritage*). However, it is a difficult question whether a risk of 'initial interest confusion' makes the use not 'in accordance with honest commercial practices', for example if a website markets accessories for a well-known brand using a domain name incorporating the brand, such as 'nokiafaceplates.com', but makes it clear on the site that the operator of the website is not connected with Nokia and that the faceplates are not made by Nokia.

Own name or address D2.14

The minutes of the Council meetings which adopted the relevant EU legislation indicate that the exception for a person's own name was intended to be limited to the names of individuals. However, it is controversial whether these minutes can be used; the English High Court (Laddie J) held that the minutes were not admissible to interpret the legislation in *Wagamama v City Centre Restaurants*, and this view was supported by Advocate-General Jacobs in *Sabel v Puma*. However, this is suspect since it is based on the premise that the minutes are not accessible to the public, whereas in fact they have been officially published in the Official Journal of the OHIM (1/95 and 4/95), and on observations of the ECJ regarding Council minutes at a time when they were not accessible to the public (whereas in the more recent case *Bowden v Tuffnells Parcels Express* the ECJ supported its conclusion on the interpretation of a Directive by reference to the minutes of the Council meeting.)

The English courts have held that the exception does extend in principle to the names of companies. For example, it was held to provide an arguable defence to the Irish shop called 'Crate and Barrel' when it put up a website at crateandbarrel-ie.com and crateandbarrel.ie (*Euromarket Designs v Peters*. A similar view was being taken in *Scandecor v Scandecor* which has been referred to the ECJ on other points.). On the other hand, the English Court of Appeal held that a company formed, owned and operated by William Asprey, a scion of the famous family of jewellers, was not entitled to use the name 'William R. Asprey Esquire', since the company's name was WRA (Guns) Limited (*Asprey & Garrard v WRA (Guns)*).

It is not clear whether a domain name might be regarded as a person's own name or address, on the basis that it is the person's internet name or address, even if it does not bear any relation to his/her ordinary name. The registration of a domain name in the knowledge that it incorporated a famous brand would not avoid infringement on this basis, since it would not be 'in accordance with honest practices'. However, the innocent use of a domain name which happens to be identical or similar to a mark registered by another party might be permitted on the ground that it is the 'name' or 'address' in cyberspace of the person using it. This argument was raised, but not decided, in the *fcuk.com* case (*French Connection v Sutton*), where the domain name had been used by the respondent as an e-mail address for some time before the action was brought.

Descriptive use   D2.15

The second of the exceptions summarised at D2.13 above is primarily directed at the situation where words are used generically and without reference to the trade mark owner. However, it is a controversial question whether and how far the exception also applies where a trade mark is used to describe goods or services which relate to the trade mark owner, as where a 'fan' website uses a domain name which incorporates the name of its subject. For example, does the defence apply where 'Arsenalfc.co.uk' is used for a website providing information about the club or (more controversially) advertising memorabilia? This issue was raised but not resolved in a case which settled on confidential terms (*The Arsenal Football Club v Champion Press*).

Another difficult issue is whether this exception permits the use of a mark to indicate a type of goods associated with the trade mark owner. In a case pending before the ECJ (*Holterhoff v Freiesleben*), Advocate-General Jacobs has given an opinion that it was permissible to use the names 'Spirit Sun' and 'Context Cut' to describe gems cut according to the method developed by the proprietor of these marks in circumstances where it was clear that the gems had not actually been cut by him.

Exhaustion of rights D2.16

There is another exception for use in relation to goods which have been placed on the market in the European Economic Area under the trade mark by or with the consent of the proprietor (*Directive 89/104/EC, Art 7; Regulation 40/94, Art 13; TMA 1994, s 12*). This principle is commonly referred to as 'exhaustion of rights'. EU law recognises Community-wide exhaustion, but not international exhaustion; it is no defence to a claim of trade mark infringement in the EU that the product was placed on the market with the consent of the proprietor in a country outside the EU (*Silhouette v Hartlauer; Zino Davidoff v M&S Toiletries*).

This exception does not apply where there exist legitimate reasons for the proprietor to oppose further commercialisation of the goods, especially where the condition of the goods is changed or impaired after they have been put on the market. It is a controversial question whether the exception applies to the use of a domain name incorporating a trade mark for a site marketing or selling goods placed on the market in the EU under the trade mark by the proprietor, for example the use of Nike.co.uk to sell genuine Nike goods placed on the market in the EU by Nike. One view is that Nike cannot complain of trade mark infringement in this situation since it has no legitimate reason to oppose the further commercialisation of the goods. Another view is that such use may mislead consumers into believing that the website is operated by Nike or an official distributor, and that this gives Nike legitimate reasons to oppose the further commercialisation of the goods in this way. The second view is more difficult to maintain if the website makes it clear that it is unofficial. There have been differing decisions on this point under the ICANN UDRP: see the discussion in *Philips-Indonesia.com*.

TMA 1994 also provides that it is not an infringement to use a trade mark for the purpose of identifying goods or services as those of the proprietor or a licensee, unless the use is not in accordance with honest practices and without due cause takes unfair advantage of or is detrimental to the distinctive character or repute of the mark. There is no corresponding express provision in the EU legislation. If this UK provision adds anything which is not implicit under the EU legislation, it would appear to be contrary to the 1989 Directive, which has been held to lay down an exhaustive regime as regards what constitutes infringement (*Silhouette v Hartlauer;* see Jonathan DC Turner, *Plus Royaliste que le Roi – Glaxo v Dowelhurst* [*2000*] *EIPR 434*).

Invalidity **D2.17**

Another defence to infringement is that the complainant's trade mark is invalid. The fact that a trade mark has been registered confers a presumption of validity but is not conclusive (*Regulation 40/94, Art 95(1)*; *TMA 1994, s 72*). Validity can be challenged, in particular in infringement proceedings, except where the same challenge by the same party has already been rejected by the Community Trade Mark Office (*Regulation 40/94, Art 96(2)*). If the challenge is upheld, not only will the infringement claim fail, but the trade mark will also be revoked, and this is a risk which has to be faced by a complainant in bringing trade mark infringement proceedings. Questions of validity can also arise in connection with the defence that the respondent is using its own trade mark for goods or services for which it is validly registered. The requirements for valid registration of a trade mark in the EU are outlined at D2.18 *et seq* below.

Registrability and validity **D2.18**

The registrability and validity of a trade mark in the EU depends on several factors, set out at D2.19–2.23 below.

Distinctiveness **D2.19**

The purpose of trade mark law is to enable the goods or services of one undertaking to be distinguished from those of another undertaking. Accordingly, to be validly registered as a trade mark in EU countries, a name must be capable of distinguishing goods or services of one undertaking from those of other undertakings (*Directive 89/104/EC, Art 2, 3(1)(a)*; *Regulation 40/94, Art 4, 7(1)(a)*; *TMA 1994, s 1(1), 3(1)(a)*). It must not be devoid of distinctive character and it must not consist exclusively of a sign or indication which may serve, in trade, to designate some characteristic of the goods or services, or which has become customary in the current language or in the *bona fide* and established practices of the trade (*Directive 89/104/EC, Art 3(1)(b)–(d)*; *Regulation 40/94, Art 7(1)(b)–(d)*; *TMA 1994, s 3(1)(b)–(d)*).

A descriptive name may acquire a distinctive character as a result of use. For example, the indication 'British Telecom' may serve to designate the characteristics of services, but as a result of its use as the name of a company, it has acquired a distinctive character and is, no doubt, validly registered as a trade mark.

The standard of distinctiveness required to be met for a valid registration has been set at a relatively low level by the ECJ: 'Baby Dry' has been held to be registrable as a trade mark for nappies (*Procter & Gamble v OHIM*), as has 'New Born Baby' for dolls (*Zapf Creation v OHIM*), and a refusal to register 'Das Prinzip der Bequemlichkeit' ('the principle of comfort') for tools, vehicles and furniture was overturned on appeal (*Erpo Möbelwerk v OHIM*).

In some cases a trade mark may be used to identify a product as a memento rather than as an indication of who made it – for example 'Elvis Presley' for deodorant. It was held under the old English law (prior to European harmonisation) that this trade mark was invalid since it was descriptive of the product as a memento rather than distinctive. This approach was held to be correct in principle under the new law in *Arsenal v Reed*, but the challenge to the validity of the registration of 'Arsenal' for clothing was rejected since it had been used not only in the form of a memento, but also as an indication of origin on swing tickets, packaging and neck labels. This still leaves open the possibility that the registration of 'Arsenal' for (say) beer mats, is invalid. This issue was raised but not decided in a case brought by Arsenal and other Premier League clubs against the registrant of Arsenalfc.co.uk and similar domain names.

A trade mark which was distinctive when registered may be revoked if it has become the common name in the trade for a product or service for which it is registered in consequence of the acts or inactivity of the proprietor (*Directive 89/104/EC, Art 12(2)(a)*; *Regulation 40/94, Art 50(1)(b)*; *TMA 1994, s 46(1)(c)*). This may apply to names which have become generic such as 'Hoover', but only if the generic use can be said to be a consequence of acts or inactivity of the proprietor.

Public policy and morality D2.20

A trade mark is not registrable under EU law if it is contrary to public policy or accepted principles of morality (*Directive 89/104/EC, Art 3(1)(f)*; *Regulation 40/94, Art 7(1)(f)*; *TMA 1994, s 3(3)(a)*). National laws may also provide that signs of high symbolic value, such as religious symbols, are unregistrable as national marks (*Directive 89/104/EC, Art 3(2)(b)*), but this optional provision has not been adopted in relation to UK or Community marks. It was argued in the *fcuk.com* case (*French Connection v Sutton*) that French Connection's registration of 'fcuk' was invalid on this ground, particularly as the Advertising Standards Authority had objected to French Connection's advertisements on the basis of consumer research showing that a significant majority found them offensive. The judge held that this argument should be investigated fully at trial. An application to register 'Tiny Penis' for swimwear and clothing was recently refused registration by the UK Trade Marks Office on this ground (*Ghazilian's application*).

Deceptive marks   D2.21

A trade mark is not registrable if it is of such a nature as to deceive the public (*Directive 89/104/EC, Art 3(1)(g)*; *Regulation 40/94, Art 7(1)(g)*; *TMA 1994, s 3(3)(b)*). A registration which was valid when made may cease to be valid if the mark has become liable to mislead in consequence of the use made of it by the proprietor or with his consent (*Directive 89/104/EC, Art 12(2)(b)*; *Regulation 40/94, Art 50(1)(c)*; *TMA 1994, s 46(1)(d)*). Whether a trade mark became liable to mislead when it was licensed to an unconnected company is the subject of a case pending before the ECJ (*Scandecor*). National trade mark laws may also provide that a national trade mark is unregistrable if its use is prohibited by law or if the application is made in bad faith (*Directive 89/104/EC, Art 3(2)(a), (d)*; *TMA 1994, s 3(4), (6)*).

Conflict with prior rights   D2.22

A trade mark is unregistrable under UK law if its use constitutes unfair competition (passing off), and hence is prohibited by law, having regard to the reputation already acquired by another party under the same or a similar mark, whether registered or not (*TMA 1994, ss 3(4), 5(4)*). However, there is a separate ground of objection if the trade mark conflicts with an 'earlier mark'.

An 'earlier mark' is a mark which was already well known at the priority date of the mark in issue or which has been or will be registered with an earlier application or priority date. The priority date is the date which may be claimed from an application made in the previous six months in another country; Community trade mark applications may also claim 'seniority' from earlier registrations or applications in member states.

There is a conflict if:

- the mark in issue is *identical* to an earlier mark and is registered or sought to be registered for *identical* goods or services;

- the mark in issue is *identical* to an earlier mark for *similar* goods or services, or *similar* to an earlier mark for *identical* or *similar* goods or services, and as a result there is a likelihood of confusion; or

- the mark in issue is *identical* or *similar* to an earlier mark for goods or services which are *not similar*, and the earlier mark has a reputation, and the use of the mark in issue without due cause would take unfair advantage of, or be detrimental to, the distinctive character or repute of the earlier trade mark (*Directive 89/104/EC, Art 4; Regulation 40/94, Art 8; TMA 1994, ss 5–6*). The third objection is optional under the Directive and is not applicable in relation to national trade marks of some member states. (See D2.11 above.)

These grounds of invalidity correspond to the definition of infringement (see D2.7–D2.11 above) and should be interpreted in the same way. In essence a trade mark whose use infringes an earlier trade mark cannot be validly registered for such use.

Non-use D2.23

Finally, a trade mark registration may be revoked if the trade mark has not been put to genuine use by or with the consent of the proprietor for five years and there are no proper reasons for non-use (*Directive 89/104/EC, Arts 10, 11; Regulation 40/94, Art 50; TMA 1994, s 46(1)(a), (b)*). To avoid revocation, use must take place in the territory of the relevant registration. Thus in the *Crateandbarrel* case it was held that the US complainant's UK trade mark registration was probably invalid since it had not been used by the complainant to any significant extent in the UK. The use must also be for the goods or services for which the mark is registered. In *Avnet v Isoact* the English High Court held that the complainant's registration of its name 'Avnet' for advertising services was probably invalid even though this name was used on its catalogue and website. This was considered to be use for the goods sold by the complainant rather than for advertising services provided to its suppliers.

Procedure and consequences of infringement D2.24

Registered trade marks are most commonly protected by civil proceedings (see D2.25 below), but infringement can also constitute a criminal law (see D2.26 below).

Civil proceedings D2.25

In civil proceedings a successful complainant can normally obtain an injunction restraining infringement. UK courts may also order that the infringing domain name be transferred to the complainant if they are satisfied that this is necessary to prevent further infringement, as in the *One in a Million* case (the text of the order in this case has been placed on the Nominet UK website at www.nic.uk/news/legal/oiam–order.html). In the USA, *ACPA 1999* provides for the transfer of a domain name in cases to which it applies, for example where there has been registration, trafficking or use with a bad faith intent to profit.

In very clear cases of infringement, the complainant may be able to obtain summary judgment, as in the *One in a Million* case (*British Telecommunications v One in a Million*). Other cases which are not so clear-cut may take a year or more to be tried. In such cases it may be possible to obtain an interim injunction if there is a risk of irreparable damage pending trial, provided the complainant does not delay bringing the proceedings. However, in deciding whether to grant an injunction, the court will also take into account the damage which may be done to the respondent if an injunction is wrongly granted against it. If freedom of speech is involved, this may be a particularly important consideration (as to the current position in the UK, see *Human Rights Act 1998, s 12(3)*; *Douglas v Hello*).

A domain name to which the UDRP (see D1.7 above) applies may not be transferred to another holder during a pending court proceeding or arbitration unless the transferee agrees in writing to be bound by the decision (UDRP, para 8a). A .uk domain name may not be transferred to another holder during a pending court proceeding or arbitration (Nominet DRP, para 12(a)(ii)).

A successful complainant in civil proceedings is normally awarded compensation for any damage caused by the infringement, although this is often difficult to prove. In the USA, a complainant can obtain triple damages for a deliberate or reckless infringement, or punitive damages under *ACPA 1999* in cases to which it applies (registration, trafficking or use with a bad faith intent to profit).

In proceedings in England, the losing party is normally required to pay most of the costs of the winning party. The position is often different in other jurisdictions; in some jurisdictions costs may be awarded only in some cases, or only a limited amount may be awarded by way of costs. In practice, damages and costs may be irrecoverable against a party without significant assets, particularly if it is in another jurisdiction.

Note: Court procedures can be complicated and expensive; parties should normally consult specialist lawyers before commencing or responding to legal action.

Criminal proceedings D2.26

Infringement of a registered trade mark can also be a criminal offence under English law, but only where the false mark is applied to goods or to material intended to be used for labelling or packaging goods, as a business paper in relation to goods, or for advertising goods (*TMA 1994, s 92*). It appears from the wording that the mark must be placed on physical material, and hence that the use of a domain name which infringes a mark could not be a criminal infringement under this section.

However, use of an infringing domain name could constitute a criminal offence under the *Trade Descriptions Act 1968* (*TDA 1968*). Although this Act similarly provides that it is an offence to apply a false trade description to goods, it goes on to specify that a person applies a trade description to goods if he uses the trade description in any manner likely to be taken as referring to the goods (*TDA 1968, ss 1(1), 4(1)(c)*). It is clear that this extends to advertising (*TDA 1968, s 5* specifically refers to advertisements), including the marketing of goods through a website with a misleading domain name. *TDA 1968* also provides that it is an offence knowingly or recklessly to make a false statement as to the provision of services or the person by whom they are provided (*TDA 1968, s 14*). This offence could be committed where services are offered or provided through a website with a misleading domain name. Criminal offences under *TDA 1968* are punishable by fines or imprisonment.

D3 – Unfair Competition Laws

Applicable laws D3.1

Unfair competition laws differ from country to country and, in contrast to the position regarding registered trade marks, there has been no harmonisation of national competition laws under EU law. UK passing off law remains similar or identical to that of commonwealth countries and is similar in many respects to US federal and states' unfair competition law. The laws of some other European countries have a broader scope in that they are not limited to appropriation of identity by deceptive trading, but may also provide protection against appropriation of innovation or design even in the absence of any deception (see generally Anselm Kamperman Sanders, *Unfair Competition Law – The Protection of Intellectual and Industrial Creativity*, Clarendon Press, Oxford, 1997). This chapter will focus on the position under UK and similar laws.

In view of the differences between national laws, it can be important to establish which law or laws apply if the events constituting what is alleged to be unfair competition occur in different countries. Under UK rules the applicable law is probably the law of the country where the complainant has goodwill which is damaged or liable to be damaged by the unfair competition, since the action is for damage to goodwill caused by misrepresentation (*Warnink v Townend*) (see *section 11(2)(b)* of the *Private International Law (Miscellaneous Provisions) Act 1995*). However, the position is unclear where goodwill in several countries is damaged or liable to be damaged. The conventional rules assume that only one country's law should apply in relation to any given conduct, but in a case of alleged unfair competition it may be appropriate to consider whether the act is wrongful under the law of any of the countries where the complainant's goodwill is likely to be damaged. Alternatively, it could be argued that a claim for unfair competition should not be regarded as a cause of action in respect of damage to property, and that the applicable law should be that of the country where the alleged wrongful act took place.

Jurisdiction D3.2

Proceedings for unfair competition can be brought against a respondent in the EU in the respondent's home country or the country where the wrongful act or damage occurs (*Bier v Mines de Potasse d'Alsace*; *Dumez France v Hessiche Landesbank*). It was held in the *Internet World* case (*Mecklermedia v DC Congress*) that the English High Court had jurisdiction because there was an arguable case that damage was caused to the complainant's goodwill by misrepresentations to its customers in the UK, even though the communications in question originated in another member state.

Accordingly, where a party in the EU is responsible for a website with a misleading domain name, it is likely that the courts of any EU member state where customers or potential customers of the complainant are liable to be misled will have jurisdiction in proceedings for unfair competition. The courts of the countries where the registrar is located or the website hosted would probably also have jurisdiction, being the countries where the harmful event occurred. As in the case of concurrent proceedings for trade mark infringement, courts other than the first seized may stay the proceedings or decline jurisdiction and must do so if the proceedings are for the same cause of action between the same parties (*EC Regulation on jurisdiction and the recognition and enforcement of judgments in civil and commercial matters No 44/2001, Art 27–8*).

Where the respondent is not in an EU state, the jurisdiction of the courts in EU countries depends on national procedural rules. Under UK rules, proceedings can be brought in the UK courts if the respondents can be served in the UK or if the wrongful act or damage occurred or is likely to occur in the UK (*Civil Procedure Rules 1998 (SI 1998/3132), Rule 6.20(1), (2), (8), (10)*). UK courts therefore have jurisdiction if deception occurs or is likely to occur in the UK even if the respondents are outside the UK. In addition, since putting instruments of deception into circulation in the UK is actionable even if the deception take place outside the UK (*Walker v Ost*), it appears that UK courts have jurisdiction where a misleading domain name is registered or sold in the UK whether it is a .uk TLD or not (instruments of deceptions are discussed further at D3.11 below).

As regards jurisdiction in the US, see the observations made at D2.6 above in relation to trade mark infringement.

Basic requirements of passing off   D3.3

To succeed under UK law in a complaint of passing off relating to a name, a complainant must establish:

- that it owns goodwill in a name, in that the name is recognised as identifying the complainant;

- that the respondent's use of the same or similar name amounts to a misrepresentation that the goods, services or business of the respondent are those of the complainant or connected with it; and

- that the complainant has suffered or is likely to suffer damage as a result of the misrepresentation.

(Adapted from Lord Oliver's speech in *Reckitt & Colman v Borden* at 406.)

Goodwill D3.4

For the purposes of passing off, goodwill refers to the commercial benefit of a reputation under a particular name or other indication. In the present state of English law, the action for passing off cannot be used to protect a merely personal reputation (*McCullock v May*; *Kaye v Robertson*), but it can be used to protect an author's commercial interest in his name, as where the politician and author, Alan Clark, successfully objected to a parody of his work which was not so obviously a spoof as to avoid confusion (*Clark v Associated Newspapers*).

English courts have upheld claims for passing off brought by charities (*British Legion v British Legion Club*; *The British Diabetic Association v The Diabetic Society*) and professional associations (*Society of Accountants and Auditors v Goodway*; *The Law Society of England and Wales v Griffith*), but have rejected claims in relation to the name of a house (*Day v Brownrigg*) and a political party ('Social Democratic Party') (*Kean v McGiven*) on the ground that there was no protectable interest in the nature of goodwill. The position in UK law may be contrasted with the USA and Germany, where specific protection for individual names is provided, as mentioned in the first section of this chapter.

Relevant date D3.5

The complainant must show that it has goodwill under the name at the date when the respondent's use of the name in question commenced (*Cadbury Schweppes v Pub Squash*). Thus in the *fcuk.com* case (*French Connection v Sutton*), the respondent registered and started using the domain name for e-mail some two months after the complainant, French Connection, commenced an advertising campaign using the slogan 'fcuk fashion'. The advertisements in this period contained little or nothing to indicate that 'fcuk' was supposed to be a brand name, and research commissioned by the Advertising Standards Authority found that a majority of the public understood them to mean 'f*** fashion'. It was held that the complainant's evidence of its goodwill at the relevant date was insufficient to provide a basis for summary judgment.

Distinctiveness D3.6

It is necessary for the complainant to show that the name under which it claims to have goodwill is distinctive, in the sense that it is recognised by a significant number of people dealing or likely to deal with the complainant as referring to the complainant or its business, goods or services. Where a name is inherently distinctive, relatively little use by the complainant will suffice to make it distinctive and relatively little evidence of distinctiveness will be required. By contrast, where the name is inherently descriptive, greater use and clearer evidence of distinctiveness will be required, but it is never impossible for a descriptive name to acquire sufficient reputation to found a passing off action (*Reckitt & Colman v Borden*).

Requirement for goodwill in the jurisdiction D3.7

It has been held in a series of English cases that the complainant must have goodwill in the English market to bring a passing off action under English law and that goodwill is situated where the business is carried on (*Bernardin v Pavilion Properties*; *Athlete's Foot v Cobra*; *Anheuser Busch v Budejovicky Budvar*; and see also *Star Industrial v Yap Kwee Kor* (Privy Council on appeal from Singapore)). On this basis, it is not enough for a business to have a reputation under the name in England; its products or services must actually be supplied in England under the name at the relevant date. Thus it was held by the Court of Appeal that the American Budweiser company did not have sufficient goodwill in England to found a claim for passing off when its sales in England prior to the relevant date had been largely confined to US military bases, which were physically located in England but not part of the English market (*Anheuser Busch v Budejovicky Budvar*).

This territorial approach is inconsistent with the globalisation of commerce and with an international medium such as the internet. It has been rejected or ignored by courts in a number of other countries: *Orkin Exterminating v Pest Co of Canada* (Canada); *ConAgra v McCain Foods* (Australia); *Dominion Rent A Car v Budget Rent A Car System* (New Zealand); *Tan-Ichi v Jancar* (Hong Kong); *Apple Computer v Apple Leasing Industries*; *Calvin Klein v International Apparel Syndicate*; *Yahoo v Akash Arora* (India); *C&A* (Eire).

The deficiencies of the territorial approach were also recognised by a senior English judge in *The Hit Factory* case (*Pete Waterman v CBS*), and it has been held to be incompatible with EU law to the extent that it discriminates against businesses established in other EU countries which have a reputation but no trade in England at the relevant date (*Maxim's v Dye*). At the present time, it can only be said that English courts may still feel bound by precedent to follow the restrictive traditional approach but will probably be ready to find that any form of trade in England in conjunction with international reputation produces sufficient goodwill to found a claim for passing off.

Misrepresentation   D3.8

The next requirement of a passing off claim is that the respondent is making a misrepresentation by using a name which is likely to mislead a significant number of people into believing that the respondent or its business, goods or services are those of the complainant or are connected with it.

The misrepresentation need not be deliberate. However, if there is an intention to deceive the court will readily infer that the respondent knows what he is doing and that there is a likelihood of deception being achieved (*Ash (Claudius) v Invicta*).

Nature and degree of confusion required   D3.9

There is no quantitative definition of the degree of confusion which must be established; it depends on the circumstances and the impression made on the judge. The question is whether typical consumers or others dealing with the complainant are likely to be misled. If the goods are such that consumers are unlikely to pay a great deal of attention, this must be taken into account (*Reckitt & Colman v Borden*), but the possibility of confusing a 'moron in a hurry' is insufficient (*Morning Star v Express Newspapers*). Where a name is descriptive the court may expect members of the public to pay more attention to small differences and may be more willing to ascribe any instances of confusion to carelessness or indifference than to misrepresentation (*Office Cleaning Services v Westminster Window and General Cleaners*). Where the complainant is operating in a niche or exclusive market, confusion of a relatively small number of people in absolute terms may be a relatively significant section of the relevant market sufficient to satisfy the requirement (*Neutrogena v Golden*).

135

As has been discussed in connection with registered trade marks (see D2.10 above), an authoritative court has held that initial interest confusion is insufficient to constitute passing off in a case relating to the appearance of supermarket products (*Cadbury Schweppes v Pub Squash*). On this basis it was held in the *fcuk.com* case (*French Connection v Sutton*) that the complainant, French Connection, had not shown that the respondent's use of the name was bound to cause confusion amounting to passing off. Anyone who went to the respondent's website or located it using a search engine would immediately realise that it was nothing to do with the fashion retailer. This approach was also followed as regards the passing off claim in the *BP Petrol Station* case (but see D2.10 above regarding the opposite conclusion reached on the claim for trade mark infringement).

It could be argued that a lesser degree of confusion may suffice in a case of an inherently distinctive name, but it is difficult to justify a fundamental difference of approach. On the other hand, in the *Roadtech* case (*Roadtech Computer Systems v Mandata*), the defendant was held liable for passing off by using the claimant's mark in metatags to attract users to its site. However, as explained in D2.10 above, this decision cannot be regarded as authoritative.

Confusion may result from the fact that two companies are using the same descriptive term to describe their product, particularly if one company has until recently had a monopoly in the product in question. Such confusion does not mean that there is any misrepresentation, unless the term had become distinctive of one of the companies before the other started to use it. Thus a claim brought by the Chicago Pizza Pie Factory against Grunt's Chicago Pizza Company failed on the ground that the term 'Chicago Pizza' described the principal offering of the restaurants and was not distinctive of the complainant (*My Kinda Town v Soll*). By contrast, in the well-known *Jif Lemon* case, Colmans succeeded because the plastic-lemon packaging was held to have become distinctive of its brand (*Reckitt & Colman v Borden*).

The misrepresentation need not lead people to believe that the respondent is the same as the complainant. It is sufficient that it leads people to believe that the respondent is connected with the complainant in the sense that the complainant is responsible for the quality of the respondent's goods (*Harrods v The Harrodian*). On the other hand, the fact that people are led to believe that there is some other form of connection, for example that the complainant sponsored or founded the respondent, is not enough to meet this requirement.

It was held in the *One in a Million* case (*British Telecommunications v One in a Million*) that the registration of domain names incorporating well-known brands itself amounted to misrepresentations actionable as passing off, since the entries on the registry's WHOIS database were liable to mislead. This finding has to be understood in the light of the fact that the respondents held themselves out in correspondence as carrying on a business of registering domain names on behalf of blue-chip clients such as British Telecommunications plc (this being a gloss on the fact that, when challenged previously by this company, they had released domain names which they had speculatively registered). In these circumstances, the respondents' registration of further domain names incorporating the names of well-known companies misrepresented that these companies were their clients. The case should not be regarded as holding that any registration of a domain name incorporating a well-known brand of itself represents that the registrant has been authorised by the owner of the brand, although as a general rule courts will try to find some way of holding cybersquatters liable.

Damage   D3.10

The third requirement for a valid passing off claim under UK law is damage, or the likelihood of damage, to the complainant's business or goodwill as a result of the misrepresentation. The damage may take several forms. The simplest is diversion of business, where consumers acquire the respondent's goods or services in the mistaken belief that they are the complainant's. However, loss of business due to the respondent's competition is not a valid cause for complaint. Furthermore, as discussed at D3.9 above, it appears that a complainant may not be entitled to object where initial interest confusion enables the respondent to put its offering to consumers, even if this results in some of them taking it instead of the complainant's product.

Another well-recognised form of damage is injury to the reputation of the complainant's product where it is associated with the respondent's inferior product. However, it is more controversial whether damage in the form of erosion of distinctiveness ('dilution') of the complainant's mark is relevant. Damage of this nature was taken into account by the English Court of Appeal in the *Elderflower Champagne* case (*Taittinger v Allbey*), but Millett LJ appeared to cast some doubt on this point in *The Harrodian School* case (*Harrods v The Harrodian*).

It was thought at one time that a complaint of passing off could only be made against a respondent operating in the same field as the complainant. However, damage to reputation can be caused by confusion with a party operating in a different field, and it is now clear that a respondent in a different field can be guilty of passing off if the three requirements are met (see D3.5 above). On the other hand, 'where there is no or only a tenuous degree of overlap between the parties' respective fields of activity the burden of proving the likelihood of confusion and resulting damage is a heavy one'. Cases brought by Harrods against The Harrodian School and by Stringfellow's Nightclub against McCain's 'Stringfellow' chips failed on this ground (*Harrods v The Harrodian*; *Stringfellow v McCain Foods*). Clearly this point may be relevant where the respondent's domain name is the same as or similar to a major brand, but the respondent is using or proposing to use it in a different field, as in the *fcuk.com* case (see D3.9 above).

Instruments of fraud   D3.11

A claim for threatened passing off can be brought where the respondent has equipped itself or intends to equip another with an 'instrument (or tool) of fraud (or deception)'. This was the main basis for the decision in the *One in a Million* case (*British Telecommunications v One in a Million*). Aldous LJ explained in that case that a name may be an 'instrument of fraud' if it will inherently lead to passing off because of its similarity with a distinctive and well-known name, or if it is likely to be used to pass off, taking into account the respondent's intention. Effectively references to 'instrument of fraud' are another way of saying that a valid claim can be brought against a respondent who has provided or threatens to provide another party with means which are likely to be used to pass off.

In the *One in a Million* case, *marksandspencer.com* was held to be inherently an instrument of deception in the hands of anyone other than Marks & Spencer plc or a connected company, since it had no meaning other than this company's name. On the other hand the domain name *bt.org*, which was also registered by the respondents, was not inherently a tool of deception, but the evidence was held to show that the respondents intended to deceive and to hold British Telecommunications plc's goodwill under the name 'BT' to ransom, so that in the hands of the respondents *bt.org* was also an instrument of deception.

By contrast, in the *fcuk.com* case (*French Connection v Sutton*), this domain name was not held to be an instrument of deception. 'Fcuk' was not a household word, particularly at the relevant date, and had other meanings, as indicating other companies or organisations in other fields or as an alternative to 'f***'. Furthermore, it was not shown that the respondent intended to mislead or to exploit the complainant's goodwill.

Defences D3.12

The use by an individual of his own name in good faith does not constitute passing off, even if the requirements for passing off are otherwise met (*Turton v Turton*). However, this defence does not apply to a company's name, even if the company is named after its founder, unless the company acquires existing goodwill of the founder under his name (*Fine Cotton Spinners v Cash*). Nor does the defence allow a company to use the name of its founder where this is not the name of the company (*Asprey & Garrard v WRA (Guns)*).

It is also a defence to a claim for passing off that the complainant's own use of the mark has been deceptive or contrary to public policy (*Leather Cloth v American Leather Cloth*; *Ford v Foster*; *Bile Bean v Davidson*). Thus it was argued in the *fcuk.com* case (*French Connection v Sutton*) that even if the complainant established the basic requirements of passing off, it would not be entitled to relief because its own use of the mark had been offensive and contrary to the standards sought to be enforced by the Advertising Standards Authority. The point was left undecided.

Procedure and remedies for passing off D3.13

Proceedings and remedies for passing off are generally similar to those for trade mark infringement outlined in D2.24–D2.26 above.

D4 – The ICANN Dispute Resolution Policies (UDRP and STOP)

Uniform Domain Name Dispute Resolution Policy   D4.1

As noted at D1.7 above, the ICANN Uniform Domain Name Dispute Resolution Policy ('UDRP') (reproduced in APPENDIX 2) applies to the existing gTLDs (.com, .net, .org, .biz, .info and .name) and a considerable number of ccTLDs, and will apply to the new gTLDs (.aero, .coop, .museum and .pro) once they are available.

In the case of the .biz TLD, a proceeding under the UDRP cannot be brought in respect of a domain name which is, or can be, subject to a proceeding under STOP (see D4.23 below). A proceeding under the RDRP (see D1.9 above) can be brought in conjunction with a proceeding under the UDRP (if not precluded by the availability of STOP) by a single complaint.

Under the policy, complaints are examined by independent panels appointed by accredited dispute resolution service providers. If the panel concludes that the complaint satisfies the requirements specified in the policy, it directs that the domain name should be cancelled or transferred to the complainant. If not, the complaint is rejected.

Requirements for a complaint to succeed   D4.2

To succeed in a complaint, the complainant must prove that:

- the domain name is identical or confusingly similar to a trade mark in which the complainant has rights;

- the respondent holder has no rights or legitimate interests in respect of the domain name; and

- the domain name has been registered and is being used in bad faith (UDRP, para 4(a)).

These requirements are further explored at D4.3–D4.13 below.

Although the procedure is a summary one, and the requirements of a valid complaint include 'bad faith', it has been held to be sufficient for the complainant to prove the requirements on the balance of probabilities; it is not necessary to meet a higher standard such as proof beyond all reasonable doubt (*iriefm.com* (disapproving the standard indicated in the earlier decision *WIPO Case D2000-0158* relating to the same domain name)).

The panel must decide the complaint in accordance with the ICANN UDRP, the ICANN Rules for Uniform Domain Name Dispute Resolution Policy ('UDRP Rules') and 'any rules and principles of law that it deems applicable' (UDRP Rules, para 15(a)). The UDRP, and the UDRP Rules are reproduced in APPENDIX 2. Further information can be found on the ICANN website at www.icann.org/udrp/.

Note: Decisions under the UDRP relating to gTLDs can be accessed or downloaded through the alphabetical and numerical lists on the ICANN website, as well as by using the search engine (at www.icann.org/udrp/udrpdec.htm). WIPO decisions under the UDRP relating to ccTLDs can be accessed or downloaded from the WIPO website at http://arbiter.wipo.int/domains/decisions/index–cctld.html.

The domain name is identical or confusingly similar to a trade mark in which the complainant has rights D4.3

The early decisions in *jeanettewinterson.com* and *juliaroberts.com* confirmed that the marks protected under the policy include unregistered marks recognised by the laws of unfair competition, including the names of authors and actors. However, the policy probably does not protect the rights conferred by some countries' laws (see D1.5 above) in personal names which are not used for a commercial purpose of any kind, since these are not normally regarded as trade marks.

Since the internet is global, the rights relied upon by the complainant need not be in the country where the respondent's website is hosted. Thus in *thetimesofindia.com* case, the complainant was able to rely on trade mark registrations in the USA, even though the respondent was in India (see also *kcts.com*). However, the rights claimed must exist under some law. In *pointmail.com* the complainant was based in California and its limited use and promotion of the name 'Pointmail.com' had taken place in California. The panel held that the complainant had not shown that the name 'Pointmail.com' had acquired sufficient distinctiveness (secondary meaning) to be protected under US federal or Californian unfair competition law. Although the complainant had applied to register 'Pointmail' and 'Pointmail.com' as US trade marks, these applications had not been granted at the time of the complaint and so did not constitute rights as required by the policy. Accordingly the complaint was rejected.

It has been held that a complainant can rely on rights in marks used by the group even if the goodwill or registered trade marks are owned by a subsidiary (*firstdirect.tv*). However, it is safer to ensure that the complaint is made in the name of the company which owns the most relevant trade mark rights. Although the policy and rules only refer to complainant in the singular, it has been accepted that two or more connected companies can be complainants (*directlinesucks.com, garrards.com*), and this is appropriate if the relevant trade mark rights are or may be owned by different companies in the group.

Identical to the complainant's mark   D4.4

If the domain name is identical to the complainant's mark, the complainant does not have to prove a likelihood of confusion to establish the first requirement of the policy. It may therefore be important to determine whether the name is identical or merely similar to the complainant's mark. In this connection, it has been held in a number of cases that the gTLD suffix should be disregarded (for example *deriskit.com, kcts.com, boffi.com, firstdirect.tv, celinedion.com*).

This view appears to be supported by the observations of Advocate-General Jacobs in the ECJ in *LTJ Diffusion v SADAS (judgment pending)* to the extent that the rules and principles of EU trade mark law are considered applicable. A domain name may also be regarded as identical to the complainant's mark if the only differences are minor variants such as hyphens between words, as in the *deriskit.com* case (the complainant's mark being 'de-riskit').

On the other hand, it appears that a material addition to the complainant's mark in the second level domain ('SLD') avoids identity, with the consequence that the complainant has to prove a likelihood of confusion. Thus cases such as *nokiagirls.com* and numerous 'sucks' cases, where 'sucks.com' is added to a famous brand, have been decided on the basis that the domain name was confusingly similar, rather than identical, to the complainant's mark.

Confusingly similar to the complainant's mark **D4.5**

If the name is not identical to the complainant's mark, it is necessary to decide whether it is confusingly similar within the meaning of the policy. This raises the question of whether (*a*) an abstract comparison is made in which it is sufficient that potential use would cause confusion, or (*b*) the actual use of the name must be likely to cause confusion. The first approach accords with that traditionally followed under UK trade mark law (*Origins*), whereas the ECJ appears to have inclined towards the second approach (*Canon*).

It is thought that in the context of UDRP the first approach is likely to be followed. In this context, the requirement that the name is identical or confusingly similar to the complainant's mark determines whether the complainant has a legitimate interest (*locus standi*); the test of whether the name is objectionable is provided in the second and third requirements (see D4.2 above and *celinedion.com*). Moreover, it is clear from the examples of 'bad faith' use mentioned in the policy (see D4.8 below), and the WIPO report which led to its adoption, that the policy is intended to catch respondents who have registered domain names primarily with a view to selling them to complainants at a profit, regardless of whether they are using the names in a way which is likely to cause confusion. Indeed, it would be difficult to justify finding against a typical cybersquatter if the complainant had to show that the actual use made of the domain name was likely to cause confusion.

The hypothetical use approach has been approved explicitly in *philips-indonesia.com* and *philipssucks.com*, as well as implicitly in the many cases where complainants have succeeded even though the respondent was not using the domain name in a way which was likely to cause confusion.

The first requirement has been held to be satisfied in a number of cases where the likelihood of confusion would appear to have been relatively low, as for example in many of the *sucks.com* cases mentioned above. This approach can be justified on the basis that the function of the first requirement is to establish that the complainant has a relevant interest, with the respondent's entitlement to retain the name being assessed by reference to the second and third requirements. On the other hand, where the complainant's mark is inherently descriptive, it may be held that relatively small differences are sufficient for the domain name not to be confusingly similar. Thus, for example, a complaint by 'Digital City' in respect of *Digitalcitymap.com* was rejected.

The holder has no rights or legitimate interests   D4.6

The second requirement which must be established by the complainant is that the holder has no rights or legitimate interests in respect of the domain name. The policy goes on to specify a number of circumstances which, if proven, demonstrate that the holder has rights or legitimate interests for this purpose (UDRP, Para 4(c)). It seems clear from the wording of the policy that if these circumstances are proved, the complaint must fail, but also that these circumstances are not exhaustive of the rights or legitimate interests which may defeat a complaint.

The circumstances specified by the policy as providing the respondent with rights or legitimate interests are:

- before any notice to the holder of the dispute, it has used or made demonstrable preparations to use the domain name or a name corresponding to the domain name in connection with a *bona fide* offering of goods or services;

- the holder has been commonly known by the domain name, even if it has acquired no trade mark rights; and

- the holder is making legitimate non-commercial or fair use of the domain name, without intent for commercial gain, to misleadingly divert consumers or to tarnish the complainant's trade mark.

Use must be genuine to provide legitimate interest   D4.7

It is common for more experienced speculators in domain names to develop some use of the domain names so as to be able to rely on the first or third of these specified types of legitimate interest. In such cases, the panel has to decide whether the use is genuine or not. Thus, in a series of cases, an entity called Hanna Law Firm established consumer complaint websites at domain names which it had registered based on well-known brands, such as *esteelauder.com*, *esteelauder.net*, *bartlesandjaymes.com*, *bartlesandjaymes.net* and *searsroebuck.com*. Hanna Law Firm's claim to a legitimate interest was rejected.

Similar decisions were reached in relation to Purge IT's registration and use of *natwestsucks.com*, *directlinesucks.com*, *dixonssucks.com* and *standardcharteredsucks.com*. In these cases, the operation by the same registrant of a number of similar sites was regarded as a significant indication that they were not genuine. It was also noted that Purge IT's motives were not wholly altruistic since it had indicated that it was willing to transfer the domain names to the owners of the relevant brands for a substantial consideration. By contrast, in *bridgestone-firestone.net*, the respondent had been engaged since 1990 in a dispute about pension payments with his former employer, a company in the Bridgestone Firestone group. It was held that he had a right or legitimate interest in establishing a website criticising the complainant at this address.

Use by resellers, repairers etc. D4.8

Another issue is whether a registrant has a legitimate interest in a domain name based on a well-known mark where it is used for a website genuinely offering products or services supplied by the brand owner or related products or services, such as spare parts or repairs. Complaints succeeded in cases of this nature in *heelquick.com, fanuc.com* and *cunardcruise.com*, but failed in *militec.com, drawtite.com, kittinger.com* and *philips-indonesia.com*.

In the *philips-indonesia.com* case, the respondent, based in Indonesia, had established a website with a homepage which said 'Welcome To Unofficial Indonesia Philips Electronics Store Online . . . Enter Store'. This linked to further pages with pictures and descriptions of various Philips products and details of how to order them from the respondent. It appeared that this website was established prior to the complainant's first letter of complaint. After noting that the principle of exhaustion of trade mark rights was widely recognised in the trade mark laws of different countries, the panel concluded that the complainant had not shown that the respondent was not entitled under Indonesian law to use the Philips mark to advertise genuine goods placed on the market by the Philips group. Accordingly, the complainant had not shown that the respondent did not have a right or legitimate interest on the basis of use in connection with a *bona fide* offering of goods as recognised in Article 4(c)(i) of the UDRP.

Burden of proof D4.9

In *euro2000.com*, the respondent established an unofficial website relating to the Euro 2000 football championship at this domain name. The panel would have found for the complainants but for the fact that an application for an injunction to prevent the respondent using the name had been rejected by the Paris court. It was held that this gave the respondent at least a temporary right or legitimate interest within the meaning of the policy to use the name in a significant and relevant country.

Paragraph 4(a) of the UDRP specifies that the complainant must prove that each of the three elements of a valid complaint are present. However, paragraph 4(c) refers to the respondent proving circumstances which demonstrate its rights or legitimate interests. It has been held in a number of cases that these provisions can be reconciled on the basis that it is for the complainant to establish a *prima facie* case that the respondent has no right or legitimate interest in respect of the domain name, but that if this is established, it is for the respondent to rebut it by proving that it does have a right or legitimate interest (see for example *neusiedler.com*).

The domain name has been registered and is being used in bad faith   D4.10

The third requirement of a valid complaint is that the domain name has been registered and is being used in bad faith. It was confirmed in early cases such as *worldwrestlingfederation.com*, *telstra.org* and *jeanettewinterson.com* that bad faith registration and bad faith use are cumulative requirements, although bad faith use may be evidence of bad faith registration.

At the same time, it was held in *telstra.org* and subsequent cases, for example *toshibastore.com*, *revlon.net*, *guerlain.net*, *lladro-retired.com*, *ingersoll-rand.net* that 'use' can include passively holding a domain name. According to these cases, it is necessary to consider all the circumstances, for example the strength of the reputation of the trade mark, any explanation provided by the respondent for its registration and subsequent failure to activate the domain name, any concealment of the respondent's identity or provision of false contact details, and whether any legitimate use of the domain name by the respondent is plausible.

On a literal interpretation of the policy, the domain name must be being used in bad faith at the time of the complaint. However, it is thought that a respondent who has registered and used a domain name in bad faith cannot circumvent the policy by commencing a legitimate use in advance of the submission of a complaint under the policy. As noted above, one of the specified examples of a right or legitimate interest which may defeat a complaint is where the holder has used or made demonstrable preparations to use the domain name for a *bona fide* offering of goods or services *before* notice of the dispute. It would seem to be inconsistent with this provision if a complaint could be defeated by use after notice of the dispute but before the filing of a formal complaint. Indeed, the sudden commencement of use following notice of a dispute may itself be evidence of bad faith, particularly if it does not appear to be genuine.

Specified circumstances D4.11

The policy specifies various circumstances which, if found by the panel to be present, are evidence of registration and use in bad faith. These are:

- circumstances indicating that the respondent registered or acquired the domain name primarily for the purpose of selling, renting, or otherwise transferring it to the complainant, or a competitor of the complainant, for valuable consideration in excess of documented out-of-pocket costs directly related to the domain name;

- the respondent registered the domain name in order to prevent the owner of the trademark or service mark from reflecting the mark in a corresponding domain name, provided that it has engaged in a pattern of such conduct;

- the respondent registered the domain name primarily for the purpose of disrupting the business of a competitor; and

- by using the domain name, the respondent intentionally attempted to attract, for commercial gain, internet users to its website, by creating a likelihood of confusion with the complainant's mark as to the source, sponsorship, affiliation, or endorsement of the respondent's website or of a product or service on it.

The fact that these circumstances are described as 'evidence' of bad faith registration and use might suggest that a finding that they are present is not necessarily conclusive. However, in practice if one of the specified circumstances is found it is likely that the complaint will be upheld, assuming that the other requirements of the policy are met.

The specified circumstances refer to bad faith on the part of the respondent. However, bad faith by another party may be taken into account, for example where cybersquatter A registers famousbrand.com then transfers it to the respondent, cybersquatter B. In *broadcastamerica.tv* the registration was effected in the name of the respondent without her authority by a party who then offered it for sale to the complainant. It was held that the bad faith of the third party was sufficient to meet the requirement of the policy.

Is 'bad faith' limited to conduct targeted at the complainant? D4.12

It is clear from the wording of the policy that the above examples are not exhaustive of the circumstances which may amount to bad faith. However, it is noteworthy that the specified circumstances all refer to conduct which takes unfair advantage of, or unfairly damages, the particular complainant. It can be argued that this indicates that the concept of bad faith is limited to conduct targeted in some way at the complainant.

The decision in *kcts.com* provides some support for this view. In this case, the panel was not convinced by the respondent's use of the domain name for a website covering 'Kensington & Chelsea Tourism Sites', but held that the complainant, a public television broadcaster called KCTS based in Seattle, had not shown that the domain name was registered in bad faith, since there was no evidence that the UK-based respondent was likely to have heard of the complainant when the domain name was registered.

Similarly, in *fastnet.com* the evidence was that the domain name was acquired by the respondent, who lived near Fastnet, with the intention of creating a website about the famous Fastnet lighthouse. He subsequently offered it for sale to the complainant and other companies using the name 'Fastnet' for $100,000. The complaint was rejected, the panel observing that: 'Attempting to sell a legitimately acquired domain name is not of itself illegitimate, whatever the price being sought.'

On the other hand, it was held in *plazahotel.com* that the existence of several Plaza Hotels around the world does not justify acquiring a domain name containing that name with a view to selling it at a profit to one or other of them.

General evidence of bad faith   **D4.13**

It is not clear how far general evidence of bad faith may be taken into account. In *deriskit.com* the respondent copied the complainant's business model, which had been disclosed to the respondent in the course of confidential discussions about its possible participation in the complainant's venture. The panel commented that both parties had confused the issue with arguments based on allegations of breach of confidence, breach of copyright, passing off and breach of trade mark, and stated that the evidence relating to these matters had largely been ignored except to the extent to which it bore on the issue of the respondent's *bona fides*.

The provision of false or inadequate information upon registering the domain name has been regarded as evidence of bad faith in a number of cases, for example *ticket-master.com*, *quixtar-sign-up.com*, *cabletronsystems.com*, *eResolution.com*. However, what appeared to be an accidental failure to correct a default country field in an otherwise apparently correct address was not regarded as justifying a finding of bad faith in *philips-indonesia. com*.

The way in which a domain name holder replies to a complaint may be evidence of bad faith. For example, in *attglobalsecurity.com* the panel found evidence of bad faith in that:

'The tone of the respondent's correspondence has been inconsistent with that of someone seeking to ensure that the dispute is dealt with quickly, fairly and expeditiously. His letters were downright dismissive in circumstances where the complainant clearly had grounds for complaint. His attack on the validity of the complainant's underlying rights in the mark AT&T in particular were doomed to failure, yet he pursued the attack to absurd lengths. His attack on the *bona fides* of the complainant went well beyond what was reasonable . . .'

'Without prejudice' correspondence has been taken into account in determining whether the domain name was being used in bad faith (see for example *walmartcanadasucks.com*). This contrasts with the position in court proceedings in the UK, in which such correspondence is generally inadmissible, as was confirmed in the *whsmith.com* case (*WH Smith v Colman*). Setting aside such rules of national law can be justified in proceedings under the policy on the basis of an implied term of the policy, which is accepted by the registrant as part of the contract governing the registration. One of the main objects of the policy, reflected in the first of the specified examples of bad faith, is to prevent the registration of domain names incorporating trade marks with the intention of sale at a profit to the trade mark owner. It would be inconsistent with this object to allow registrants to seek payment with impunity by marking their correspondence 'without prejudice'.

Procedure   D4.14

The procedure for determining complaints under the policy is set out partly in the UDRP itself, but mainly in the ICANN UDRP Rules and in Supplementary Rules of the accredited Dispute Resolution Service Providers.

Accredited providers   D4.15

The following providers have been accredited by ICANN and are currently accepting cases under the UDRP.

- The Asian Domain Name Dispute Resolution Centre.

- CPR Institute for Dispute Resolution ('CPR').

- The National Arbitration Forum ('NAF').

- The World Intellectual Property Organization ('WIPO').

A complainant under the UDRP may submit the complaint to any of these providers. The majority the of complaints to date have been submitted to the WIPO. (See APPENDIX 3 for the WIPO and NAF supplemental rules to the ICANN UDRP.)

Fees D4.16

A fixed fee, set by the service provider, is payable by the complainant unless the respondent elects for the complaint to be heard by a three member panel, in which case the respondent must pay half of the fee (UDRP Rules, para 19(a)). No action is to be taken by the provider on the complaint until the fee is paid and, if it is not paid within 10 days of receipt of the complaint, the complaint is deemed to have withdrawn. In exceptional circumstances, for example a hearing, the provider may request additional fees which must, however, be agreed with the parties and the panel (UDRP Rules, para 19(b)–(d)). Fees may be partly refunded if the complaint is withdrawn before a decision (details are set out on the providers' websites).

A single complaint may relate to more than one domain name registered by the same holder (UDRP Rules, para 3(c)). WIPO's fees, in US dollars, are:

No. of disputed domain names in complaint	1 Member Panel	3 Member Panel
1–5	1500	3000
6–10	2000	4000
More than 10	To be decided in consultation with the WIPO	

NAF's fees are slightly cheaper and are set out below.

No. of disputed domain names in complaint	1 Member Panel	3 Member Panel
1	1,150	2,500
2	1,300	2,600
3–5	1,400	2,800
6–10	1,750	3,500
11–15	2,000	4,000
More than 15	To be determined in consultation with NAF	

Composition of the panel   D4.17

Each of the providers maintains a list of panellists able to determine complaints. The panel comprises one member appointed by the provider from its list of panellists unless either party elects to have a three member panel, in which case the procedure is as follows.

- Each party submits the names and contact details of three proposed panellists; these may be taken from the lists of panellists of any of the accredited providers.

- The provider endeavours to appoint one of each party's candidates, unless it is unable to do so on its customary terms within five days, in which case it makes that appointment from its own list of panellists.

- The provider submits a list of five candidates for the third member, for the parties to indicate their preferences within five days; the provider then selects one of the five in a manner which reasonably balances the preferences of both parties (UDRP Rules, para 6). The third member will normally be the presiding panellist (WIPO Rules, para 7(b); NAF Rules, para 9(b)).

It is generally considered that a respondent has a greater prospect of success if he elects a three member panel. He can then influence the composition of the panel so that it is more likely to have a balance of pro-complainant and pro-respondent sympathies. Accordingly, it may be worthwhile for a respondent to make this election, even though he must then share the provider's fee to which he would otherwise not have to contribute. However, it should be noted that majority decisions of three member Panels (under UDRP Rules, para 15(c)) are not uncommon and it is possible that the panellist appointed from the respondent's list will be in a minority. Furthermore, while an indication of the views of particular panellists may be gathered from their previous decisions, past performance is not necessarily a guide to the future.

Panellists are required to be impartial and independent. Before accepting appointment in any case they must disclose to the provider any circumstances giving rise to justifiable doubt as to their impartiality or independence. Once appointed they must disclose promptly any new circumstances giving rise to such doubt, in which case the provider may appoint a substitute panel (UDRP Rules, para 7).

Language D4.18

The language of the procedure must be the language of the registration agreement under which the domain name was registered, unless otherwise agreed by the parties, specified in the registration agreement or determined by the panel having regard to the circumstances of the case. The panel may order any documents submitted in languages other than that of the procedure to be accompanied by a translation into the language of the procedure (UDRP Rules, para 11).

It appears that there is no requirement that a complaint must be in the same language as the registration agreement (see the decision in *niveasun.com*). However, a complainant who files in a different language runs the risk that the panel may decline to change the language of the procedure and may require the complainant to translate the complaint and other documents for the benefit of the respondent and the panel.

It is, of course, wrong to assume that the registration agreement will be in English, particularly if the registrar is in a country in which English is not the first language. A complainant should check the position before filing a complaint and decide whether to file in the language of the registration agreement or to file in some other language and argue that this should be the language of the procedure.

Establishing the language of the registration agreement is not always straightforward. For example, in *niveasun.com,* the registration had been made online through a website which provided alternative versions of the registration agreement in English and Korean. Since the registrant was Korean, the panel held that it was more likely that the agreement was in Korean. In *bmwassist.net* the registration agreement was in both German and English, specifying that both versions 'are to be considered as one' and cross-referring to a version of the UDRP in English. The panel concluded that the language of the registration agreement should be taken as English for the purposes of the UDRP Rules. Furthermore, while it may be relatively easy to find out the registrar's current practice, it is possible that a different practice operated at the time of registration of the domain name in question.

It was observed by the panel in *niveasun.com* that where a complaint is filed in a language other than that of the registration agreement, it should normally contain reasons as to why the language of the procedure should be changed, so that the respondent has an opportunity to reply. In that case, the panel considered it appropriate to make a procedural order requesting the parties to make submissions as to whether the language of the procedure should be English (the language of the complaint) and, if not, how the power to order translations should be exercised.

The panel also indicated in the *niveasun.com* case that some form of notice of the proceeding should be given to the respondent in the language of the registration agreement, unless it was clear that it had no difficulty with the language of the complaint, so as to ensure that it appreciated the nature of the proceeding and was not deprived of a fair opportunity of putting its case. WIPO's Supplementary Rules (para 4(a)) require the complainant to use a standard-form coversheet in the language of the registration agreement where available. However, at the time of writing it appears that this is only available from the WIPO website in English, French or Spanish. NAF's coversheet is only in English.

The complaint   D4.19

The complaint must comply with various formal requirements, which are mainly set out in UDRP Rules at para 3. Compliance with these requirements is facilitated by using the model forms provided by the service providers.

Amongst other things, the complaint must specify the mark or marks relied upon and describe the goods or services with which each mark is used. The latter is a somewhat odd requirement given that a complainant does not have to show that the respondent is using the domain name in relation to the same or similar goods or services. Copies of trade mark registrations relied upon must also be annexed, as must a copy of the applicable policy. The requirement to annex a copy of the policy appears to be superfluous given that the provider has to check with the registrar that the UDRP applies.

The complaint must state that the complainant will submit, with respect to any challenge to the decision under the UDRP cancelling or transferring the domain name, to the jurisdiction of the courts at the location of either:

- the principal office of the registrar (if the domain-holder has submitted to this jurisdiction in the registration agreement); or

- the respondent's address according to the registrar's WHOIS database.

This requirement has given rise to confusion in some cases. For example, some complaints have conflated a reference to the principal office of the registrar with the WHOIS record for the respondent's address (see *niveasun.com, boffi.com*). Unless the complainant has checked that the registration agreement contains a submission to the jurisdiction of the registrar, the submission should be made to the jurisdiction of the respondent.

The complaint must also state (in prescribed terms) that the complainant:

- agrees that its claims and remedies concerning the registration, the dispute or the dispute's resolution will be solely against the respondent; and

- waives all claims and remedies against the provider and panellists (except in the case of deliberate wrongdoing), the registry administrator, and ICANN, as well as their directors, officers, employees and agents.

The first part of this requirement appears to go too far. On the face of it the complainant is required to forego, for example, any legal claims against a previous registrant who has sold the domain name to the respondent or any remedies against the registrar requiring it to transfer or cancel the registration. It is debatable whether the previous registrant or the registrar could rely on this statement in subsequent court proceedings.

Finally, the complaint must certify, again in prescribed terms, that:

- the information in the complaint is, to the best of the complainant's knowledge, complete and accurate;

- the complaint is not presented for any improper purpose; and

- the assertions in it are warranted under the UDRP Rules and applicable law as it now exists or may be extended by good-faith and reasonable argument.

In *Fantasychannel.tv* the complainant provided a misleading selection of correspondence which implied that a sale of the domain name was first suggested by the respondent whereas it had been raised by the complainant. However, the panel considered that it would not be right to dismiss the complaint, since the use of the domain name by anyone other than the complainant would be likely to lead to confusion, and the respondent had himself sought to deceive the panel. The panel reluctantly concluded that there was no sanction available to penalise the complainant's lack of candour.

In complaints to WIPO, the grounds must not exceed 5000 words (WIPO Rules, para 10). Complaints to NAF must not exceed ten pages (NAF Rules, para 4(a)). In practice these limits can be circumvented by material in annexes, although excess material may be ignored in a case of obvious evasion.

Notification of complaint and response   **D4.20**

The provider must review the complaint for administrative compliance with the policy and rules. If compliant, the complaint must be forwarded by the provider to the respondent with three days of payment of the fee by the complainant. If the complaint is found deficient, the provider must notify the parties, and the complainant then has five days to correct deficiencies, failing which the complaint is deemed to be withdrawn.

The respondent must submit a response within 20 days of the forwarding of the complaint by the provider. This rather tight time limit may be extended by written agreement between the parties approved by the provider, or in exceptional circumstances by the provider on request by the respondent (UDRP Rules, para 5(a), (d)).

Again, there are various formal requirements (UDRP Rules, para 5(b)) and use of the provider's model form is recommended. Amongst other things, the response is required to respond specifically to the statements and allegations in the complaint, to include all bases for the respondent to retain registration and use of the disputed domain name, and to annex any documentary or other evidence relied upon. Sworn statements on contentious points may be given additional weight; on the other hand, statements of unidentified witnesses may be disregarded (*kcts.com*).

Like the complaint, the response must certify that:

- the information is, to the best of the respondent's knowledge, complete and accurate;

- the response is not presented for any improper purpose; and

- the assertions in it are warranted under the rules and applicable law as it now exists or may be extended by good faith and reasonable argument.

In *talk-city.com* the panel declined to take into account a late-filed response because of its failure to contain this mandatory certification.

The same length limits apply to the response as to the complaint (see D4.19 above).

In many cases the respondent does not submit any response. In these cases and in the absence of exceptional circumstances the panel is required to decide the dispute on the basis of the complaint (UDRP Rules, para 5(e)).

Further submissions D4.21

The panel may request further statements or documents from the parties, but this is entirely at the panel's discretion (UDRP Rules, para 12). A party may invite the panel to exercise this power, but cannot apply directly for the admission of additional evidence or submissions.

In *plazahotel.com* the panel emphasised that the policy and rules had deliberately avoided a right of reply in the interest of rapid and cost-effective dispute resolution. The panel considered that if a party wishes to submit a further statement, the proper practice is to seek consent from the panel, explaining why it considers that a further statement is warranted, for example because of new, pertinent facts or legal authority arising after the original submissions were filed, or to comment on factual or legal misstatements which are so horrendous as to justify a reply. If, in the light of the request, the panel concludes that further statements are desirable, it can then make a ruling enabling both parties to make further statements within appropriate and fair time limits.

This ruling has been followed in subsequent cases, for example *htmlease.com*, *tdwatergouse.com*, *goldline.com*, *wwfauction.com*, *kcts.com*. In some of these cases, it has been stated that further submissions may be appropriate where the other party has raised arguments which could not reasonably have been anticipated. Simple references to new decisions under the policy, without comment, have occasionally been accepted. In most other cases, applications to admit further statements have been refused. On the other hand, it has been held that where a panel suspects that a complaint has merit, but has not been sufficiently proved, the panel should avoid the practice of dismissing the complaint without prejudice, but should instead invite further statements (see *creo-scitex.com*).

Since the complainant will not normally have an opportunity to reply to the response, it is important for it to seek to anticipate and address the respondent's likely arguments in the complaint. Any point which the respondent has raised in correspondence should be covered and the complainant should try to consider whether any other points might be raised. This is particularly important because a complainant may not be permitted to make a further complaint under the policy if an earlier complaint has been rejected (see D4.22 below).

The panel is required to decide a complaint on the basis of the statements and documents submitted and in accordance with the UDRP, the UDRP Rules and any rules and principles of law that it deems applicable. This appears to exclude inquiries by the panel on its own initiative, other than by requesting further statements or documents from the parties. However, it is probably appropriate for a panel to view any website at the disputed domain name, and in the *plazahotel.com* case, the panel checked the status of the registered trade marks relied on by the complainant through the United States Patent and Trademark Office (USPTO) website even though this had not been indicated in the complaint.

The rules further provide that there are to be no in-person hearings unless the panel determines, in its sole discretion and as an exceptional matter, that such a hearing is necessary for deciding the complaint (UDRP Rules, para 13). It should also be noted that no party is permitted to have unilateral communications with the panel; all communications must be made through a case administrator appointed by the provider (UDRP Rules, para 8).

The parties are required to state in the complaint and the response whether any other legal proceedings have been commenced or terminated in connection with the disputed domain name, and to inform the provider if any are commenced during the procedure (UDRP Rules, para 3(b)(xi), 5(b)(vi), 18(b)). If legal proceedings are initiated in respect of the dispute prior to or during the procedure under the UDRP, the panel has a discretion to suspend or terminate the procedure or proceed to a decision (UDRP, para 18(a)). If it proceeds to a decision, it may take the outcome of the proceedings into account, as in the *euro2000.com* case, where the complainant's unsuccessful application for an injunction in a French court led to the rejection of the complaint.

The panel's decision   **D4.22**

In the absence of special circumstances, the panel is required to forward its decision to the provider within 14 days of its appointment. If the complaint is found to be justified in accordance with the policy, the remedy is the cancellation or transfer of the domain name. The policy and rules do not identify any criteria for determining which of these remedies is appropriate. It is arguable from the wording of the policy that it is for the complainant to choose (UDRP, para 4(i)). In practice, transfer is normally ordered if the complaint succeeds. Damages and costs cannot be recovered under the policy.

If the panel finds that the complaint was brought in bad faith (reverse domain name hijacking) or primarily to harass the respondent, it is required to state this in its decision (UDRP Rules, para 15(e)). Apart from rejection of the complaint, there is no sanction for such conduct under the policy, but the finding may perhaps assist the respondent in court proceedings.

A decision of the panel that the domain name should be cancelled or transferred is not implemented for ten business days after its notification by the provider to the registrar. If the registrar receives official documentation in this period that the respondent has commenced legal action against the complainant in a jurisdiction to which the complainant submitted in the complaint in accordance with the UDRP Rules, the decision will not be implemented until the registrar receives satisfactory evidence that the dispute has been resolved between the parties or that the legal action has been dismissed.

A domain name may not be transferred to another holder or registrar during a proceeding under the UDRP or for 15 business days after it has concluded (UDRP, para 8). This is intended to prevent the procedure being frustrated by a transfer to a different registrar or registrant which is not a party to the proceeding before a decision is implemented. A crafty respondent could commence a legal proceeding within the ten business day period following an adverse decision and transfer the domain name immediately after the expiry of the 15 business day period before the complainant has time to react. However, such conduct would be unlikely to impress a court or panel in the event of a further complaint under the policy.

It appears that a domain name holder wishing to challenge an adverse finding under the policy can bring a contractual claim on the basis that the requirements of the policy were not in fact met (see *Sallen v Corinthians*), or a claim for a declaration that the complainant's trade mark rights have not been infringed. There is no definition in the policy of the type of legal proceeding which would forestall implementation of a decision to transfer or revoke the domain name, and it seems that any proceeding between the same parties relating to the right to use the domain name would suffice for this purpose.

Conversely, an unsuccessful complainant may bring proceedings for trade mark infringement or unfair competition, and may be able to bring a contractual claim on the basis that the requirements of the policy were met.

It has generally been held that a complainant may not make a further complaint under the policy if an earlier complaint between the same parties has been rejected, unless there are special circumstances (such as serious misconduct, perjured evidence, discovery of credible, material evidence which could not reasonably have been foreseen or known by the party at the time of the previous proceeding, or a breach of natural justice), or the new complaint is based on conduct subsequent to the previous decision which differs materially from conduct prior to the decision. However, in some cases a further complaint has been permitted where an earlier complaint was denied expressly 'without prejudice to re-filing' or on the ground that parties should not be precluded by normal principles of *res judicata* in a new and evolving field.

The position is different where the subsequent complaint is made by a different party. Thus in *talalabughazaleh.com* it was held that the complainant companies were not barred on account of an earlier complaint by their principal shareholder which had been rejected on the ground that he did not own the trade mark rights relied upon. In *euro2000.com* it was held that the complaint was not barred by an earlier unsuccessful complaint, partly because there was an additional complainant which was not a party to the earlier decision and partly because the previous complaint had been under Network Solutions' old dispute resolution policy prior to the UDRP. However, it is thought that a further complaint by an assignee, licensee or other party whose rights in the mark derive from the complainant in an earlier, unsuccessful complainant might well be barred.

Start-up Trademark Opposition Policy ('STOP') D4.23

The operator of the .biz registry provided an Intellectual Property ('IP') Claim Service to owners of trade marks (including service marks, i.e. trade marks for services). To benefit from this service, a trade mark owner had to submit an IP claim form for the .biz domain name matching the exact alphanumeric string contained in the trade mark in which the claimant had rights.

A claimant who has submitted an IP claim form is notified of any registration of a domain name matching identically the domain name specified in the form. The claimant then has a right to challenge the registration under STOP by submitting a complaint to one of the accredited service providers (currently WIPO or NAF) within 20 days of the notification.

The period for submitting IP claim forms has expired, but disputes under STOP may still arise whenever anyone registers a .biz domain name specified in an existing IP claim form. Furthermore, proceedings under the UDRP cannot be brought against a domain name as long as it is, or *can be*, subject to a proceeding under STOP (STOP, para 5).

The Policy, Rules and Supplemental Rules for STOP, as well as model forms and decisions, are posted on the websites of WIPO (http://arbiter.wipo.int/domains/gtld/biz/stop/) and NAF (www.arbitration-forum.com/domains/STOP/index.asp).

Differences between STOP and UDRP   D4.24

The provisions of STOP are essentially the same as the UDRP, but there are the following differences.

- Under the STOP policy, the disputed domain name must be *identical* to the claimant's mark, in contrast to the UDRP where confusing similarity suffices (STOP, para 4(a)(i)). It seems clear that the requirement of identity under the STOP policy refers to the SLD and that the .biz suffix can be disregarded, and many cases have been decided on this basis.

- Assuming the first requirement is met, a domain name can be challenged under STOP if it was registered *or* used in bad faith (STOP, para 4(b)), in contrast to the position under the UDRP where it is necessary to show registration *and* use in bad faith (although 'use' has been interpreted very broadly for the purposes of the UDRP: see D4.10 above). In this respect, STOP is similar to the Nominet DRP (see D5.3 below).

- STOP specifies that registration of the domain name in order to prevent the complainant from reflecting its mark in a corresponding domain name constitutes evidence of bad faith, even if the registrant has not engaged in a pattern of such conduct (STOP, para

4(b)(ii) – in contrast to the corresponding provision of the UDRP which requires a pattern of such conduct.

- STOP provides that being the owner or beneficiary of a trade or service mark identical to the domain name demonstrates that the holder of the domain name has rights or legitimate interests in it. On a literal interpretation, it appears that a trade mark registration would thus defeat a complaint regardless of the merits, but it is thought that a trade mark registration made for this purpose without any real justification would be disregarded. Nevertheless, registrants of domain names which are subject to IP claims should consider whether to seek to strengthen their position by applying to register a corresponding trade mark.

- Legitimate non-commercial or fair use of the domain name is not identified in STOP as demonstrating a right or legitimate interest – this is no doubt because a person intending such use should not register a .biz name.

- In all cases where STOP applies, the registrant has received notification of an IP claim before the registration was completed. Therefore the registrant cannot say that he had no notice of the claim at the time of registration and it may be difficult to resist an allegation of bad faith where the registrant intends to engage in activities similar to the complainant's (see *genelogic.biz*).

- Disputes under STOP are submitted to a single panellist (STOP, para 4(e)); there is no provision for a three member panel as under the UDRP.

- The only remedy which can be obtained by a successful challenge under STOP is the transfer of the contested domain name (STOP, para 4(i)); cancellation is not available.

- A domain name cannot be transferred to another registrant or registrar until all pending *or prospective* challenges under STOP have been resolved, except to a sole claimant in a pending proceeding (STOP, para 8(a)). Similarly, a settlement between the claimant and holder is only allowed if there are no other pending or prospective challenges to the domain name under STOP. 'Prospective challenges' are presumably challenges which may be made by any IP claimants who have specified the relevant domain name.

- There are special provisions for domain names for which more than one IP claim form has been filed (see D4.25 below).

Multiple IP claims   **D4.25**

The same mark may belong to different parties, for example in different territories or in respect of different products/services (see D1.1).

Accordingly, it is possible to have multiple IP claim forms in respect of the same domain name, and special provisions for dealing with this situation are set out in para 4(i) of STOP.

- The Registry Operator is responsible for establishing the challenge priority among the multiple claimants on a randomised basis.

- If the priority claimant demonstrates that it has legitimate rights to the domain name, that the registrant does not have legitimate rights, and that the registrant has registered or used the domain name in bad faith, then the domain name is awarded to that claimant, and no further challenges under STOP are permitted.

- If the registrant demonstrates that it has legitimate rights to the domain name, then the complaint is dismissed, and no further challenges under STOP are permitted.

- If the priority complainant is unable to demonstrate that it has legitimate rights, or that the domain name was registered in bad faith, and the registrant is unable to demonstrate that it has legitimate rights, the complaint is dismissed; further challenges under STOP are permitted by other IP claimants but not by the one who has failed.

- A domain name cannot be transferred to any of the claimants until all pending or prospective challenges under STOP have been resolved (STOP, para 8(a)).

The random choice of first challenger can thus have significant implications.

- If successful, the priority claimant is awarded the domain name, notwithstanding the interests of other claimants.

- Since a complaint may be defeated by bona fide use before notice of the dispute (STOP, para 4(c)(ii)), the choice of claimant may have implications for the date of notice of 'the dispute' and hence whether the complaint succeeds or fails.

D5 – The Nominet Dispute Resolution Service Policy

Basic requirements   D5.1

The Nominet Dispute Resolution Service Policy ('Nominet DRP') is based to a considerable extent on the ICANN UDRP but there are a number of significant differences. The discussion in this chapter will concentrate on the points of divergence and should be read together with the discussion of the ICANN UDRP at D4 THE ICANN UNIFORM DOMAIN NAME DISPUTE RESOLUTION POLICY above. (The Nominet DRP is included, along with the Procedure for the Conduct of Proceedings under the Dispute Resolution Service ('Nominet procedure'), in APPENDIX 4. Further information, including decisions, can be found on the Nominet website at www.nic.uk.)

The requirements of a valid complaint under the Nominet DRP are:

- the complainant has rights in respect of a name or mark which is identical or similar to the contested domain name; and

- in the hands of the respondent, the domain name is an abusive registration, that is one which was registered or otherwise acquired or has been used in a manner which took unfair advantage of, or was unfairly detrimental to, the complainant's rights (Nominet DRP, para 2, in conjunction with the definition of 'abusive registration' in para 1).

The first requirement is similar, but not identical, to the first requirement of the UDRP (that the domain name is identical or confusingly similar to a trade mark in which the complainant has rights (see D4.3–D4.5 above)). The second requirement is similar in some respects to the third requirement of the UDRP (that the domain name has been registered and is being used in bad faith (see D4.10–D4.13 above)), but is also defined so as to include some of the considerations which arise under the second requirement of the UDRP (that the respondent has no right or legitimate interest in respect of the domain name, see D4.6–D4.9 above).

The Nominet DRP expressly provides that the complainant is required to prove both elements on the balance of probabilities. This is similar to the position reached in decisions under the UDRP (see D4.2 above).

The complainant has rights in a name or mark identical or similar to domain name D5.2

The Nominet DRP makes it clear that the rights which may be relied upon are not limited to rights enforceable under English law (Nominet DRP, para 1).

In contrast to the UDRP, there is no requirement that the complainant's rights must be trade mark rights. As well as registered and 'common law' trade mark rights, it would appear that rights in names of the kind recognised in German law and under the US *Anti-cybersquatting Consumer Protection Act 1999* (*ACPA 1999*) (see D1.5 above) may be relied upon. However, it is not clear whether an individual resident in the UK can claim 'rights' in his personal name for the purpose of the Nominet Policy, if he is not engaged in any trade or profession so as to have legally protected goodwill under his name. Under UK law, a person has a right to use his name in the sense that he is free to use it, but he does not have a right to claim against others using it (see D3.4 above).

One view is that the purpose of the Nominet DRP is merely to provide a cheap and speedy means of protecting rights which can be claimed under the general law in cases of clear abuse in relation to domain names. On this view, individuals' names are not protected under the policy any more than under the general law.

The alternative view is that the policy provides a specific means of redress against misuse of the first-come, first-served system of registration, and this should include abusive registration of individuals' names even if equivalent protection is not provided under the general law. It appears to have been assumed that this view is correct in applying the Nominet DRP to the new .me.uk domain without any modification of the definition of 'rights'. This view is also supported by the consideration that there could be discrimination against individuals resident in England if individuals resident in, for example, Germany or the US could rely on their rights protected under German or US law.

The Nominet DRP also specifies that a complainant may not rely on rights in a name or term which is wholly descriptive of its business (Nominet DRP, para 1). It should be noted that this exclusion does not apply to the many names which are partly descriptive, such as 'Burger King'. However, it could apply to names which are wholly descriptive even if they are also distinctive and protectable as trade marks or by the law of passing off. For example, 'British Telecommunications' might be regarded as 'wholly descriptive' of its business. Names such as 'Hoover' which have become generic might also be excluded under this provision.

It is not clear at what date the complainant is required to have the rights it is relying upon – should it be the date when the domain name was registered, or when it was first used, or when the complaint was made, or when the complaint is determined? This issue was discussed in *aviance.co.uk* where the expert held that the rights had to exist at the date of the complaint. He also held, in line with the *pointmail.com* decision under the UDRP, that a pending application for a registered trade mark did not constitute a right for the purpose of the Nominet policy.

It appears that the complainant's rights do not have to be rights of ownership. In *montesa.co.uk* it was held that the complainant could rely on its exclusive right under a distribution agreement with Honda to distribute motorcycles under the unregistered mark 'Montesa'.

The complainant's name or mark must be identical or similar to the contested domain name. The Nominet DRP does not expressly require that they be *confusingly* similar, but it is not clear how it should be determined whether they are 'similar'. It could be argued that this should be determined in line with EU trade mark law, in which the concept of similarity is interpreted in relation to the likelihood of confusion (*Directive on the approximation of trade mark laws in the Member States (89/104/EC), Recital 10*; *EC Regulation on the Community Trade Mark No 40/94*; *Canon*; *Lloyd Schuhfabrik Meyer v Klijsen Handel*). Alternatively, it could be argued that the omission of 'confusingly' must be deliberate and that 'similar' must be understood as a different concept, not dependent on likelihood of confusion. This view is supported by the function of the first requirement in the context of the Nominet DRP, namely of ensuring that the complainant has a legitimate interest, the issue of whether the registration is objectionable being determined under the second requirement. For the reasons discussed above in relation to the UDRP (see D4.5 above), it appears that it should not be necessary for a complainant to show that the domain name is actually being used in a way which is likely to cause confusion.

It has been held (in line with decisions under the UDRP (see D4.4 above)) that the ccTLD and generic SLD suffixes (.co.uk etc) should be discounted in considering whether the complainant's name or mark is identical or similar to the contested domain name (for example see *xigris.co.uk, telstra.org.uk, montesa.co.uk*).

Abusive registration D5.3

The Nominet DRP requires a complainant to prove that the contested domain has been registered, acquired *or* used in an abusive manner

(Nominet DRP, para 1). This differs from the UDRP under which both registration *and* use in bad faith must be shown, although 'use' has been interpreted very broadly under the UDRP (see D4.10 above). On the other hand, under the Nominet policy the domain name must be shown to be abusive 'in the hands of the respondent'. Thus a domain name originally registered abusively could cease to be abusive if acquired by a person who used it legitimately. For example, 'arsenalfc.co.uk' might be abusive in the hands of a person intending to sell it to Arsenal, but arguably not abusive if acquired by a person operating a genuine, unofficial fan site.

As well as providing a statement of the concept of 'abusive registration' in terms of unfair advantage or unfair detriment to the complainant's rights, the Nominet DRP provides lists of factors which may be evidence that the domain name is or is not an abusive registration (Nominet DRP, paras 3, 4). It seems clear that these lists in the main Nominet DRP are neither exhaustive (other conduct may be abusive) (see for example *telstra.org.uk, tarmacvandal.co.uk*); nor conclusive (the presumption which they raise may be rebutted by other evidence). However, the rules for the .me.uk domain specify a situation which is conclusively taken as abusive (see D5.4 below).

There is a potentially significant difference from the UDRP in relation to the last point. Under the UDRP, if one of the circumstances demonstrating a right or legitimate interest of the respondent is established, it appears that the complaint should be dismissed. By contrast, under the Nominet DRP, the presence of one of the specified indications that the registration is not abusive is not conclusive, and the expert must still consider whether in all the circumstances the use of the domain name takes unfair advantage of or is unfairly detrimental to the complainant's rights.

Thus in *gefanuc.co.uk*, the respondent was genuinely using a website at the contested domain name to sell products made by the complainant, GE Fanuc. It was held that the use of the domain name to attract customers to the site took unfair advantage of the name, even though they would not be confused after looking at the site. Although a similar decision was reached under the UDRP in *fanuc.com* (where the respondent was selling unauthorised, reconditioned parts for the complainant's products), other decisions under the UDRP have rejected complaints where the domain name was used for a website genuinely selling products as placed on the market by the complainant (see D4.8 above).

Circumstances indicating abusive registration D5.4

The specific circumstances identified in the Nominet DRP as indicating that the domain name is an abusive registration are:

- the respondent has registered or acquired the domain name:

  ○ for the purposes of selling, renting or otherwise transferring it to the complainant or a competitor of the complainant for valuable consideration in excess of documented out-of-pocket costs directly associated with acquiring or using it,

  ○ as a blocking registration against a name or mark in which the complainant has rights, or

  ○ primarily for the purpose of unfairly disrupting the complainant's business;

- the respondent is using the domain name in a way which has confused people or businesses into believing that the domain name is registered to, operated or authorised by, or otherwise connected to the complainant;

- in combination with other circumstances indicating that the registration is abusive, the respondent is engaged in a pattern of making abusive registrations; or

- the respondent has given false contact details to Nominet.

However, the Nominet policy expressly provides that failure to use a domain name for the purpose of e-mail or a website is not in itself evidence that the registration is abusive. In *fiatfinance.co.uk* a complaint was rejected on the basis of this provision in circumstances where a complaint under the UDRP would probably have succeeded in accordance with the *telstra.org* line of decisions (see D4.10 above).

In the case of .me.uk registrations, there is a separate provision in the rules for this domain that abusive registration is demonstrated without exclusion if the registrant is not a natural person and cannot demonstrate that it registered the domain name with the agreement at a time of a specific natural person, and that the domain name was a reasonably faithful representation of that person's legal name.

Circumstances indicating non-abusive registration D5.5

The specified circumstances indicating that the registration is not abusive are that:

- before being informed of the dispute, the respondent has:

  ○ used or made demonstrable preparations to use the domain name or a similar domain name in connection with a genuine offering of goods or services,

  ○ been commonly known by the name or legitimately connected with a mark identical or similar to the domain name, or

  ○ made legitimate non-commercial or fair use of the domain name; or

- the domain name is generic or descriptive and the respondent is making fair use of it.

Burden of proof   D5.6

As with the UDRP's examples of legitimate rights or interests, the Nominet DRP's examples of contraindications to abusive registration are prefaced by the statement 'How the respondent may demonstrate in its response that the domain name is not an abusive registration', suggesting that the burden of proof may lie on the respondent. As under the UDRP, it is thought that the general burden of proof under the Nominet policy is on the complainant, but if the complainant establishes a *prima facie* case, the onus lies on the respondent to rebut it by establishing one of the specified circumstances indicating that the registration is not abusive or in some other way.

The Nominet policy goes on to provide that 'fair use' may include fan or criticism sites, but if the domain name (apart from the generic suffix) is identical to the name in which the complainant has rights, without any addition, and the respondent is using it without the complainant's authorisation, the burden shifts to the respondent to show that the domain name is not abusive. Thus, if the domain name 'Natwestsucks.co. uk' were being used ostensibly for a non-commercial criticism site, the burden of proof would remain with the complainant to show that the use was not legitimate and genuine. On the other hand, if the domain name 'Natwest.co.uk' were being used for such a site without the bank's consent, the burden would lie on the respondent to show that it was not abusive. In *pharmacia.co.uk* it was held that the risk of even fleeting confusion caused a criticism site using a domain name identical the complainant's mark to be an abusive registration. This may be contrasted with the *bridgestone-firestone.net* decision under the UDRP (see D4.7 above).

Procedure   D5.7

The procedure for the Nominet DRP is set out in the Nominet Dispute Resolution Service Procedure (see APPENDIX 4). The main points are as follows.

The complaint   D5.8

The complaint must satisfy a number of formal requirements, many of which are similar to those under the UDRP, and use of Nominet's model form is recommended (Nominet procedure, para 3). The complaint must not exceed 2000 words (a considerably lower limit than under the ICANN UDRP). As under the UDRP, a complaint may relate to more than one domain name registered in the name of the same respondent. Unlike the UDRP, no fee is payable on submission of the complaint.

The complaint must state that the complainant submits to the exclusive jurisdiction of the English courts with respect to any legal proceedings seeking to reverse the effect of a decision in its favour, and that it agrees that such proceedings will be governed by English law (Nominet procedure, para 3(b)(viii)). The latter point could be problematic if the complainant is relying on a right under the law of another country; it is thought that to this extent the law of that other country must apply.

Nominet checks the complaint for compliance with its policy and procedure (Nominet procedure, para 4) (including the word limit (Nominet procedure, para 15)). If found to be compliant, it is forwarded to the respondent with Nominet's explanatory coversheet. If it is found to be non-compliant, the deficiencies are notified to the complainant, which then has three days to rectify them, failing which the complaint is deemed withdrawn.

Response, reply and mediation   D5.9

The respondent is required to submit a response within 15 days of receipt (or deemed receipt) of the complaint. Again, there are formal requirements (Nominet procedure, para 5) and use of Nominet's model form is recommended. The response must not exceed 2000 words; if the limit is exceeded, Nominet notifies the respondent, which must return a submission complying with the limit within three days, failing which Nominet proceeds as if no response has been submitted (Nominet procedure, para 15).

If no response is submitted, Nominet notifies the parties that, unless there are exceptional circumstances, it will appoint an expert to determine the dispute on payment by the complainant of the applicable fee (Nominet procedure, para 5(d)) (currently £750 plus VAT for 1–5 names; and a fee to be set in consultation with the complainant for more (Nominet procedure, para 21)). If a response is submitted, the complainant may submit a reply (not exceeding 2000 words) within five days of receiving it (Nominet procedure, para 6). This may be contrasted with the UDRP procedure, under which the complainant has no right to reply.

Whether a reply is received or not, Nominet then proceeds to conduct an informal mediation to attempt to resolve the dispute by agreement (Nominet procedure, para 7). This is another feature which differentiates the Nominet process from the UDRP. The negotiations are without prejudice and confidential. If an acceptable resolution is not reached within ten days, Nominet notifies the parties that it will appoint an expert to determine the dispute on payment by the complainant of the applicable fee (Nominet procedure, para 7(c)).

Appointment of the expert D5.10

If Nominet does not receive the complainant's request to refer the dispute to an independent expert within ten days of its notice to do so, the complaint is deemed withdrawn, but this will not prevent the complainant submitting a different complaint (Nominet procedure, para 8(a)). The terms of this provision do not cover the position where notification to refer is given following a default by the respondent, and it is not clear whether the time limit and sanction of deemed withdrawal is applicable in this situation. It is not clear whether a further complaint in respect of the same domain name would have to be justified by matters such as new evidence which could not have been obtained previously or new and different conduct by the respondent. By analogy with the position where a legal proceeding is withdrawn without a determination on the merits, it would appear that no special justification is required, but it could be argued that the reference to a 'different complaint' indicates that it is not permissible to resubmit the same complaint.

If the complainant requests that the dispute be referred to an expert and pays the applicable fee within the time limit, Nominet then appoints a single expert selected from its list in rotation (Nominet procedure, para 8). This is intended to avoid the criticism made of the WIPO's procedure for selecting panellists under the UDRP that some panellists are selected more often than others, resulting in a systemic pro-complainant bias. On the other hand, the Nominet procedure does not provide for three member panels, except for appeals (see D5.12 below).

Unless exceptional circumstances apply, the expert must decide the complaint on the basis of the parties' submissions, the policy and the procedure within ten days of appointment (Nominet procedure, para 16). The expert may request further statements or documents from the parties, but is not obliged to consider any statements or documents other than those received according to the policy or procedure or requested by him (Nominet procedure, para 13). As under the UDRP, no hearings are held unless the expert determines in his sole discretion in an exceptional case that a hearing is necessary to enable him to come to a decision (Nominet procedure, para 14).

If legal proceedings relating to a domain name are commenced before or during proceedings under the Nominet DRP, the Nominet proceedings will be suspended pending the outcome of the legal proceedings; this differs from the UDRP where the panel has a discretion to proceed to a determination (Nominet procedure, para 20). Parties are required to inform Nominet of any legal proceedings in connection with the disputed domain name (Nominet procedure, paras 3(b)(vii), 5(c)(iv), 20(b)). A respondent may not transfer a disputed domain name to another holder during a dispute under the Nominet policy or for ten days after its conclusion (except to the complainant under a settlement) or during court proceedings or an arbitration (Nominet policy, para 12).

The expert's decision   D5.11

If the expert finds in favour of the complainant, he may decide that the domain name should be cancelled, suspended, transferred or otherwise amended. Although this is not expressly stated in the policy or procedure, it is implicit from para 17(c) of the Nominet procedure and other provisions. However, it is not clear whether the choice of remedy depends on which of these options is specified in the complaint (Nominet procedure, para 3(b)(vi)). In practice, transfer to the complainant is directed in nearly all cases where the complaint is upheld.

The decision will then be implemented after ten days, unless Nominet has received either an appeal under the Nominet procedure (as to which see D5.12 below) or official documentation showing that the respondent has issued legal proceedings seeking to reverse the effect of the expert's decision and served them on the complainant (or, if the complainant is outside the UK, has commenced the process of serving them on the complainant).

If the expert finds that the complaint was brought in bad faith (reverse domain name hijacking), this must be stated in the decision. In the unlikely event that a complainant is found to have brought a complaint in bad faith on three occasions within two years, no further complaints will be accepted from that complainant for a period of two years (Nominet procedure, para 16(d)).

Further proceedings D5.12

In contrast to the position under the UDRP, either party can appeal from a decision of the single expert by submitting grounds of appeal (not exceeding 2000 words) (Nominet procedure, para 18), together with the appeal fee of £3,000 plus VAT (Nominet procedure, para 21(e)). The appeal is determined by a panel of three experts appointed by Nominet from its list.

If there is an appeal, Nominet will take no further action until the appeal is concluded. If the respondent duly notifies legal proceedings (see D5.11 above), Nominet will take no further action unless it receives satisfactory evidence that a settlement has been reached or that the proceedings have been dismissed, withdrawn or are otherwise unsuccessful (Nominet procedure, para 17).

It is not clear whether 'proceedings seeking to reverse the effect of the expert's decision' must be proceedings based on the terms of the Nominet policy as a contract, or whether an application for a declaration of non-infringement of the trade mark rights relied upon would qualify. If the latter, it may be possible to prevent implementation of a correct decision under the policy, since it is possible for a registration to be abusive within the meaning of the policy without infringing the complainant's rights.

Part E: FAQs

Part III: EEOC

E1 – FAQs

Q: **I engaged a web design company to design my website. As part of the job it also bought a domain name for me. The site has been operational for some time now, but I have suddenly found out that the domain name is still registered in the web design company's name and it has gone bust. How can I get the domain name transferred to me to ensure that I own it?**

A: First you must ensure that the liquidator has not sold it as part of the design company's assets. If not, you must write to the liquidator staking your claim to the name. If you have an invoice showing that you paid for it, you should send a copy of it to the liquidator and request the immediate transfer of the name to you on the basis that the design company was holding it for you as trustee. Ideally, the liquidator should transfer the domain name to you and record the transfer at the appropriate domain name registry. At the same time as you write to the liquidator, you should write to the registry telling them what the position is, enclosing a copy of the invoice and asking it to transfer the domain name into your company's name. The registrar may or may not do so depending on its transfer policy. You should also update the ISP's hosting records.

Q: **I have had a website for almost two years now but I have suddenly found that the domain name I was using has been registered by someone else and my site is no longer operational. What can I do to get the name back?**

A: Domain names tend to be registered for two years at a time. It may be that you did not re-register the domain name in time and consequently your registration has lapsed. If your web designer or hosting company agreed to re-register the domain name for you, then you should contact it immediately indicating that you hold it responsible for failure to renew. You should also approach the new owner as soon as possible to see if it is willing to transfer the name to you. You may find that you have to pay more for it than just the

177

registration fee to cover the new owner's purchase costs and any out of pocket expenses, but such fees may be open to negotiation. If you have forgotten to re-register, you should follow the approach of writing to the new owner described above. If you suspect bad faith on the part of the new owner, you should take legal advice before initiating contact.

Q: **We are a company registered in England and Wales. Someone else has registered the domain name of our company name. What can we do to get the name from it?**

A: Limited company registration confers many legal benefits, but from a 'trade name' perspective it simply prevents another limited company or plc registering the same name. Company registration does not prevent a partnership or sole trader from using that name and does not prevent any person from registering that company name as a domain name. The general exception to this is if your company is well known and the person who registered the domain name cannot reasonably say that it did not know of your company at the time of registration. If this is the case, you may be able to prove that, by registering the name, the registrant has been cybersquatting. If you feel this has happened you may wish to use an appropriate name dispute resolution policy to try to get the name transferred to you. Registration of your company name as a domain name by another person may also constitute passing off. You will have the opportunity to prove both of these offences by commencing court proceedings.

Q: **I have spent a considerable amount of time preparing a website using a domain name which I now understand is the same as somebody else's registered trade mark. I am willing to transfer the domain name to them, but can I get compensation for the registration fee and time and effort I have put into the site?**

A: If the trade mark owner has a genuine registration and you do agree to transfer, you can ask for your out-of-pocket expenses to be covered. These include the registration fee, the cost of site development, the cost of buying a new domain name, the cost of reprinting stationery etc. Be wary about asking for an inflated price or one not based on fact, however, as the trade mark owner may think you are cybersquatting and commence proceedings against you for trade mark infringement.

Q: **I have been contacted by the solicitors acting for a services retailer called 'Simple'. They have told me that my website at 'simpleadvertising.com' infringes its client's registered trade mark and copyright. They say that it is impossible**

that I have not heard about their client's business; I have, but did not know that it undertook advertising and I am not even sure that it does. I think it is trying to get every 'simple' domain it can. What can I do?

A: Trade marks registered for common or generic words like 'simple' often do not guarantee the owner an exclusive right to use that name as this would take that word out of common parlance. It is worth making this point to Simple. Also, having a trade mark registered does not automatically mean that the trade mark owner will have the domain name transferred to it simply by virtue of its trade mark registration. In this case you should respond to the solicitors emphasising the point that the word 'simple' is a generic and descriptive one, and thus you are entitled to use it for goods and services unrelated to their clients. You might also refer to the UDRP in your response, stating that you did not register the name in bad faith and that Simple would have to prove bad faith if the matter were heard under UDRP.

Q: I was wondering whether in ICANN's view registering a generic domain name with the sole intention of selling it later on for a profit would amount to 'bad faith registration'? Or does bad faith only occur where the intention is to sell to a party I know has a legitimate interest in the domain name?

A: If a name is truly generic, such as 'car.com' or 'business.net', then registration of it for the purpose of onward sale would not be bad faith. In fact, domain names are considered a valuable asset in an intellectual property portfolio. Having said that, if a generic name has been registered as a trade mark, the trade mark owner may still try and may succeed in a claim for trade mark infringement. The outcome will depend on the precise trade mark registered, the domain name used and the conduct of the registrant in offering it for sale.

Q: I have received a letter from a solicitor claiming that the domain name for my website breaches its client's trade mark and is passing off. The domain name I have registered is 'bikesrus.com'. I do intend to go ahead with the site launch, but do not want to completely close the door to the other company if it will offer me a sensible fee for this domain name.

A: As you know, trade mark owners have a right to use their mark on their products and services and to prevent others from using the same (or very similar mark) on the same or similar goods or services. The mark this company has registered is a device mark, meaning that it protects the logo as it is presented, not the words contained in it, and the registration does not grant that company an exclusive right to use the words contained in the mark. Generally a device trade mark will not protect the owner against registration and use of the words as a domain name. None of the classes of registration this company has relate to the provision of information or services via the internet, but the wide registration would probably mean that you could not brand such products yourself with 'bikesrus' or the domain name.

If this company is not able to establish that its trade mark is being infringed by your registration and use of the domain name, there are two other approaches which it may take to get the name transferred to it, and you should be aware of these. The first is that it may claim that use of the words 'bikesrus' is passing off, namely that you are representing your site as being associated with its products or otherwise using its reputation to enhance your own business. Whether it will be able to prove this comes down to whether it has sufficient evidence to show that the name 'bikesrus' is linked with it in the minds of the public. Passing off proceedings are quite costly both to bring and to defend, but if this company is minded to do so it may issue proceedings against you on this ground. The second approach it may take is to use UDRP to get the domain name transferred to it. Such arbitrations are quick and relatively cheap, but the arbitrator's decisions are not always easy to predict and consequently the company may decide not to use this avenue.

Q: I am a director of a business called 'Gardens Only,' a garden design company. We are very well-known and our head office is in the USA. We do not have a trade mark registered for our business. The top level and country code domain names for 'gardensonly' have been registered by someone else, who is not using them. We would like to get these names transferred to us. What can we do?

A: Under ICANN's UDRP a claimant who believes it has a better right to the name than the registrant, by virtue of its own long use of that domain name as its business name or the name of its product, can use UDRP to attempt to compel transfer of the name to it. To succeed in this, the claimant must show that:

- the domain name is identical or confusingly similar to a trade mark or service mark in which it has rights;

- the registrant has registered and is using the domain name 'in bad faith'; and

- the registrant does not have a 'legitimate reason' to use it.

If a claimant can prove these basic issues, then the domain name will almost certainly be transferred to it. In the case of famous names, you should also be aware that in the USA it might be possible to commence proceedings under the *Anticybersquatting Consumer Protection Act 1999* against a person who warehouses domain names which are also famous business names.

Q: **I own a national chain of flower shops called 'Bloomers' which has been established for 18 years. I instructed my web designers to buy 'bloomers.co.uk' for me and they said they had done so. I have now discovered that an online lingerie shop is using this domain name as a brochure site, which is potentially quite damaging to my business. I have written to it asking for it to sell the domain name to me but it will not do so. Can I refer the matter to Nominet and get them to transfer the name to me?**

A: Under Nominet's DRS you can complain to Nominet if the registration by the lingerie shop is an 'abusive registration', in that it has been acquired or is being used in a manner which takes unfair advantage of or which is unfairly detrimental to your rights to that domain name. If you believe that it is, you should apply to Nominet who will appoint an expert to hear the matter and decide whether the registration should be cancelled, suspended, transferred or amended. If you do not want to use Nominet's arbitration service, or feel that the registration is not an 'abusive' one because the lingerie shop might also have a right to use the name, you might consider upping your offer; this is obviously a commercial decision for you to make. You might also want to consider making a claim against your web designers if they promised to register this domain name for you and did not do so in a timely manner.

Q: **My business buys and sells furniture. Last year I registered the business name as a trade mark in the UK. Having recently performed a domain name search for the business name, I was horrified to learn that someone else with the same business name has registered the .co.uk version of my trade mark as a domain name. Is this an offence and what rights do I have as the holder of the registered trade mark?**

A: As trade marks can be registered in 42 classes of goods and services, having a name registered as a trade mark in respect of your goods or services does not mean that someone will not have the same name registered in respect of different goods and services. As Nominet's dispute resolution procedure favours trade mark owners, if you wish to seek to have the domain name transferred to you, your first course of action should be to contact Nominet to initiate its dispute resolution procedure. At this stage, it is worth contacting the domain name owner to find out whether it also has a registered trade mark for this name. If the domain name owner has a trade mark or a justifiable reason to use the domain name you may find that you are unable to have it transferred to you. If however Nominet believes you have a better right to the domain name, it may order its transfer to you. If you are unsuccessful using Nominet and the domain name owner does not have a trade mark registered for its goods/services you may wish to consider trade mark infringement proceedings against it.

Q: **We are the registered owners of disc-sync.com. We have been contacted by a document storage company, which says that it has a US trade mark registered 'disc-sync' and that we are cybersquatting. We planned to use the domain name ourselves for our mobile disco website. Do we have to give this company the domain name?**

A: A trade mark is a mark or sign which distinguishes the goods and services of one person from the goods and services of another. Having a trade mark registered effectively gives the owner of it a monopoly right to use that mark for its goods or services in the country where the mark is registered. In the case of words which are in common use and which are registered as trade marks, the trade mark owner will generally not be able to prevent a person from using the same word in relation to different goods/services, but will probably be able to prevent a person using the same word for the same goods and services. As your services are dissimilar from those of the trade mark owner, you may be able to argue in favour of keeping the domain name, in which case you might reply to the trade mark owner telling it that if it wants the domain name, it should seek return via UDRP. It may of course choose not to use this route and instead commence trade mark infringement proceedings against you in the USA. As trade marks are national in nature, it may have difficulty proving infringement and because such proceedings are expensive it may not be inclined to do so. To ensure that it cannot claim that you are passing off, you might wish to put a disclaimer on your website which states you are not related to the US company and provide a link to its website.

Q: **I have registered the domain name 'cine360.co.uk' for use on a website providing information about films shown at the 'cine' cinema chain and offering online booking for these cinemas as there is no central information and booking point. I contacted Cine's head office to tell them my intentions and its solicitors wrote to me demanding I transfer the domain name to Cine. Do I have to?**

A: There is certainly an argument that you are entitled to use this
      domain name, as you are offering an 'add-on' or information
      service which increases the business of Cine. It is possible however
      that Cine may take the view that you are depriving it of revenue,
      such as an online booking fee. Also it may argue that use of its
      listings is in breach of its copyright or database rights. The position
      may be different if you had registered the .com version of it, as such
      registration might have been considered to have been made in bad
      faith.

Q: **I have registered the name 'Tomcruz.com' for a tribute site.
      His lawyers have written to me saying that this is
      cybersquatting and defamation. Are they right?**

A: There has been a lot of controversy about fan sites which use the
      famous person's name in their URL. Generally speaking, celebrities
      have been able to reclaim their domains if their name is a given one
      or an adopted one, for example Julia Roberts and Madonna, but
      this is not always the case, as Sting recently discovered. On the
      whole, to avoid any liability it is best to make it clear that the site is
      a fan site and to add a disclaimer stating that it is not sanctioned by
      the star. As far as defamation is concerned, the defence of 'truth'
      exists in English law, but because you have chosen to misspell his
      surname you would need specific advice on this aspect.

Q: **We are an aircraft courier company called 'In the Air' and
      we have registered the domain name 'Intheairontime.com'
      for our online courier booking service. We are registering it
      as a trade mark in the UK and the mark was published last
      week. We have received correspondence from a very large
      multi-national courier company which claims that it has
      rights in the name 'Air On Time' and is asking us to transfer
      the domain name to it free of charge. Must we do so?**

A: Has the other courier company told you where it has registered its
      trade mark and given you details of it? If not, you should ask for
      these first. Trade mark registrations are national in nature so you
      should establish where this company's mark is registered. If you
      offer the courier service in a country where it has registered its
      mark, you may potentially be infringing its trade mark, but I would
      need more information on this. You should not let the other
      courier company know about your trade mark application,
      however, as that might alert it to the need to object to your
      registration on the grounds of its prior registration. If its mark is
      registered, but you believe that you have a right to use this domain
      name, stand your ground and tell the other courier company that
      you are prepared to go to UDRP on this and let an arbitrator
      decide who has a better right to the domain name.

Q: **We are a limited company which established a website about a year ago. The domain name we are using was bought by one of the directors on behalf of the company. He has since left but still owns the domain name. How can we get it back?**

A: As the director registered it for the company's benefit, he can probably be said to be holding it in trust for the company. The English courts have recently decided that a director cannot register and keep a trade mark which is the same as his employer's company name. The same is almost certainly true of domain names. You should write to him making these points and asking him to transfer the domain name to the company.

Q: **I have recently purchased a domain name which is the same as another company's name. The domain name resolves to my website. I presumed this was legal. The other company has told me what I am doing is illegal and is 'passing off'. Is this correct and can I sell it the domain name?**

A: Passing off occurs when one person passes off its goods or services as those of another person. If you were aware of the company and did intend to pass your site off as a site owned or associated with that company, you may be passing off and you should be particularly careful to avoid selling similar services or products with similar brand names as the other company's. You should not offer to sell it the domain name as this could be construed as cybersquatting.

Q: **I have registered the domain name 'pangalactic.co.uk' and have used it for almost a year. I have received a letter from Pangalactic World Studios' English solicitor saying that I have to give it this name free of charge or it will take action against me for passing off, trade mark infringement, cybersquatting, creating an instrument of fraud and deception! A day later I also received a separate letter from Pangalactic Stores Ltd's solicitors saying the same sort of thing. I do not want to take on these corporate giants, but I have spent a lot of money on promotion and business stationery, what should I do?**

A: The fact that these two corporations already trade using the same name, albeit for different businesses means there may be scope to argue your case stating that the domain name is different from Pangalactic World Studios' trade mark, that that there is no likelihood of confusion and thus no passing off, that you have not cybersquatted and countering its other claims. Similar arguments could be used to counter the claims made by Pangalactic Stores.

Q: I use a company called Big Band for website hosting. I recently registered the domain name 'bigband.co.uk' as I could not believe that Big Band forgot to register this domain and so and wrote to it offering to sell it the domain name for £10,000. In response it has written to me accusing me of cybersquatting. Is it right?

A: As you were aware of Internetters existence when you registered the domain name, and you offered to sell it to Internetters for a price in excess of what you paid for it, you would probably be found by a court to be cybersquatting. If Big Band is also the owner of a registered trade mark, you might find that it sues you for trade mark infringement. In this case, we recommend that you agree to transfer the domain name to Internetters for your out of pocket expenses only.

Q: If I have got a domain name registered but am not using it, and then a company registers the trade mark, could it take me to court over this?

A: The answer to your question is 'it depends' as this is a nebulous area. If you registered the domain name before the company registered its trade mark, and the mark is not one that is famous or recognisable, then it is unlikely that the registrant will be able to claim that you have no right to the domain name. This is even more likely to be the case if you have a justifiable reason to use it for your business.

Q: Should I register my domain name as a trade mark?

A: It is sensible to register your domain name as a trade mark to prevent anyone else claiming that they have a better right to the domain than you have. Also, most domain name dispute resolution policies favour trade mark owners and certainly sunrise period registrations do so. Registering your domain name as a trade mark will not necessarily ensure that you are permitted to continue to use that name if you have registered it for the purposes of warehousing. Nor will it ensure you can keep the domain name if another person has an identical mark registered in the same country for different goods/services and seeks transfer of the domain name to it, or if an identical mark is registered in another country. Furthermore, registration of your domain name as a trade mark is not guaranteed. Most registries will not permit you to register the TLD or ccTLD part of the domain name and will not permit registrations of 'e' or 'm' words where the 'e' or 'm' stands for electronic or mobile. Also, a third party may object to your registration on the grounds that the mark is the same as or similar to its name or registration. Finally, you need to consider where to register your domain name, as trade marks are only local in protection whereas domain names are global in application.

Q: **I hope to open a small private nursery. Are there any restrictions to using .edu?**

A: The .edu top level domain is reserved for degree-granting educational institutions in the United States granting four-year degrees and is registrable only through Network Solutions. There are a number of national registries which operate .edu as a second level ccTLD, such as edu.bm (Bermuda) .edu.my (Malaysia), .edu.za (South Africa) and it may be possible to register a .edu second level in these countries depending on national registry requirements. In the UK and certain other countries it is possible to register .ac to indicate that the site relates to an academic institution. You can find eligibility criteria at www.ja.net/documents/naming/ac.uk-naming-rules.html, but I think it is unlikely that this will apply to your business unless all or part of your activities is publicly funded. You may wish to consider registering the .net or .org versions of the domain name you have chosen. In the past, .net and .org have been used for commercial businesses rather than .com, but this has changed and they tend to indicate sites offering information and services as well as e-commerce. Have you considered registering a .biz domain name?

Q: **We are a charitable golfing foundation called 'Golf for Grannies'. We recently decided to publicise our activities online. We have discovered that the .org domain name of our charity name has been registered by a commercial enterprise for its leisure breaks. We thought that .org was reserved for public bodies and charities. Is this not the case?**

A: .org was initially intended for use by public bodies and charities, but has come to be used widely by companies and other businesses. You may wish to seek the transfer of the domain name using UDRP if you believe you have a better right to the domain name than the registrant.

Q: **We wish to market our product in Australia and want to set up a website using a .com.au ccTLD. The Australian agent we are using has told us we cannot use this country code unless we have a commercial base in Australia. Is this true?**

A: This is correct, in order to register .com.au you must be a commercial entity registered to trade in Australia. Different national domain name registries have different rules for registration using ccTLDs. You can save time and money by investigating these before launching any product or site.

Appendices

Appendices

Appendix 1 – Glossary and Abbreviations

Administrative contact	The general administrative contact for a domain name registration as recorded on a WHOIS record. This tends to be a person who is intended to be the first point of call in relation to queries regarding domain name use or contents of a website.
ADNDRC	Asian Domain Name Dispute Resolution Centre – based in Beijing and with an office in Hong Kong; arbitrators engaged by this body hear domain name disputes brought under UDRP.
Affinity domain	Please refer to section B3.13 for full description.
ccTLD	Country code top level domain name – the part of the domain name indicating the national registry where the domain name was registered, e.g. .co.uk, .us or .au
CPR	CPR Institute for Dispute Resolution – arbitrators engaged by this body hear domain name disputes brought under UDRP.
Crypt-PW	A security system protecting domain names and preventing details relating to them from being changed without authority. This system requires a password to be entered in order for changes to be made to a domain name.
CTM	Community Trade Mark – refers to a trade mark which is registered centrally in respect of all countries in the European Community.
Cybersquatting	Registration of a domain name to which another person or business (usually a well-known or famous one) has rights. Cybersquatting is usually (though not always) characterised by such a registration followed by an offer by the registrant to sell the domain name to the other person or business which has rights to it for a price in excess of the registrant's registration expenses.

Domain name	A unique name used to locate a particular website which when entered into a browser will direct the user to that particular website. Domain names are a more memorable form of a long string of numbers (known as an IP address), which locates a certain website on the internet. Domain names are divided into a series of 'domains', starting with the top level domain (TLD) at the right after the last full stop, then the second level domain (SLD) to the left of the last full stop, the third level domain to the left of the SLD and so on.
DRPs	Dispute resolution policies applying to domain names, including Nominet's DRS Policy and ICANN's UDRP etc (see APPENDICES 2–4).
Escrow	A procedure by which a third party holds funds/data/documents/computer code for release to a specified party upon the occurrence of a specified event. Computer code relating to a website is often held in 'escrow' so that if the host ceases to trade, the escrow agent will release the code to the website owner.
Escrow agent (see also stakeholder)	A person or entity which holds funds/data/ documents/computer code for release to a specified party upon the occurrence of a specified event.
FAQ	Frequently Asked Question.
gTLD	Global top level domain name – a top level domain name such as .com, .net, .org, .edu, .gov, .mil, .biz, .info, .name, .pro, .coop, .aero, .museum
Host	An entity with one or more computers ('servers') connected to the www which enables websites to be accessible via the internet.
http	Hypertext Transfer Protocol – a standardised methodology (and language) used for transferring documents across the internet.
Hypertext	Text which is written so as to digitally enable a web user to click on the text and link to another website to a different place on the internet (or within the same site).
ICANN	Internet Corporation for Assigned Names and Numbers – the body which regulates creation and allocation of TLDs and ccTLDs.

Internet	A collection of computers across the world which use identical internet protocol addressing so as to enable users of the internet system to locate them.
IP address	Internet Protocol address — a unique numeric address for a particular website which enables computers to locate a particular website on the web.
ISO	International Standards Organisation.
ISP	Internet Service Provider — an entity which provides access to the internet and other services, usually for a fee. Examples of ISPs include British Telecom and Freeserve.
Link	A hypertext enabled connection which takes a user from one place to another on the internet.
Metatag	Key words which through use of hypertext code are embedded in websites which assist search engines to locate information on the www for web users.
NAF	National Arbitration Forum — based in the USA, arbitrators engaged by this body hear domain name disputes brought under UDRP.
Name server	A computer on which data relating to domain names is stored.
Nice Classification	An internationally recognised system of classifying goods and services into 42 different classes for the purposes of trade mark registration.
NSI	Network Solutions Incorporated — now owned by Verisign — the Registry for the .com .net and .org TLDs.
OHIM	Office for the Harmonisation of the Internal Market — the official name of the CTM trade marks registry.
Online	A term used to indicate that a person is connected to the internet or www — when not connected or when referring to matters not related to the internet or www the term 'offline is used.
PGP *or* **Pretty Good Privacy**	An encryption based security system which can be used to prevent domain names (and details relating to them) from being changed without authority. PGP requires a previously advised digital signature to be used before any changes can be made.

Protection domain	Please refer to section B3.10 for full description.
Referrer domain	Please refer to section B3.9 for full description.
Registrar	A Registrar is an organisation accredited by ICANN, which can register domain names with the various Registries on behalf of clients. Registrars have access to the various Registries' Shared Registry Systems.
Registration certificate	A certificate which records ownership of a domain name.
Registry	A Registry is an organisation accredited by ICANN, which maintains the register of domain names for any given TLD. There are separate registries for each gTLD and ccTLD. gTLD Registries do not deal directly with the public and only work with Registrars.
Registry key	An alphanumeric password, usually supplied by the domain name Registry which enables an authorised user to access a domain record and change the address and contact details of the registrant.
Reverse domain hijacking	A term used to describe a claim brought against a *bona fide* registrant of a domain name who is using a name with good reason, but which the claimant claims entitlement to. Such claims are usually brought by large businesses for domain names which include parts of their own business names which are generic.
RNCA	Registrant Name Change Agreement – an agreement required to change details of domain name ownership with NSI.
Search engine	An internet tool which operates as a directory of internet subjects and which enables users to find information by ranking key phrases and making them available, usually in perceived order of relevance, to the user upon request.
Server	A computer which gives multiple users simultaneous access to a computer system or the internet.
Shop front domain	Please refer to section B3.8 for full description.

SLD	Second level domain – the SLD is to the left of the full stop before the top level domain (TLD). For example, the 'internetters' part of 'internetters.com' is the SLD.Subsequent third and fourth level domains are to the left of the full stop after the SLD.
Sponsored domain	Please refer to section B3.11 for full description.
Stakeholder	A person who holds domain name purchase monies or a proportion thereof and only releases the money to the vendor when it has received confirmation of the transfer of a domain name to a purchaser.
Sucks site	A site which uses the same name as a genuine or authentic website but which adds the word 'sucks' (or similar word) to that domain name. Such sites tend to be used for sites which are derogatory of the 'genuine' site or which list complaints about their goods/services/website/treatment of staff/aftersales etc.
Surf	A colloquial phrase meaning to use the internet and in particular to visit a number of websites whilst online.
Tag holder	A tag holder is a member of Nominet, the UK domain registry. Tag holders register and manage their clients' domain names. Most UK ISPs are tag holders.
Technical contact	The technical contact for a domain name registration as recorded on a WHOIS record. This tends to be the name of a person in the company who registered the domain name or a technician at the domain name owner's business who can deal with IT related domain name issues.
TLD	Top level domain – .com, .net, .org, .edu, .biz, .info .name, .aero, .museum, .pro
Trade mark	Any sign which is capable of being represented graphically (usually a word or logo or a word and logo) which distinguishes the goods and services of one entity from those of another.
Trawl	To search a number of websites on the www simultaneously or consecutively – usually used to describe the exercise of looking for a particular piece of information.
Trawling domain	Please refer to section B3.12 for full description.

UDRP	The Uniform Domain Name Dispute Resolution Policy – ICANN's domain name dispute resolution policy as described in Part 4.
url	Uniform Resource Locator – the standard system of addressing websites located on the internet. Urls are strings of numbers separated by full stops which are converted into words or 'website addresses' (i.e. domain names) for ease of recollection/relevance for website users.
Vanity domain	Please refer to section B3.14 for full description.
Web/www	The World Wide Web – a collection of interconnected computers linked through the use of hypertext and located by using a url.
WHOIS	A record of who owns which domain names maintained by NSI/Verisign. The word 'WHOIS' has come to describe any such directory maintained by a Registry.
WIPO	The World Intellectual Property Organisation – based in Geneva, arbitrators engaged by this body hear domain name disputes brought under UDRP.

Appendix 2 – ICANN Uniform Domain Name Dispute Resolution Policy and Rules for Uniform Domain Name Dispute Resolution Policy

Uniform Domain Name Dispute Resolution Policy

(As Approved by ICANN on October 24, 1999)

1. Purpose. This Uniform Domain Name Dispute Resolution Policy (the "Policy") has been adopted by the Internet Corporation for Assigned Names and Numbers ("ICANN"), is incorporated by reference into your Registration Agreement, and sets forth the terms and conditions in connection with a dispute between you and any party other than us (the registrar) over the registration and use of an Internet domain name registered by you. Proceedings under Paragraph 4 of this Policy will be conducted according to the Rules for Uniform Domain Name Dispute Resolution Policy (the "Rules of Procedure"), which are available at www.icann.org/udrp/udrp-rules-24oct99.htm, and the selected administrative-dispute-resolution service provider's supplemental rules.

2. Your Representations. By applying to register a domain name, or by asking us to maintain or renew a domain name registration, you hereby represent and warrant to us that (a) the statements that you made in your Registration Agreement are complete and accurate; (b) to your knowledge, the registration of the domain name will not infringe upon or otherwise violate the rights of any third party; (c) you are not registering the domain name for an unlawful purpose; and (d) you will not knowingly use the domain name in violation of any applicable laws or regulations. It is your responsibility to determine whether your domain name registration infringes or violates someone else's rights.

3. Cancellations, Transfers, and Changes. We will cancel, transfer or otherwise make changes to domain name registrations under the following circumstances:

a. subject to the provisions of Paragraph 8, our receipt of written or appropriate electronic instructions from you or your authorized agent to take such action;

b. our receipt of an order from a court or arbitral tribunal, in each case of competent jurisdiction, requiring such action; and/or

c. our receipt of a decision of an Administrative Panel requiring such action in any administrative proceeding to which you were a party and which was conducted under this Policy or a later version of this Policy adopted by ICANN. (See Paragraph 4(i) and (k) below.)

We may also cancel, transfer or otherwise make changes to a domain name registration in accordance with the terms of your Registration Agreement or other legal requirements.

4. Mandatory Administrative Proceeding. This Paragraph sets forth the type of disputes for which you are required to submit to a mandatory administrative proceeding. These proceedings will be conducted before one of the administrative-dispute-resolution service providers listed at http://www.icann.org/dndr/udrp/approved-providers.htm (each, a "Provider").

a. **Applicable Disputes.** You are required to submit to a mandatory administrative proceeding in the event that a third party (a "complainant") asserts to the applicable Provider, in compliance with the Rules of Procedure, that

(i) your domain name is identical or confusingly similar to a trademark or service mark in which the complainant has rights; and

(ii) you have no rights or legitimate interests in respect of the domain name; and

(iii) your domain name has been registered and is being used in bad faith.

In the administrative proceeding, the complainant must prove that each of these three elements are present.

b. **Evidence of Registration and Use in Bad Faith.** For the purposes of Paragraph 4(a)(iii), the following circumstances, in particular but without limitation, if found by the Panel to be present, shall be evidence of the registration and use of a domain name in bad faith:

(i)   circumstances indicating that you have registered or you have acquired the domain name primarily for the purpose of selling, renting, or otherwise transferring the domain name registration to the complainant who is the owner of the trademark or service mark or to a competitor of that complainant, for valuable consideration in excess of your documented out-of-pocket costs directly related to the domain name; or

(ii)   you have registered the domain name in order to prevent the owner of the trademark or service mark from reflecting the mark in a corresponding domain name, provided that you have engaged in a pattern of such conduct; or

(iii)   you have registered the domain name primarily for the purpose of disrupting the business of a competitor; or

(iv)   by using the domain name, you have intentionally attempted to attract, for commercial gain, Internet users to your web site or other on-line location, by creating a likelihood of confusion with the complainant's mark as to the source, sponsorship, affiliation, or endorsement of your web site or location or of a product or service on your web site or location.

c.   **How to Demonstrate Your Rights to and Legitimate Interests in the Domain Name in Responding to a Complaint.** When you receive a complaint, you should refer to Paragraph 5 of the Rules of Procedure in determining how your response should be prepared. Any of the following circumstances, in particular but without limitation, if found by the Panel to be proved based on its evaluation of all evidence presented, shall demonstrate your rights or legitimate interests to the domain name for purposes of Paragraph 4(a)(ii):

(i)   before any notice to you of the dispute, your use of, or demonstrable preparations to use, the domain name or a name corresponding to the domain name in connection with a bona fide offering of goods or services; or

(ii)   you (as an individual, business, or other organization) have been commonly known by the domain name, even if you have acquired no trademark or service mark rights; or

(iii)   you are making a legitimate noncommercial or fair use of the domain name, without intent for commercial gain to misleadingly divert consumers or to tarnish the trademark or service mark at issue.

d.   **Selection of Provider.** The complainant shall select the Provider from among those approved by ICANN by submitting the complaint to that Provider. The selected Provider will administer the proceeding, except in cases of consolidation as described in Paragraph 4(f).

e. **Initiation of Proceeding and Process and Appointment of Administrative Panel.** The Rules of Procedure state the process for initiating and conducting a proceeding and for appointing the panel that will decide the dispute (the "Administrative Panel").

f. **Consolidation.** In the event of multiple disputes between you and a complainant, either you or the complainant may petition to consolidate the disputes before a single Administrative Panel. This petition shall be made to the first Administrative Panel appointed to hear a pending dispute between the parties. This Administrative Panel may consolidate before it any or all such disputes in its sole discretion, provided that the disputes being consolidated are governed by this Policy or a later version of this Policy adopted by ICANN.

g. **Fees.** All fees charged by a Provider in connection with any dispute before an Administrative Panel pursuant to this Policy shall be paid by the complainant, except in cases where you elect to expand the Administrative Panel from one to three panelists as provided in Paragraph 5(b)(iv) of the Rules of Procedure, in which case all fees will be split evenly by you and the complainant.

h. **Our Involvement in Administrative Proceedings.** We do not, and will not, participate in the administration or conduct of any proceeding before an Administrative Panel. In addition, we will not be liable as a result of any decisions rendered by the Administrative Panel.

i. **Remedies.** The remedies available to a complainant pursuant to any proceeding before an Administrative Panel shall be limited to requiring the cancellation of your domain name or the transfer of your domain name registration to the complainant.

j. **Notification and Publication.** The Provider shall notify us of any decision made by an Administrative Panel with respect to a domain name you have registered with us. All decisions under this Policy will be published in full over the Internet, except when an Administrative Panel determines in an exceptional case to redact portions of its decision.

k. **Availability of Court Proceedings.** The mandatory administrative proceeding requirements set forth in Paragraph 4 shall not prevent either you or the complainant from submitting the dispute to a court of competent jurisdiction for independent resolution before such mandatory administrative proceeding is commenced or after such proceeding is concluded. If an Administrative Panel decides that your domain name registration should be canceled or transferred, we will wait ten (10) business days (as observed in the location of our principal office) after we are informed by the applicable Provider of the Administrative Panel's decision before implementing that decision. We will then implement the decision unless we have received from you during that ten (10) business day period official documentation (such as a copy of a complaint, file-stamped by the clerk of the court) that you have commenced a lawsuit against the complainant in a jurisdiction to which the complainant has submitted under Paragraph 3(b)(xiii) of the Rules of Procedure. (In general, that jurisdiction is either the location of our principal office or of your address as shown in our Whois database. See Paragraphs 1 and 3(b)(xiii) of the Rules of Procedure for details.) If we receive such documentation within the ten (10) business day period, we will not implement the Administrative Panel's decision, and we will take no further action, until we receive (i) evidence satisfactory to us of a resolution between the parties; (ii) evidence satisfactory to us that your lawsuit has been dismissed or withdrawn; or (iii) a copy of an order from such court dismissing your lawsuit or ordering that you do not have the right to continue to use your domain name.

5. All Other Disputes and Litigation. All other disputes between you and any party other than us regarding your domain name registration that are not brought pursuant to the mandatory administrative proceeding provisions of Paragraph 4 shall be resolved between you and such other party through any court, arbitration or other proceeding that may be available.

6. Our Involvement in Disputes. We will not participate in any way in any dispute between you and any party other than us regarding the registration and use of your domain name. You shall not name us as a party or otherwise include us in any such proceeding. In the event that we are named as a party in any such proceeding, we reserve the right to raise any and all defenses deemed appropriate, and to take any other action necessary to defend ourselves.

7. Maintaining the Status Quo. We will not cancel, transfer, activate, deactivate, or otherwise change the status of any domain name registration under this Policy except as provided in Paragraph 3 above.

8. Transfers During a Dispute.

a.   **Transfers of a Domain Name to a New Holder.** You may not transfer your domain name registration to another holder (i) during a pending administrative proceeding brought pursuant to Paragraph 4 or for a period of fifteen (15) business days (as observed in the location of our principal place of business) after such proceeding is concluded; or (ii) during a pending court proceeding or arbitration commenced regarding your domain name unless the party to whom the domain name registration is being transferred agrees, in writing, to be bound by the decision of the court or arbitrator. We reserve the right to cancel any transfer of a domain name registration to another holder that is made in violation of this subparagraph.

b. **Changing Registrars.** You may not transfer your domain name registration to another registrar during a pending administrative proceeding brought pursuant to Paragraph 4 or for a period of fifteen (15) business days (as observed in the location of our principal place of business) after such proceeding is concluded. You may transfer administration of your domain name registration to another registrar during a pending court action or arbitration, provided that the domain name you have registered with us shall continue to be subject to the proceedings commenced against you in accordance with the terms of this Policy. In the event that you transfer a domain name registration to us during the pendency of a court action or arbitration, such dispute shall remain subject to the domain name dispute policy of the registrar from which the domain name registration was transferred.

9. Policy Modifications. We reserve the right to modify this Policy at any time with the permission of ICANN. We will post our revised Policy at [URL] at least thirty (30) calendar days before it becomes effective. Unless this Policy has already been invoked by the submission of a complaint to a Provider, in which event the version of the Policy in effect at the time it was invoked will apply to you until the dispute is over, all such changes will be binding upon you with respect to any domain name registration dispute, whether the dispute arose before, on or after the effective date of our change. In the event that you object to a change in this Policy, your sole remedy is to cancel your domain name registration with us, provided that you will not be entitled to a refund of any fees you paid to us. The revised Policy will apply to you until you cancel your domain name registration.

The ICANN Uniform Domain Name Dispute Resolution Policy is subject to copyright and is reproduced here with ICANN's permission. It can also be found on the internet at www.icann.org/dndr/udrp/policy.htm.

Rules for Uniform Domain Name Dispute Resolution Policy

(the "Rules")

(As Approved by ICANN on October 24, 1999)

Administrative proceedings for the resolution of disputes under the Uniform Dispute Resolution Policy adopted by ICANN shall be governed by these Rules and also the Supplemental Rules of the Provider administering the proceedings, as posted on its web site.

1. Definitions

In these Rules:

Complainant means the party initiating a complaint concerning a domain-name registration.

ICANN refers to the Internet Corporation for Assigned Names and Numbers.

Mutual Jurisdiction means a court jurisdiction at the location of either (a) the principal office of the Registrar (provided the domain-name holder has submitted in its Registration Agreement to that jurisdiction for court adjudication of disputes concerning or arising from the use of the domain name) or (b) the domain-name holder's address as shown for the registration of the domain name in Registrar's Whois database at the time the complaint is submitted to the Provider.

Panel means an administrative panel appointed by a Provider to decide a complaint concerning a domain-name registration.

Panelist means an individual appointed by a Provider to be a member of a Panel.

Party means a Complainant or a Respondent.

Policy means the Uniform Domain Name Dispute Resolution Policy that is incorporated by reference and made a part of the Registration Agreement.

Provider means a dispute-resolution service provider approved by ICANN. A list of such Providers appears at http://www.icann.org/dndr/udrp/approved-providers.htm.

Registrar means the entity with which the Respondent has registered a domain name that is the subject of a complaint.

Registration Agreement means the agreement between a Registrar and a domain-name holder.

Respondent means the holder of a domain-name registration against which a complaint is initiated.

Reverse Domain Name Hijacking means using the Policy in bad faith to attempt to deprive a registered domain-name holder of a domain name.

Supplemental Rules means the rules adopted by the Provider administering a proceeding to supplement these Rules. Supplemental Rules shall not be inconsistent with the Policy or these Rules and shall cover such topics as fees, word and page limits and guidelines, the means for communicating with the Provider and the Panel, and the form of cover sheets.

2. Communications

(a) When forwarding a complaint to the Respondent, it shall be the Provider's responsibility to employ reasonably available means calculated to achieve actual notice to Respondent. Achieving actual notice, or employing the following measures to do so, shall discharge this responsibility:

  (i) sending the complaint to all postal-mail and facsimile addresses (A) shown in the domain name's registration data in Registrar's Whois database for the registered domain-name holder, the technical contact, and the administrative contact and (B) supplied by Registrar to the Provider for the registration's billing contact; and

  (ii) sending the complaint in electronic form (including annexes to the extent available in that form) by e-mail to:

   (A) the e-mail addresses for those technical, administrative, and billing contacts;

   (B) postmaster@[the contested domain name]; and

   (C) if the domain name (or "www." followed by the domain name) resolves to an active web page (other than a generic page the Provider concludes is maintained by a registrar or ISP for parking domain-names registered by multiple domain-name holders), any e-mail address shown or e-mail links on that web page; and

    (iii)   sending the complaint to any address the Respondent has notified the Provider it prefers and, to the extent practicable, to all other addresses provided to the Provider by Complainant under Paragraph 3(b)(v).

(b)   Except as provided in Paragraph 2(a), any written communication to Complainant or Respondent provided for under these Rules shall be made by the preferred means stated by the Complainant or Respondent, respectively (see Paragraphs 3(b)(iii) and 5(b)(iii)), or in the absence of such specification

    (i)   by telecopy or facsimile transmission, with a confirmation of transmission; or

    (ii)   by postal or courier service, postage pre-paid and return receipt requested; or

    (iii)   electronically via the Internet, provided a record of its transmission is available.

(c)   Any communication to the Provider or the Panel shall be made by the means and in the manner (including number of copies) stated in the Provider's Supplemental Rules.

(d)   Communications shall be made in the language prescribed in Paragraph 11. E-mail communications should, if practicable, be sent in plaintext.

(e)   Either Party may update its contact details by notifying the Provider and the Registrar.

(f)   Except as otherwise provided in these Rules, or decided by a Panel, all communications provided for under these Rules shall be deemed to have been made:

    (i)   if delivered by telecopy or facsimile transmission, on the date shown on the confirmation of transmission; or

    (ii)   if by postal or courier service, on the date marked on the receipt; or

    (iii)   if via the Internet, on the date that the communication was transmitted, provided that the date of transmission is verifiable.

(g)   Except as otherwise provided in these Rules, all time periods calculated under these Rules to begin when a communication is made shall begin to run on the earliest date that the communication is deemed to have been made in accordance with Paragraph 2(f).

(h)   Any communication by

(i) a Panel to any Party shall be copied to the Provider and to the other Party;

(ii) the Provider to any Party shall be copied to the other Party; and

(iii) a Party shall be copied to the other Party, the Panel and the Provider, as the case may be.

(i) It shall be the responsibility of the sender to retain records of the fact and circumstances of sending, which shall be available for inspection by affected parties and for reporting purposes.

(j) In the event a Party sending a communication receives notification of non-delivery of the communication, the Party shall promptly notify the Panel (or, if no Panel is yet appointed, the Provider) of the circumstances of the notification. Further proceedings concerning the communication and any response shall be as directed by the Panel (or the Provider).

3. The Complaint

(a) Any person or entity may initiate an administrative proceeding by submitting a complaint in accordance with the Policy and these Rules to any Provider approved by ICANN. (Due to capacity constraints or for other reasons, a Provider's ability to accept complaints may be suspended at times. In that event, the Provider shall refuse the submission. The person or entity may submit the complaint to another Provider.)

(b) The complaint shall be submitted in hard copy and (except to the extent not available for annexes) in electronic form and shall:

    (i) Request that the complaint be submitted for decision in accordance with the Policy and these Rules;

    (ii) Provide the name, postal and e-mail addresses, and the telephone and telefax numbers of the Complainant and of any representative authorized to act for the Complainant in the administrative proceeding;

    (iii) Specify a preferred method for communications directed to the Complainant in the administrative proceeding (including person to be contacted, medium, and address information) for each of (A) electronic-only material and (B) material including hard copy;

    (iv) Designate whether Complainant elects to have the dispute decided by a single-member or a three-member Panel and, in the event Complainant elects a three-member Panel, provide the names and contact details of three candidates to serve as one of the Panelists (these candidates may be drawn from any ICANN-approved Provider's list of panelists);

(v) Provide the name of the Respondent (domain-name holder) and all information (including any postal and e-mail addresses and telephone and telefax numbers) known to Complainant regarding how to contact Respondent or any representative of Respondent, including contact information based on pre-complaint dealings, in sufficient detail to allow the Provider to send the complaint as described in Paragraph 2(a);

(vi) Specify the domain name(s) that is/are the subject of the complaint;

(vii) Identify the Registrar(s) with whom the domain name(s) is/are registered at the time the complaint is filed;

(viii) Specify the trademark(s) or service mark(s) on which the complaint is based and, for each mark, describe the goods or services, if any, with which the mark is used (Complainant may also separately describe other goods and services with which it intends, at the time the complaint is submitted, to use the mark in the future.);

(ix) Describe, in accordance with the Policy, the grounds on which the complaint is made including, in particular,

(1)   the manner in which the domain name(s) is/are identical or confusingly similar to a trademark or service mark in which the Complainant has rights; and

(2)   why the Respondent (domain-name holder) should be considered as having no rights or legitimate interests in respect of the domain name(s) that is/are the subject of the complaint; and

(3)   why the domain name(s) should be considered as having been registered and being used in bad faith

(The description should, for elements (2) and (3), discuss any aspects of Paragraphs 4(b) and 4(c) of the Policy that are applicable. The description shall comply with any word or page limit set forth in the Provider's Supplemental Rules.);

(x) Specify, in accordance with the Policy, the remedies sought;

(xi) Identify any other legal proceedings that have been commenced or terminated in connection with or relating to any of the domain name(s) that are the subject of the complaint;

(xii) State that a copy of the complaint, together with the cover sheet as prescribed by the Provider's Supplemental Rules, has been sent or transmitted to the Respondent (domain-name holder), in accordance with Paragraph 2(b);

(xiii) State that Complainant will submit, with respect to any challenges to a decision in the administrative proceeding canceling or transferring the domain name, to the jurisdiction of the courts in at least one specified Mutual Jurisdiction;

(xiv) Conclude with the following statement followed by the signature of the Complainant or its authorized representative:

> "Complainant agrees that its claims and remedies concerning the registration of the domain name, the dispute, or the dispute's resolution shall be solely against the domain-name holder and waives all such claims and remedies against (a) the dispute-resolution provider and panelists, except in the case of deliberate wrongdoing, (b) the registrar, (c) the registry administrator, and (d) the Internet Corporation for Assigned Names and Numbers, as well as their directors, officers, employees, and agents."

> "Complainant certifies that the information contained in this Complaint is to the best of Complainant's knowledge complete and accurate, that this Complaint is not being presented for any improper purpose, such as to harass, and that the assertions in this Complaint are warranted under these Rules and under applicable law, as it now exists or as it may be extended by a good-faith and reasonable argument."; and

(xv) Annex any documentary or other evidence, including a copy of the Policy applicable to the domain name(s) in dispute and any trademark or service mark registration upon which the complaint relies, together with a schedule indexing such evidence.

(c) The complaint may relate to more than one domain name, provided that the domain names are registered by the same domain-name holder.

4. Notification of Complaint

(a) The Provider shall review the complaint for administrative compliance with the Policy and these Rules and, if in compliance, shall forward the complaint (together with the explanatory cover sheet prescribed by the Provider's Supplemental Rules) to the Respondent, in the manner prescribed by Paragraph 2(a), within three (3) calendar days following receipt of the fees to be paid by the Complainant in accordance with Paragraph 19.

(b) If the Provider finds the complaint to be administratively deficient, it shall promptly notify the Complainant and the Respondent of the nature of the deficiencies identified. The Complainant shall have five (5) calendar days within which to correct any such deficiencies, after which the administrative proceeding will be deemed withdrawn without prejudice to submission of a different complaint by Complainant.

(c) The date of commencement of the administrative proceeding shall be the date on which the Provider completes its responsibilities under Paragraph 2(a) in connection with forwarding the Complaint to the Respondent.

(d) The Provider shall immediately notify the Complainant, the Respondent, the concerned Registrar(s), and ICANN of the date of commencement of the administrative proceeding.

5. The Response

(a) Within twenty (20) days of the date of commencement of the administrative proceeding the Respondent shall submit a response to the Provider.

(b) The response shall be submitted in hard copy and (except to the extent not available for annexes) in electronic form and shall:

(i) Respond specifically to the statements and allegations contained in the complaint and include any and all bases for the Respondent (domain-name holder) to retain registration and use of the disputed domain name (This portion of the response shall comply with any word or page limit set forth in the Provider's Supplemental Rules.);

(ii) Provide the name, postal and e-mail addresses, and the telephone and telefax numbers of the Respondent (domain-name holder) and of any representative authorized to act for the Respondent in the administrative proceeding;

(iii) Specify a preferred method for communications directed to the Respondent in the administrative proceeding (including person to be contacted, medium, and address information) for each of (A) electronic-only material and (B) material including hard copy;

(iv) If Complainant has elected a single-member panel in the Complaint (see Paragraph 3(b)(iv)), state whether Respondent elects instead to have the dispute decided by a three-member panel;

(v) If either Complainant or Respondent elects a three-member Panel, provide the names and contact details of three candidates to serve as one of the Panelists (these candidates may be drawn from any ICANN-approved Provider's list of panelists);

(vi) Identify any other legal proceedings that have been commenced or terminated in connection with or relating to any of the domain name(s) that are the subject of the complaint;

(vii) State that a copy of the response has been sent or transmitted to the Complainant, in accordance with Paragraph 2(b); and

(viii) Conclude with the following statement followed by the signature of the Respondent or its authorized representative:

> "Respondent certifies that the information contained in this Response is to the best of Respondent's knowledge complete and accurate, that this Response is not being presented for any improper purpose, such as to harass, and that the assertions in this Response are warranted under these Rules and under applicable law, as it now exists or as it may be extended by a good-faith and reasonable argument."; and

(ix) Annex any documentary or other evidence upon which the Respondent relies, together with a schedule indexing such documents.

(c) If Complainant has elected to have the dispute decided by a single-member Panel and Respondent elects a three-member Panel, Respondent shall be required to pay one-half of the applicable fee for a three-member Panel as set forth in the Provider's Supplemental Rules. This payment shall be made together with the submission of the response to the Provider. In the event that the required payment is not made, the dispute shall be decided by a single-member Panel.

(d) At the request of the Respondent, the Provider may, in exceptional cases, extend the period of time for the filing of the response. The period may also be extended by written stipulation between the Parties, provided the stipulation is approved by the Provider.

(e) If a Respondent does not submit a response, in the absence of exceptional circumstances, the Panel shall decide the dispute based upon the complaint.

6. Appointment of the Panel and Timing of Decision

(a) Each Provider shall maintain and publish a publicly available list of panelists and their qualifications.

(b) If neither the Complainant nor the Respondent has elected a three-member Panel (Paragraphs 3(b)(iv) and 5(b)(iv)), the Provider shall appoint, within five (5) calendar days following receipt of the response by the Provider, or the lapse of the time period for the submission thereof, a single Panelist from its list of panelists. The fees for a single-member Panel shall be paid entirely by the Complainant.

(c) If either the Complainant or the Respondent elects to have the dispute decided by a three-member Panel, the Provider shall appoint three Panelists in accordance with the procedures identified in Paragraph 6(e). The fees for a three-member Panel shall be paid in their entirety by the Complainant, except where the election for a three-member Panel was made by the Respondent, in which case the applicable fees shall be shared equally between the Parties.

(d) Unless it has already elected a three-member Panel, the Complainant shall submit to the Provider, within five (5) calendar days of communication of a response in which the Respondent elects a three-member Panel, the names and contact details of three candidates to serve as one of the Panelists. These candidates may be drawn from any ICANN-approved Provider's list of panelists.

(e) In the event that either the Complainant or the Respondent elects a three-member Panel, the Provider shall endeavor to appoint one Panelist from the list of candidates provided by each of the Complainant and the Respondent. In the event the Provider is unable within five (5) calendar days to secure the appointment of a Panelist on its customary terms from either Party's list of candidates, the Provider shall make that appointment from its list of panelists. The third Panelist shall be appointed by the Provider from a list of five candidates submitted by the Provider to the Parties, the

Provider's selection from among the five being made in a manner that reasonably balances the preferences of both Parties, as they may specify to the Provider within five (5) calendar days of the Provider's submission of the five-candidate list to the Parties.

(f)   Once the entire Panel is appointed, the Provider shall notify the Parties of the Panelists appointed and the date by which, absent exceptional circumstances, the Panel shall forward its decision on the complaint to the Provider.

7. Impartiality and Independence

A Panelist shall be impartial and independent and shall have, before accepting appointment, disclosed to the Provider any circumstances giving rise to justifiable doubt as to the Panelist's impartiality or independence. If, at any stage during the administrative proceeding, new circumstances arise that could give rise to justifiable doubt as to the impartiality or independence of the Panelist, that Panelist shall promptly disclose such circumstances to the Provider. In such event, the Provider shall have the discretion to appoint a substitute Panelist.

8. Communication Between Parties and the Panel

No Party or anyone acting on its behalf may have any unilateral communication with the Panel. All communications between a Party and the Panel or the Provider shall be made to a case administrator appointed by the Provider in the manner prescribed in the Provider's Supplemental Rules.

9. Transmission of the File to the Panel

The Provider shall forward the file to the Panel as soon as the Panelist is appointed in the case of a Panel consisting of a single member, or as soon as the last Panelist is appointed in the case of a three-member Panel.

10. General Powers of the Panel

(a)   The Panel shall conduct the administrative proceeding in such manner as it considers appropriate in accordance with the Policy and these Rules.

(b) In all cases, the Panel shall ensure that the Parties are treated with equality and that each Party is given a fair opportunity to present its case.

(c) The Panel shall ensure that the administrative proceeding takes place with due expedition. It may, at the request of a Party or on its own motion, extend, in exceptional cases, a period of time fixed by these Rules or by the Panel.

(d) The Panel shall determine the admissibility, relevance, materiality and weight of the evidence.

(e) A Panel shall decide a request by a Party to consolidate multiple domain name disputes in accordance with the Policy and these Rules.

11. Language of Proceedings

(a) Unless otherwise agreed by the Parties, or specified otherwise in the Registration Agreement, the language of the administrative proceeding shall be the language of the Registration Agreement, subject to the authority of the Panel to determine otherwise, having regard to the circumstances of the administrative proceeding.

(b) The Panel may order that any documents submitted in languages other than the language of the administrative proceeding be accompanied by a translation in whole or in part into the language of the administrative proceeding.

12. Further Statements

In addition to the complaint and the response, the Panel may request, in its sole discretion, further statements or documents from either of the Parties.

13. In-Person Hearings

There shall be no in-person hearings (including hearings by teleconference, videoconference, and web conference), unless the Panel determines, in its sole discretion and as an exceptional matter, that such a hearing is necessary for deciding the complaint.

14. Default

(a) In the event that a Party, in the absence of exceptional circumstances, does not comply with any of the time periods established by these Rules or the Panel, the Panel shall proceed to a decision on the complaint.

(b) If a Party, in the absence of exceptional circumstances, does not comply with any provision of, or requirement under, these Rules or any request from the Panel, the Panel shall draw such inferences therefrom as it considers appropriate.

15. Panel Decisions

(a) A Panel shall decide a complaint on the basis of the statements and documents submitted and in accordance with the Policy, these Rules and any rules and principles of law that it deems applicable.

(b) In the absence of exceptional circumstances, the Panel shall forward its decision on the complaint to the Provider within fourteen (14) days of its appointment pursuant to Paragraph 6.

(c) In the case of a three-member Panel, the Panel's decision shall be made by a majority.

(d) The Panel's decision shall be in writing, provide the reasons on which it is based, indicate the date on which it was rendered and identify the name(s) of the Panelist(s).

(e) Panel decisions and dissenting opinions shall normally comply with the guidelines as to length set forth in the Provider's Supplemental Rules. Any dissenting opinion shall accompany the majority decision. If the Panel concludes that the dispute is not within the scope of Paragraph 4(a) of the Policy, it shall so state. If after considering the submissions the Panel finds that the complaint was brought in bad faith, for example in an attempt at Reverse Domain Name Hijacking or was brought primarily to harass the domain-name holder, the Panel shall declare in its decision that the complaint was brought in bad faith and constitutes an abuse of the administrative proceeding.

16. Communication of Decision to Parties

(a) Within three (3) calendar days after receiving the decision from the Panel, the Provider shall communicate the full text of the decision to each Party, the concerned Registrar(s), and ICANN. The concerned Registrar(s) shall immediately communicate to each

Party, the Provider, and ICANN the date for the implementation of the decision in accordance with the Policy.

(b)   Except if the Panel determines otherwise (see Paragraph 4(j) of the Policy), the Provider shall publish the full decision and the date of its implementation on a publicly accessible web site. In any event, the portion of any decision determining a complaint to have been brought in bad faith (see Paragraph 15(e) of these Rules) shall be published.

17. Settlement or Other Grounds for Termination

(a)   If, before the Panel's decision, the Parties agree on a settlement, the Panel shall terminate the administrative proceeding.

(b)   If, before the Panel's decision is made, it becomes unnecessary or impossible to continue the administrative proceeding for any reason, the Panel shall terminate the administrative proceeding, unless a Party raises justifiable grounds for objection within a period of time to be determined by the Panel.

18. Effect of Court Proceedings

(a)   In the event of any legal proceedings initiated prior to or during an administrative proceeding in respect of a domain-name dispute that is the subject of the complaint, the Panel shall have the discretion to decide whether to suspend or terminate the administrative proceeding, or to proceed to a decision.

(b)   In the event that a Party initiates any legal proceedings during the pendency of an administrative proceeding in respect of a domain-name dispute that is the subject of the complaint, it shall promptly notify the Panel and the Provider. See Paragraph 8 above.

19. Fees

(a)   The Complainant shall pay to the Provider an initial fixed fee, in accordance with the Provider's Supplemental Rules, within the time and in the amount required. A Respondent electing under Paragraph 5(b)(iv) to have the dispute decided by a three-member Panel, rather than the single-member Panel elected by the Complainant, shall pay the Provider one-half the fixed fee for a three-member Panel. See Paragraph 5(c). In all other cases, the Complainant shall bear all of the Provider's fees, except as prescribed under Paragraph 19(d). Upon appointment of the Panel, the Provider shall refund the appropriate portion, if any, of the initial fee to the Complainant, as specified in the Provider's Supplemental Rules.

(b) No action shall be taken by the Provider on a complaint until it has received from Complainant the initial fee in accordance with Paragraph 19(a).

(c) If the Provider has not received the fee within ten (10) calendar days of receiving the complaint, the complaint shall be deemed withdrawn and the administrative proceeding terminated.

(d) In exceptional circumstances, for example in the event an in-person hearing is held, the Provider shall request the Parties for the payment of additional fees, which shall be established in agreement with the Parties and the Panel.

20. Exclusion of Liability

Except in the case of deliberate wrongdoing, neither the Provider nor a Panelist shall be liable to a Party for any act or omission in connection with any administrative proceeding under these Rules.

21. Amendments

The version of these Rules in effect at the time of the submission of the complaint to the Provider shall apply to the administrative proceeding commenced thereby. These Rules may not be amended without the express written approval of ICANN.

The ICANN Rules for Uniform Domain Name Dispute Resolution Policy are subject to copyright and are reproduced here with ICANN's permission. They can also be found on the internet at www.icann.org/dndr/udrp/uniform-rules.htm.

Appendix 3 – World Intellectual Property Organization Supplemental Rules and the National Arbitration Forum's Supplemental Rules to ICANN's Uniform Domain Name Dispute Resolution Policy

World Intellectual Property Organization Supplemental Rules for Uniform Domain Name Dispute Resolution Policy

(the "Supplemental Rules")

(In effect as of December 1, 1999)

1. Scope

(a) **Relationship to Rules**. These Supplemental Rules are to be read and used in connection with the Rules for Uniform Domain Name Dispute Resolution Policy, approved by the Internet Corporation for Assigned Names and Numbers (ICANN) on October 24, 1999 (the "Rules").

(b) **Version of Supplemental Rules**. The version of these Supplemental Rules as in effect on the date of the submission of the complaint shall apply to the administrative proceeding commenced thereby.

2. Definitions

Any term defined in the Rules shall have the same meaning in these Supplemental Rules.

3. Communications

(a) **Modalities**. Subject to Paragraphs 3(b) and 5(b) of the Rules, except where otherwise agreed beforehand with the Center, any submission that may or is required to be made to the Center or to an Administrative Panel pursuant to these Rules, may be made:

    (i) by telecopy or facsimile transmission, with a confirmation of transmission;

    (ii) by electronic mail (e-mail) using the address specified by the Center; or

    (iii) where both parties agree, through the Center's Internet-based case filing and administration system.

(b) **E-Mail Address**. For the purposes of any communications by electronic mail to the Center, including those required under Paragraphs 3(b) and 5(b) of the Rules, the following address should be used: domain.disputes@wipo.int.

(c) **Copies**. When a paper submission is to be made to the Center by a Party, it shall be submitted in four (4) sets together with the original of such submission.

(d) **Archive**. The Center shall maintain an archive of all communications received or required to be made under the Rules.

4. Submission of Complaint

(a) **Complaint Transmittal Coversheet**. In accordance with Paragraph 3(b)(xii) of the Rules, the Complainant shall be required to send or transmit its complaint under cover of the Complaint Transmittal Coversheet set out in Annex A hereto and posted on the Center's web site. Where available, the Complainant shall use the version that is in the same language(s) as the registration agreement(s) for the domain name(s) that is/are the subject of the complaint.

(b) **Registrar Notification**. The Complainant shall provide a copy of the complaint to the concerned Registrar(s) at the same time as it submits its complaint to the Center.

(c) **Complaint Notification Instructions**. In accordance with Paragraph 4(a) of the Rules, the Center shall forward the complaint to the Respondent together with the instructions set out in Annex B hereto and posted on the Center's website.

5. Formalities Compliance Review

(a) **Deficiency Notification**. The Center shall, within five (5) calendar days of receiving the complaint, review the complaint for compliance with the formal requirements of the Policy, Rules and Supplemental Rules and notify the Complainant and Respondent of any deficiencies therein.

(b) **Withdrawal**. If the Complainant fails to remedy any deficiencies identified by the Center within the time period provided for in Paragraph 4 of the Rules (i.e., five (5) calendar days), the Center shall notify the Complainant, the Respondent and the concerned Registrar(s) of the deemed withdrawal of the complaint.

(c) **Fee Refunds**. Unless the Complainant confirms its intention to re-submit a complaint to the Center following a deemed withdrawal, the Center shall refund the fee paid by the Complainant pursuant to Paragraph 19 of the Rules, less a processing fee as set forth in Annex D.

6. Appointment of Case Administrator

(a) **Notification**. The Center shall advise the Parties of the name and contact details of a member of its staff who shall be the Case Administrator and who shall be responsible for all administrative matters relating to the dispute and communications to the Administrative Panel.

(b) **Responsibilities**. The Case Administrator may provide administrative assistance to the Administrative Panel or a Panelist, but shall have no authority to decide matters of a substantive nature concerning the dispute.

7. Panelist Appointment Procedures

(a) **Party Candidates**. Where a Party is required to submit the names of three (3) candidates for consideration for appointment by the Center as a Panelist (i.e., in accordance with paragraphs 3(b)(iv), 5(b)(v) and 6(d) of the Rules), that Party shall provide the names and contact details of its three candidates in the order of its preference. In appointing a Panelist, the Center shall, subject to availability, respect the order of preference indicated by a Party.

(b) **Presiding Panelist**

(i) The third Panelist appointed in accordance with Paragraph 6(e) of the Rules shall be the Presiding Panelist.

(ii) Where, under Paragraph 6(e) of the Rules, a Party fails to indicate its order of preference for the Presiding Panelist to the Center, the Center shall nevertheless proceed to appoint the Presiding Panelist.

(iii) Notwithstanding the procedure provided for in Paragraph 6(e) of the Rules, the Parties may jointly agree on the identity of the Presiding Panelist, in which case they shall notify the Center in writing of such agreement no later than five (5) calendar days after receiving the list of candidates provided for in Paragraph 6(e).

(c) **Respondent Default**

Where the Respondent does not submit a response or does not submit the payment provided for in Paragraph 5(c) of the Rules by the deadline specified by the Center, the Center shall proceed to appoint the Administrative Panel, as follows:

(i) If the Complainant has designated a single member Administrative Panel, the Center shall appoint the Panelist from its published list;

(ii) If the Complainant has designated a three member Administrative Panel, the Center shall, subject to availability, appoint one Panelist from the names submitted by the Complainant and shall appoint the second Panelist and the Presiding Panelist from its published list.

8. Declaration

In accordance with Paragraph 7 of the Rules, prior to appointment as a Panelist, a candidate shall be required to submit to the Center a Declaration of Independence and Impartiality using the form set out in Annex C hereto and posted on the Center's web site.

9. Fees

The applicable fees for the administrative procedure are specified in Annex D hereto and posted on the Center's web site.

10. Word Limits

(a) The word limit under Paragraph 3(b)(ix) of the Rules shall be 5,000 words.

(b) The word limit under Paragraph 5(b)(i) of the Rules shall be 5,000 words.

(c) For the purposes of Paragraph 15(e) of the Rules, there shall be no word limits.

11. Amendments

Subject to the Policy and Rules, the Center may amend these Supplemental Rules in its sole discretion.

12. Exclusion of Liability

Except in respect of deliberate wrongdoing, an Administrative Panel, the World Intellectual Property Organization and the Center shall not be liable to a party, a concerned registrar or ICANN for any act or omission in connection with the administrative proceeding.

Material originally provided by the World Property Organization (WIPO), the owner of the copyright. The Secretariat of WIPO assumes no liability or responsibility with regard to the transformation or translation of this data.

The World Intellectual Property Organization Supplemental Rules for Uniform Domain Name Dispute Resolution Policy are reproduced here with the permission of WIPO. They can be found on the internet at http://arbiter.wipo. int/domains/rules/supplemental.html.

The National Arbitration Forum's Supplemental Rules to ICANN's Uniform Domain Name Dispute Resolution Policy

1. Definitions

a.   **The Rules** means the Rules for the Uniform Domain Name Dispute Resolution Policy, approved by the Internet Corporation for Assigned Names and Numbers (ICANN) October 24, 1999.

b.   **The Policy** means the Uniform Domain Name Dispute Resolution Policy approved by ICANN on October 24, 1999.

c.   **The Forum** means the National Arbitration Forum.

2. Scope

The Forum will apply the Rules, the Policy and the Forum's Supplemental Rules in effect at the time a Complaint is submitted. The Forum Supplemental Rules may be amended by the Forum in its sole discretion.

3. Communications

All communications must be directed to the Forum and not to the Panel.

4. The Complaint

a.   The Complaint must include all elements listed in Paragraph 3(b) of the Rules and may not exceed ten (10) pages.

b.   The Complainant must submit three (3) copies of the Complaint to the Forum if the Complainant requests a single-member Panel. The Complainant must submit five (5) copies of the Complaint if the Complainant requests a three (3) member Panel. If the Respondent requests a three-member Panel, the Complainant may be asked to submit additional copies of the Complaint.

c.   In accordance with Paragraph 3(b)(xii) of the Rules, the Complainant must send or transmit its Complaint to the Respondent under cover of the Complaint Transmittal Cover Sheet posted on the Forum's web site.

d.   The Complaint must be sent to the Forum by e-mail (info@arb-forum.com), and either by fax or by mail.

5. The Response

a.   The Response must include all elements listed in Paragraph 5(b) of the Rules and may not exceed ten (10) pages. If no Response is submitted or if the Response fails to designate a preferred method of communication as required under Paragraph 5(b)(iii) of the Rules, the method used by the Forum to communicate to the Respondent will be:

  i.   the e-mail address Respondent provided in the Response;

  ii.   if no Response is submitted or if no e-mail address is provided in the Response, the e-mail address of the Respondent in the WHOIS on the date the Complaint was filed;

  iii.   if there is no e-mail address in the WHOIS, the facsimile address the Respondent provided in the Response or the e-mail address provided for the Respondent in the Complaint;

  iv.   if none of these addresses are provided, the facsimile address provided for the Respondent in the Complaint; or

  v.   if none of these addresses are provided, the mail address provided for the Respondent in the Complaint.

b.   The Respondent must submit three (3) copies of the Response to the Forum if the Complainant requested a single-member Panel. If the Complainant or Respondent requested a three-member Panel, the Respondent must submit (5) copies of the Response to the Forum.

c.   The Response must be sent to the Forum by e-mail (info@arb-forum.com), and by either fax or by mail.

6. Extension for Filing a Response

a.   Paragraph 5(d) of the Rules provides that the Respondent may request additional time to submit a Response, or may be given additional time if the parties stipulate to an extension and the Forum approves. Any request by the Respondent for an extension or any joint request by the parties for an extension must:

  i.   be submitted after the parties have first conferred with each other to see if they could reach an agreement concerning the requested extension;

  ii.   be submitted in writing to the Forum and the parties within the time for the Response to be submitted;

221

    iii.   state the exceptional circumstances warranting the request for an extension;

    iv.   state the length of the extension being requested (no more than twenty (20) additional days); and

    v.   be accompanied by an extension fee of $100.

b.   The Forum may exercise its discretion in determining whether exceptional circumstances exist warranting an extension and if so, the length of the extension. No request for an extension will be approved if any of the conditions set forth in Paragraph 6(a) have not been performed.

7. Submission of other Written Statements and Documents; No Amendment to the Complaint

a.   A party may submit additional written statements and documents to the Forum and the opposing party(s) within five (5) calendar days after the date the Response was submitted or the last date the Response was due to be submitted to the Forum, whichever occurs first.

b.   Each submission must:

    i.   be timely received by the Forum;

    ii.   be accompanied by an additional submission fee of $250;

    iii.   include proof of service of these submissions upon the opposing party(s);

    iv.   be submitted in either hard copy or electronic form.

c.   The opposing party may respond, in hard copy or electronic form, to an additional submission filed in accordance with Supplemental Rule 7(a); such response must be submitted to the Forum and the opposing party(s) within five (5) calendar days after the date the additional submission was submitted.

d.   Additional submissions and responses to additional submissions may not amend the original Complaint or Response.

8. The Record of the Administrative Proceeding.

The Complaint, Response, and additional written statements and documents provided in Paragraph 12 of the Rules and Paragraph 7 of these Supplemental Rules constitute the complete record to be considered by the Panel.

9. Appointment of the Panel and Timing of Decision

a.   The Forum will maintain and publish a list of Panelists and their qualifications to which any party will be directed on the Forum's web site, http://www.arbitration-forum.com/. The Forum will appoint a Panelist from this list to serve as a single-member Panel.

b.   In cases involving a three-member Panel, the Forum will select a Chair from the three-member Panel and will endeavor to select a Chair who was not from the list of Panelist candidates provided by the parties pursuant to Paragraph 6(e) of the Rules. The Chair will sign all Orders and the Decision, coordinate and preside over the proceeding, and forward to the Forum the Panel's decision, including any concurring or dissenting opinion as required by Paragraph 15 of the Rules.

c.   In cases where the Complainant requested a three-member Panel and no Response was submitted as required by Rule 5(a), the Complainant may be given the option of converting the three-member Panel to a single-member Panel:

  i.   After the time for the Response has expired, the Forum will notify the Complainant that no response was submitted and that the Complainant may convert its three-member Panel request to a single-member Panel request;

  ii.   Within five (5) calendar days of this notification, the Complainant, by e-mail to the Forum, may request that the three-member Panel be converted to a single-member Panel;

  iii. If a single-member Panel is requested, the Forum will select a Panelist from its list of Panelists, not on the list of Panelists submitted by the Complainant; and

  iv.   If a single-member Panel conducts the administrative hearing, the Complainant will be reimbursed $1,000 of its hearing fee.

d.   If the Complainant fails to request that the three-member Panel be converted to a single-member Panel as provided in paragraph 9(c)(ii) above, the selection of the three-member Panel will be as follows:

  i.   The Complainant must provide a list of three candidates and the Forum will endeavor to select a Panelist from that list as provided in Rule 6(e);

  ii.   The Forum will select a Panelist from its list of Panel members; and

  iii. The Forum will submit to the parties a list of five candidates and will select a Panelist as provided in Rule 6(e).

e.   In cases where the Respondent requested a three-member Panel and the Complaint is withdrawn prior to the appointment of a Panel, the Respondent will be reimbursed $1,000 of its hearing fee.

10. Impartiality and Independence

a.   All Forum Panelists will take an oath to be neutral and independent.

b.   A Panelist will be disqualified if circumstances exist that create a conflict of interest or cause the Panelist to be unfair and biased, including but not limited to the following:

    i.   The Panelist has a personal bias or prejudice concerning a party or personal knowledge of disputed evidentiary facts;

    ii.   The Panelist has served as an attorney to any party or the Panelist has been associated with an attorney who has represented a party during that association;

    iii.   The Panelist, individually or as a fiduciary, or the Panelist's spouse or minor child residing in the Panelist's household, has a direct financial interest in a matter before the Panelist;

    iv.   The Panelist or the Panelist's spouse, or a person within the third degree of relationship to either of them, or the spouse of such a person:

        1.   Is a party to the proceeding, or an officer, director, or trustee of a Party; or

        2.   Is acting as a lawyer or representative in the proceeding.

c.   A party may challenge the selection of a Panelist, provided that a decision has not already been published, by filing with the Forum a written request stating the circumstances and specific reasons for the disqualification.

d.   A request to challenge must be filed in writing with the Director of Arbitration within five (5) days of the date of receipt of the notice of the selection.

e.   Provided a decision has not already been published by the selected Panelist, the Forum will promptly review the challenge and determine whether circumstances exist requiring Panelist disqualification in accord with this rule.

11. Communications Between Parties and the Panel

a.   No party may directly communicate with a Panelist.

b. The parties may communicate with the Case Coordinator assigned to their proceeding by phone, fax, e-mail, or mail through the United States Postal Service.

c. Any request by a party for any type of action by the Forum or Panel must be communicated in writing to the Forum and the opposing party(s).

12. Withdrawal

a. Prior to Commencement

i. Before the five (5) day deficiency period described in Rule 4(b) expires, the Complainant may withdraw the Complaint without prejudice. A withdrawal request must be submitted to the Forum in writing and signed by the Complainant.

ii. The Complainant may re-initiate the same proceeding within thirty (30) calendar days after a pre-commencement withdrawal. A re-initiation fee of $100 must accompany the request to re-initiate the proceeding.

iii. If the Complainant does not re-initiate the Complaint, at the end of thirty (30) calendar days the Complaint is withdrawn without prejudice and the administrative proceeding is terminated. Any subsequent Complaint will be treated as a new Complaint and must be accompanied by payment of the appropriate fees.

b. After Commencement and Prior to Response: After commencement, but before the Forum has received a Response that complies with Supplemental Rule 5, the Complaint may be withdrawn without prejudice by the Complainant. A withdrawal request must be submitted to the Forum in writing and signed by the Complainant.

c. After Response Received: After a Response that complies with Supplemental Rule 5 has been received by the Forum, but before a Panel decision is published, the Complaint may be withdrawn with prejudice if both parties agree to the withdrawal. A withdrawal request must be submitted to the Forum in writing and signed by both parties.

d. The Complaint cannot be withdrawn after a Panel decision is published.

13. Panel Decisions

Panel decisions will meet the requirements set forth in Paragraph 15 of the Rules and will be of a length that the Panel deems appropriate.

14. Correction of Clerical Mistakes.

Clerical mistakes or errors in the Panel's decision arising from oversight or omission by the Panel may be corrected by the Director of Arbitration for the Forum.

15. Communication of Decision to Parties; Publication of Decision.

The Forum will publish the decision by submitting the Panel's decision to the parties, ICANN, and the Registrar as required by the Rules, and by publishing the full decision on a publicly accessible web site.

16. Fees (U.S. Dollars)

a.   Hearing Fees

Number of Disputed Domain Names	Single-Member Panel	Three-Member Panel
1	$1,150	$2,500
2	$1,300	$2,600
3 — 5	$1,400	$2,800
6 — 10	$1,750	$3,500
11 — 15	$2,000	$4,000
16 or more	To be determined in consultation with the Forum.	To be determined in consultation with the Forum.

b.   Participatory hearings:

As stated in the Rules, in exceptional circumstances (for example, in the event an in-person hearing is held), the Forum may require the Parties to pay additional fees, which will be established by agreement of the Parties and the Director of Arbitration for the Forum prior to the appointment of the Panel.

c.   Non-Refundable Fees:

Fees to be paid to the Forum as provided in these Supplemental Rules must be paid in U.S. Dollars and are non-refundable, except as provided in Supplemental Rule 9(c)(iv) and 9(e).

17. Effective Date

These Supplemental Rules apply to all cases filed on or after February 1, 2002.

The National Arbitration Forum's Supplemental Rules to ICANN's Uniform Domain Name Dispute Resolution Policy are reproduced here with the permission of the NAF. These rules were in force as of 13 May 2002, but readers should refer to the Forum's website (www.arbitration-forum.com) for the most current version.

Appendix 4 – Nominet Dispute Resolution Service Policy and Procedure

Dispute Resolution Service Policy

The New Dispute Resolution Service Procedure is set out at http://www.nic.uk/ref/drs-procedure.html.

1. Definitions

Abusive Registration means a Domain Name which either:

i. was registered or otherwise acquired in a manner which, at the time when the registration or acquisition took place, took unfair advantage of or was unfairly detrimental to the Complainant's Rights; OR

ii. has been used in a manner which took unfair advantage of or was unfairly detrimental to the Complainant's Rights;

Complainant means a third party who asserts to us the elements set out in paragraph 2 of this Policy and according to the Procedure;

Contract means the contract between us and the Respondent, made up of our Terms and Conditions, the Rules for .uk domain and sub-domains, this Policy and the Procedure;

Days means unless otherwise stated any day other than Saturday, Sunday or any Bank or public holiday in England and Wales;

Decision means the decision reached by an Expert and where applicable includes decisions of an appeal panel;

Dispute Resolution Service means the service provided by us according to this Policy and the Procedure;

Domain Name means a domain name registered in any sub-domain of the .uk domain;

Expert means the expert(s) we appoint under paragraphs 8 or 18 of the Procedure and references to Expert where applicable also refer to the Experts appointed under paragraph 18 of the Procedure;

Informal Mediation means impartial mediation which we conduct to facilitate an acceptable resolution to the dispute;

ISP means the internet service provider through which the Domain Name in dispute has been registered or is hosted;

Party means a Complainant or Respondent and 'Parties' has a corresponding meaning;

Procedure means the Procedure for the conduct of proceedings under the Dispute Resolution Service.

Respondent means the person (including a legal person) in whose name or on whose behalf a Domain Name is registered and against whom the Complainant makes a complaint;

Rights includes, but is not limited to, rights enforceable under English law. However, a Complainant will be unable to rely on rights in a name or term which is wholly descriptive of the Complainant's business.

we means Nominet UK (company no. 3203859) whose registered office is at Sandford Gate, Sandy Lane West, Littlemore, Oxford, OX4 6LB and us and our have corresponding meanings.

2. Dispute Resolution Service

a. A Respondent must submit to proceedings under the Dispute Resolution Service if a Complainant asserts to us, according to the Procedure, that:

   i. The Complainant has Rights in respect of a name or mark which is identical or similar to the Domain Name; and

   ii. The Domain Name, in the hands of the Respondent, is an Abusive Registration.

b. The Complainant is required to prove to the Expert that both elements are present on the balance of probabilities.

c. We recommend that both Parties use our model submissions, which can be found at http://www.nic.uk/drs/models.html in the preparation of evidence.

3. Evidence of Abusive Registration

a. A non-exhaustive list of factors which may be evidence that the Domain Name is an Abusive Registration is as follows:

   i. Circumstances indicating that the Respondent has registered or otherwise acquired the Domain Name:

      A. primarily for the purposes of selling, renting or otherwise transferring the Domain Name to the Complainant or to a competitor of the Complainant, for valuable consideration in excess of the Respondent's documented out-of-pocket costs directly associated with acquiring or using the Domain Name;

      B. as a blocking registration against a name or mark in which the Complainant has Rights; or

      C. primarily for the purpose of unfairly disrupting the business of the Complainant;

   ii. Circumstances indicating that the Respondent is using the Domain Name in a way which has confused people or businesses into believing that the Domain Name is registered to, operated or authorised by, or otherwise connected with the Complainant;

   iii. In combination with other circumstances indicating that the Domain Name in dispute is an Abusive Registration, the Complainant can demonstrate that the Respondent is engaged in a pattern of making Abusive Registrations; or

   iv. It is independently verified that the Respondent has given false contact details to us.

b. Failure on the Respondent's part to use the Domain Name for the purposes of e-mail or a web-site is not in itself evidence that the Domain Name is an Abusive Registration.

4. How the Respondent may demonstrate in its response that the Domain Name is not an Abusive Registration

a. A non-exhaustive list of factors which may be evidence that the Domain Name is not an Abusive Registration is as follows:

    i.   Before being informed of the Complainant's dispute, the Respondent has:

        A.   used or made demonstrable preparations to use the Domain Name or a Domain Name which is similar to the Domain Name in connection with a genuine offering of goods or services;

        B.   been commonly known by the name or legitimately connected with a mark which is identical or similar to the Domain Name;

        C.   made legitimate non-commercial or fair use of the Domain Name; or

    ii.   The Domain Name is generic or descriptive and the Respondent is making fair use of it.

b.   Fair use may include sites operated solely in tribute to or criticism of a person or business, provided that if:

    i.   the Domain Name (not including the first and second level suffixes) is identical to the name in which the Complainant asserts Rights, without any addition; and

    ii.   the Respondent is using or intends to use the Domain Name for the purposes of a tribute or criticism site without the Complainant's authorisation

then the burden will shift to the Respondent to show that the Domain Name is not an Abusive Registration.

5. Informal Mediation

a.   After we have received the Parties' submissions under the Procedure, we will initiate and conduct a period of Informal Mediation under paragraph 7 of the Procedure.

6. Appointment of Expert

a.   If an acceptable resolution cannot be found by Informal Mediation we will notify the Parties that we will appoint an Expert when the Complainant has paid the applicable fees set out in paragraph 21(a) of the Procedure and within the time specified in paragraph 21(c) of the 7. Procedure. The Expert will come to a written Decision.

7. Notification and Publication

a. We will communicate a Decision to the Parties according to paragraph 17 of the Procedure and will publish all Decisions in full on our web site at http://www.nic.uk/drs/decisions.html.

b. Fees are payable by the Complainant or otherwise according to paragraph 21 of the Procedure only if an acceptable resolution has not been reached by Informal Mediation and once we have notified the Parties that an Expert is to be appointed.

8. Exclusion of Liability

a. Neither we nor our directors, officers, employees or servants nor any Expert shall be liable to a party for anything done or omitted in connection with any proceedings under the Dispute Resolution Service unless the act or omission is shown to have been in bad faith.

9. Appeal and Availability of Court Proceedings

a. Either Party will have the right to appeal a Decision under paragraph 18 of the Procedure. The appeal panel will consider appeals both on the basis that a matter be re-examined on the facts, and that procedure has not been correctly followed.

b. We may refer questions of interpretation of the Policy and Procedure to the appeal panel. Any decision rendered as a result of our referral will not affect any Decision previously made under the Dispute Resolution Service.

c. We will publish decisions of the appeal panel. Appeal decisions will not have precedent value, but will be of persuasive value to Experts in future decisions.

d. The operation of the Dispute Resolution Service will not prevent either the Complainant or the Respondent from submitting the dispute to a court of competent jurisdiction.

10. Implementation of Expert Decisions

a. If the Expert makes a Decision that a Domain Name registration should be cancelled, suspended, transferred or otherwise amended, we will implement that Decision by making any necessary changes to the Register according to the process set out in paragraph 17 of the Procedure.

11. Other action by us

a. We will not cancel, transfer, activate, deactivate or otherwise change any Domain Name registration except as set out in paragraph 10 above and as provided under [paragraph 8] of the Terms and Conditions.

12. Transfers During a Dispute

a. A Respondent may not transfer a Domain Name registration:

    i. whilst proceedings under the Dispute Resolution Service are ongoing in relation to the Domain Name or for a period of ten (10) Days after their conclusion, unless to the Complainant as a result of a settlement reached between the Parties and approved by us whether or not pursuant to Informal Mediation; or

    ii. whilst a court proceeding or arbitration in respect of the Domain Name registration is ongoing in a court of competent jurisdiction.

    We reserve the right to reverse any transfer of a Domain Name registration which does not comply with this paragraph.

b. A Respondent may not without the Complainant's consent (which the Complainant will not unreasonably withhold) transfer the hosting of a Domain Name to another ISP whilst proceedings under the Dispute Resolution Service are ongoing in relation to the Domain Name or for a period of ten (10) Days after the conclusion of the Dispute Resolution Service.

13. Modifications to the Policy and Procedure of the Dispute Resolution Service

a. The internet is an emerging and evolving medium and the regulatory and administrative framework under which we operate is constantly developing. For these reasons we reserve the right to make reasonable modifications to the Policy and Procedure at any time. We will only do so when we have good reason. Except where we are acting in pursuance of a statutory requirement or a court order, changes will be implemented following a process of open public consultation. Each such change will be published in advance (where practicable, 30 calendar days in advance) on our web site: http://www.nic.uk/ and will become binding and effective upon the date specified therein.

b. The Respondent will be bound by the Policy and Procedure which are current at the time the Dispute Resolution Service is commenced until the dispute is concluded.

Dispute Resolution Service Procedure

The New Dispute Resolution Service Policy is set out at http://www.nic.uk/ref/drs-policy.html.

1. Definitions

Abusive Registration means a Domain Name which either:

i. was registered or otherwise acquired in a manner which, at the time when the registration or acquisition took place, took unfair advantage of or was unfairly detrimental to the Complainant's Rights; OR

ii. has been used in a manner which took unfair advantage of or was unfairly detrimental to the Complainant's Rights;

Complainant means a third party who asserts to us the elements set out in paragraph 2 of the Policy and according to this Procedure;

Contract means the contract between us and the Respondent, made up of our Terms and Conditions, the Rules for .uk domain and sub-domains, the Policy and this Procedure;

Days means unless otherwise stated any day other than Saturday, Sunday or any Bank or public holiday in England and Wales;

Decision means the decision reached by an Expert and where applicable includes decisions of an appeal panel;

Dispute Resolution Service means the service provided by us according to the Policy and this Procedure;

Domain Name means a domain name registered in any sub-domain of the .uk domain;

Expert means the expert(s) we appoint under paragraphs 8 or 18 of this Procedure and references to Expert where applicable also refer to the Experts appointed under paragraph 18 of this Procedure;

235

Informal Mediation means impartial mediation which we conduct to facilitate an acceptable resolution to the dispute;

ISP means the internet service provider through which the Domain Name in dispute has been registered or is hosted;

Party means a Complainant or Respondent and **'Parties'** has a corresponding meaning;

Policy means Nominet's Dispute Resolution Service Policy.

Respondent means the person (including a legal person) in whose name or on whose behalf a Domain Name is registered and against whom the Complainant makes a complaint;

Reverse Domain Name Hijacking means using the Policy in bad faith in an attempt to deprive a registered domain-name holder of a domain name.

Rights includes, but is not limited to, rights enforceable under English law. However, a Complainant will be unable to rely on rights in a name or term which is wholly descriptive of the Complainant's business.

we means Nominet UK (company no. 3203859) whose registered office is at Sandford Gate, Sandy Lane West, Littlemore, Oxford, OX4 6LB and **us** and **our** have corresponding meanings.

2. Communication

a. We will send a complaint (see paragraph 3) to the Respondent by using, in our discretion, any of the following means:

   i. sending the complaint by first class post, fax or e-mail to the Respondent at the contact details shown as the registrant or other contacts in our Domain Name register database entry for the Domain Name in dispute;

   ii. sending the complaint in electronic form (including attachments to the extent available in that form) by e-mail to;

   A. postmaster@[the Domain Name in dispute]; or

   B. if the Domain Name resolves to an active web page (other than a generic page which we conclude is maintained by an ISP for parking Domain Names), to any e-mail address shown or e-mail links on that web page so far as this is practicable; or

iii.   sending the complaint to any addresses provided to us by the Complainant under paragraph 3(b)(iii) so far as this is practicable.

b.   Except as set out in paragraph 2(a) above, all written communication to a Party or a Party's representative under the Policy or this Procedure shall be made by fax, first class post or e-mail.

c.   Communication shall be made in English. E-mail communications should be sent in plain text so far as this is practicable.

d.   During the course of proceedings under the Dispute Resolution Service, if either Party wishes to change its contact details it must notify us of all changes.

e.   Except as otherwise provided in this Procedure or as otherwise decided by us or if appointed, the Expert, all communications provided for under this Procedure shall be deemed to have been received:

i.   if sent by facsimile, on the date transmitted; or

ii.   if sent by first class post, on the second Day after posting; or

iii.   if sent via the Internet, on the date that the communication was transmitted; and

iv.   where communications are received by more than one method, at the earliest date received;

and, unless otherwise provided in this Procedure, the time periods provided for under the Policy and this Procedure shall be calculated accordingly.

f.   Any communication (except for communications relating to Informal Mediation) by:

i.   us to any Party shall be copied by us to the other Party and if appointed, the Expert; and

ii.   a Party to another Party shall be copied by the sender to us and we will copy such correspondence to the Expert, if appointed.

3. The Complaint

a.   Any person or entity may submit a complaint to us in accordance with the Policy and this Procedure. In exceptional circumstances, we may have to suspend our ability to accept complaints. If so, we will post a message to that effect on our web-site which will indicate when the suspension is likely to be lifted.

b. The Complainant must send the complaint to us in hard copy and (except to the extent not available for attachments) in electronic form. The complaint shall:-

  i. not exceed 2000 words (not including the text set out in paragraph 3(b)(ix) below and annexes);

  ii. specify whether the Complainant wishes to be contacted direct or through an authorised representative, and set out the e-mail address, telephone number, fax number and postal address which should be used;

  iii. set out any of the Respondent's contact details which are known to the Complainant;

  iv. specify the Domain Name which is the subject of the dispute and the name or mark which is identical or similar to the Domain Name and in which the Complainant asserts it has Rights;

  v. describe in accordance with the Policy the grounds on which the complaint is made including in particular: what Rights the Complainant asserts in the name or mark; why the Domain Name should be considered to be an Abusive Registration in the hands of the Respondent; and discuss any applicable aspects of paragraph 3 of the Policy, as well as any other grounds which support the Complainant's assertion;

  vi. specify whether the Complainant is seeking to have the Domain Name transferred, suspended, cancelled or otherwise amended;

  vii. tell us whether any legal proceedings have been commenced or terminated in connection with the Domain Name which is the subject of the complaint;

  viii. state that the Complainant will submit to the exclusive jurisdiction of the English courts with respect to any legal proceedings seeking to reverse the effect of a Decision requiring the suspension, cancellation, transfer or other amendment to a Domain Name registration, and that the Complainant agrees that any such legal proceedings will be governed by English law;

  ix. conclude with the following statement followed by the signature of the Complainant or its authorised representative:-

      "The Complainant agrees that its claims and remedies concerning the registration of the Domain Name, the dispute, or the dispute's resolution shall be solely against the Respondent and that neither Nominet UK nor its directors, officers, employees or servants nor any Expert shall be liable for anything done or omitted in connection with any proceedings under the Dispute Resolution Service unless the act or omission is shown to have been in bad faith.";

"The information contained in this complaint is to the best of the Complainant's knowledge true and complete. This complaint is not being presented in bad faith and the matters stated in this complaint comply with the Procedure and applicable law."; and

x.   attach any documentary or other evidence on which the Complainant relies including correspondence and any trade mark registration and/or evidence of use of or reputation in a name or mark, together with an index of the material attached.

c.   The complaint may relate to more than one Domain Name, provided that those Domain Names are registered in the name of the Respondent.

4. Notification of Complaint

a.   We will check that the complaint complies with the Policy and this Procedure and, if so, we will forward it to the Respondent together with our explanatory coversheet within three (3) Days of our receipt of the complaint.

b.   If we find that the complaint does not comply with the Policy and this Procedure, we will promptly notify the Complainant of the deficiencies we have identified. The Complainant shall have three (3) Days from receipt of notification within which to correct the deficiencies and return the complaint to us, failing which we will deem the complaint to be withdrawn. This will not prevent the Complainant submitting a different complaint to us.

c.   Proceedings under the Dispute Resolution Service will commence on the earliest date upon which the complaint is deemed to have been received by the Respondent in accordance with paragraph 2(e) of this Procedure. We will promptly notify the Parties of the date of commencement of such proceedings.

5. The Response

a. Within fifteen (15) Days of the date of commencement of proceedings under the Dispute Resolution Service, the Respondent shall submit a response to us.

b. Within three (3) Days following our receipt of the response, we will forward the response to the Complainant.

c   The Respondent must send the response to us in hard copy and (except to the extent not available for attachments) in electronic form to us at the addresses set out in our explanatory coversheet. The response shall:

    i.   not exceed 2000 words (not including the text set out in paragraph 5(c)(v) and annexes);

    ii. include any grounds the Respondent wishes to rely upon to rebut the Complainant's assertions under 3(b)(v) above including any relevant factors set out in paragraph 4 of the Policy;

    iii. specify whether the Respondent wishes to be contacted direct or through an authorised representative, and set out the e-mail address, telephone number, fax number and postal address which should be used;

    iv. tell us whether any legal proceedings have been commenced or terminated in connection with the Domain Name which is the subject of the complaint;

    v.   conclude with the following statement followed by the signature of the Respondent or its authorised representative:-

        "The information contained in this response is to the best of the Respondent's knowledge true and complete and the matters stated in this response comply with the Procedure and applicable law."; and

    vi. attach any documentary or other evidence on which the Respondent relies including correspondence and any trade mark registration and/or evidence of use of or reputation in a name or mark together with an index of the material attached.

d. If the Respondent does not submit a response, we will notify the Parties that we will appoint the Expert on our receipt from the Complainant of the applicable fees according to paragraph 21 and in the absence of exceptional circumstances.

6. Reply by the Complainant

a. Within five (5) Days of receiving the response from us, the Complainant may submit to us a reply to the Respondent's response, which shall not exceed 2000 words (not including annexes). If the Complainant does not submit a reply to us within five (5) Days we will proceed to Informal Mediation.

7. Informal Mediation

a. Within three (3) Days of our receipt of the Complainant's reply, we will begin to conduct Informal Mediation. Informal Mediation will be conducted in a manner which we, in our sole discretion, consider appropriate.

b. Negotiations conducted between the Parties during Informal Mediation shall be without prejudice, that is they will not affect either Party's position should an acceptable resolution not be found. Negotiations will be confidential, that is we will not reveal details of such negotiations to any third parties unless a court of competent jurisdiction orders us to do so, or we are required to do so by applicable laws or regulations.

c. If the Parties do not achieve an acceptable resolution through Informal Mediation within ten (10) Days, we will send notice to the Parties that we will appoint an Expert when the Complainant has paid the applicable fees set out under paragraph 21(a) within the time limit specified in paragraph 21(c).

8. Appointment of the Expert and Timing of Decision

a. If we do not receive the Complainant's request to refer the matter to an Expert together with the applicable fees within ten (10) Days of the Complainant's receipt of the notice referred to in paragraph 7(c) above, we will deem the complaint to be withdrawn. This will not prevent the Complainant submitting a different complaint to us.

b. Within five (5) Days of our receipt of the applicable fees from the Complainant, we will appoint an Expert on a rotational basis from our list of Experts.

c. We will maintain and publish a list of experts and their qualifications.

d.   Once we have appointed the Expert, we will notify the Parties of the name of the Expert appointed and the date by which, except in exceptional circumstances, the Expert will forward his or her Decision to us.

9. Impartiality and Independence

a.   The Expert shall be impartial and independent and both before accepting the appointment and during the proceedings will disclose to us any circumstances giving rise to justifiable doubt as to his or her impartiality or independence. We will have the discretion to appoint a substitute Expert if necessary in which case we will adjust the timetable accordingly.

10. Communication Between Parties and the Expert

a.   A Party and the Expert must not communicate directly. All communication between a Party and the Expert must be made through us.

11. Transmission of the File to the Expert

a.   We will forward the file except for documents relating to Informal Mediation to the Expert as soon as the Expert is appointed.

12. General Powers of Nominet and the Expert

a.   We, or the Expert if appointed, may in exceptional cases extend any period of time in proceedings under the Dispute Resolution Service.

b.   The Expert shall determine the admissibility, relevance, materiality and weight of the evidence.

c.   We shall decide a request by a Party to consolidate multiple Domain Name disputes in accordance with the Policy and this Procedure.

13. Further Statement

a.   In addition to the complaint, the response and if applicable the reply and any appeal, the Expert may request further statements or documents from the Parties. The Expert will not be obliged to consider any statements or documents from the Parties which he or she has not received according to the Policy or this Procedure or which he or she has not requested.

14. In Person Hearings

a.   No in person hearings (including hearings by conference call, video conference and web conference) will be held unless the Expert determines in his or her sole discretion and in exceptional cases, that such a hearing is necessary to enable him or her to come to a Decision.

15. Default

a.   If we find that a submission by a Party exceeds the word limit, we will return the submission to that Party who will within three (3) Days return a submission to us which complies with the word limits. If we do not receive the submission back from:

   i.   the Complainant, we will deem the complaint to be withdrawn, which will not stop the Complainant from submitting a different complaint; or

   ii.   the Respondent, we will notify the Parties that we will appoint the Expert when the Complainant has paid the applicable fees set out in paragraph 21 and in the absence of exceptional circumstances. Once appointed the Expert will decide the dispute based upon the complaint and evidence attached to it.

b.   If, in the absence of exceptional circumstances, a Party does not comply with any time period laid down in the Policy or this Procedure, the Expert will proceed to a Decision on the complaint. If the Expert has not been appointed Nominet shall take any action which it deems appropriate in its sole discretion, unless prescribed by this Procedure.

c.   If, in the absence of exceptional circumstances, a Party does not comply with any provision in the Policy or this Procedure or any request by us or the Expert, the Expert will draw such inferences from the Party's non compliance as he or she considers appropriate.

16. Expert Decision

a.   The Expert will decide a complaint on the basis of the Parties' submissions, the Policy and the Procedure.

b.   Unless exceptional circumstances apply, an Expert shall forward his or her Decision to us within ten (10) Days of his or her appointment pursuant to paragraph 8.

c.   The Decision shall be in writing and signed, provide the reasons on which it is based, indicate the date on which it was made and identify the name of the Expert.

d.   If the Expert concludes that the dispute is not within the scope of paragraph 2 of the Policy, he or she shall state that this is the case. If, after considering the submissions, the Expert finds that the complaint was brought in bad faith, for example in an attempt at Reverse Domain Name Hijacking, the Expert shall state this finding in the Decision. If the Complainant is found on three separate occasions within a 2 year period to have brought a complaint in bad faith, Nominet will not accept any further complaints from that Complainant for a period of 2 years.

17. Communication of Decision to Parties and Implementation of Decision

a.   Within three (3) Days of our receipt of a Decision from the Expert, we will communicate the full text of the Decision to each Party and the date for the implementation of the Decision in accordance with the Policy.

b.   We will publish the full Decision and the date that any action which the Decision requires will be taken, on our website.

c.   If the Expert makes a Decision that a Domain Name registration should be cancelled, suspended, transferred or otherwise amended, we will implement that Decision by making any necessary changes to the Domain Name register database after ten (10) Days of the date of the Decision, unless, during the ten (10) Days following the date of the Decision we receive from:

   i.   either Party an appeal complying with paragraph 18 of the Procedure, in which case we will take no further action in respect of the Domain Name until the appeal is concluded; or

   ii.   the Respondent official documentation showing that the Respondent has issued and served (or in the case of service outside England and Wales, commenced the process of serving) legal proceedings against the Complainant seeking to reverse the effect of the Decision. In this case, we will take no further action in respect of the Domain Name unless we receive:

A. evidence which satisfies us that the Parties have reached a settlement; or

B. evidence which satisfies us that such proceedings have been dismissed, withdrawn or are otherwise unsuccessful.

18. Appeal

a. Either Party shall have the right to appeal a Decision by submitting written grounds for appeal to us not exceeding 2000 words together with the appropriate fees under paragraph 21(e) within five (5) Days of the date that the Decision has been communicated to the Parties pursuant to paragraph 17 above. The appeal will be determined as soon as is practically possible by a panel of three Experts appointed by us at our sole discretion from our list of experts.

19. Settlement or Other Grounds for Termination

a. If, before a Decision is made the Parties agree and notify us of a settlement which we approve, whether or not pursuant to Informal Mediation, we will terminate proceedings under the Dispute Resolution Service.

b. If, before a Decision is made, it becomes unnecessary or impossible to continue proceedings under the Dispute Resolution Service for any reason, we will terminate proceedings under the Dispute Resolution Service unless a Party raises justifiable grounds for objection within a period of time which we will determine.

20. Effect of Court Proceedings

a. If legal proceedings relating to a Domain Name which is the subject of the complaint are issued in a court of competent jurisdiction before or during the course of proceedings under the Dispute Resolution Service and are brought to our attention, we will suspend the proceedings, pending the outcome of the legal proceedings.

b. A Party must promptly notify us if it initiates legal proceedings in a court of competent jurisdiction in relating to a Domain Name which is the subject of a complaint during the course of proceedings under the Dispute Resolution Service.

21. Fees

a. The applicable fees in respect of the referral of proceedings under the Dispute Resolution Service to an Expert are £750 + VAT for disputes involving 1-5 Domain Names. For disputes involving 6 or more Domain Names, we will set a fee in consultation with the Complainant. Fees are calculated on a cost-recovery basis, and are passed on in their entirety to the Expert(s). Nominet does not charge for its mediation or administration services in respect of the Dispute Resolution Service.

b. Fees are payable by the Complainant only if we notify the Parties that an Expert is to be appointed.

c. If we have not received the fees from the Complainant as set out in paragraph 21(a) above within ten (10) Days of receipt by the Complainant of notice from us that an Expert is to be appointed under paragraphs 5(d), 7(c) or 15(a)(ii) we will deem the complaint to be withdrawn.

d. In exceptional circumstances, for example if an in person hearing is held, we will request that the Parties pay additional fees to be agreed between us, the Parties and the Expert.

e. The applicable fees for the submission of an appeal are £3,000 + VAT.

22. Exclusion of Liability

a. Neither we nor our directors, officers, employees or servants nor any Expert shall be liable to a party for anything done or omitted in connection with any proceedings under the Dispute Resolution Service unless the act or omission is shown to have been in bad faith.

23. Modifications to the Policy and Procedure of the Dispute Resolution Service

a. The internet is an emerging and evolving medium and the regulatory and administrative framework under which we operate is constantly developing. For these reasons we reserve the right to make reasonable modifications to the Policy and Procedure at any time. We will only do so when we have good reason. Except where we are acting in pursuance of a statutory requirement or a court order, changes will be implemented following a process of open public consultation. Each such change will be published in advance (where practicable, thirty (30) calendar days in advance) on our web site: http://www.nic.uk/ and will become binding and effective upon the date specified therein.

b.   The Respondent will be bound by the Policy and Procedure which are current at the time the Dispute Resolution Service is commenced until the dispute is concluded.

Appendix 5

Table of Major ccTLDs, Their Registries and Applicable DRPs

TLD	Country	Registry and URL for Registration Services	Applicable Dispute Resolution Policy and Additional Useful Notes
.ag	Antigua and Barbuda	UHSA School of Medicine (www.nic.ag)	UDRP applies.
.as	American Samoa	ASNIC (www.nic.as)	UDRP applies.
.at	Austria	NIC.AT Internet Verwaltungs und Betriebsgesellschaft m.b.H (www.nic.at/)	A 'first come first served' policy applies, although common law applies in relation to registered or claimed intellectual property rights. NIC.AT may refuse to register domain names where it believes there is good reason.

TLD	Country	Registry and URL for Registration Services	Applicable Dispute Resolution Policy and Additional Useful Notes
.au	Australia	.au Domain Administration (auDA) (www.aunic.net)	The Registry's policy provides that the parties must attempt to settle the dispute by negotiations and conciliation. If that fails, the parties must refer the dispute to commercial arbitration or the court.
.be	Belgium	DNS BE vzw/asbl (www.dns.be)	DNS BE does not participate in or conduct any dispute resolution proceedings. Such proceedings should be referred to a 'dispute resolution entity' i.e. one of the recognised domain name dispute forums (e.g. WIPO) or court.
.bh	Bahrain	BATELCO (www.inet.com.bh)	The Court of Bahrain has jurisdiction, but BATELCO may act as an arbitrator if requested to do so by parties.
.bo	Bolivia	BolNet 9 www.nic.bo)	Disputes are dealt with by negotiation or through the courts and BOLNET's policies will apply to effect a court order.
.br	Brazil	Federative Republic of Brazil (www.registro.br)	No details regarding dispute resolution currently available.
.bs	Bahamas	The College of the Bahamas Computer Center (dns.nic.bs)	UDRP applies.

TLD	Country	Registry and URL for Registration Services	Applicable Dispute Resolution Policy and Additional Useful Notes
.bz	Belize	University College of Belize	UDRP applies.
.ca	Canada	Canadian Internet Registration Authority (www.cira.ca)	CIRA Domain Name Dispute Resolution Policy applies. This policy is similar to UDRP.
.cc	Cocos Islands	Island Internet Services (www.nic.cc)	UDRP applies.
.ch	Switzerland	SWITCH Teleinformatics Services (www.nic.ch)	SWITCH's own policy applies and domain names will be deleted upon a court order or order of a governmental or administrative body.
.cn	China	CNNIC (www.cnnic.net.cn)	CNNIC will act upon a court order but otherwise does not mediate or arbitrate disputes.
.co	Colombia	Universidad de Los Andes, NIC Columbia (www.nic.co)	No dispute resolution policy is currently in place.
.cy	Cyprus	University of Cyprus (www.nic.cy)	UDRP applies.

TLD	Country	Registry and URL for Registration Services	Applicable Dispute Resolution Policy and Additional Useful Notes
.de	Germany	DENIC eG (www.denic.de)	Denic will not act as arbitrator or mediator in disputes but will act upon a court order to transfer/cancel a registration. Under its terms and conditions Denic can refuse to register a domain name if it is in 'obvious violation' of the law.
.dk	Denmark	Dansk Internet Forum (www.dk-hostmaster.dk)	DK Hostmaster's Rules apply. Under this, a three member complaints board hears disputes based on registration in bad faith or prior trade mark rights. Other disputes regarding domain names are to be decided by the Maritime and Commercial Court in Copenhagen.
.ec	Ecuador	NIC.EC (NICEC) S.A. (www.nic.ec)	UDRP applies.
.es	Spain	Centro de Comunicactiones CSIC RedIRIRS (www.nic.es)	Registrations are made on a 'first come, first served' basis and no dispute resolution policy is in place.
.fi	Finland	Finnish Communications Regulatory Authority (www.ficora.fi)	Domain names may not be registered by individuals. In the event of dispute the parties should refer the matter to the court for determination.

TLD	Country	Registry and URL for Registration Services	Applicable Dispute Resolution Policy and Additional Useful Notes
.fj	Fiji	The University of the South Pacific (www.usp.ac.fj/DomReg)	UDRP applies.
.fm	Micronesia	FSM Telecommunications Corporation (www.fm)	No details regarding dispute resolution currently available.
.fr	France	AFNIC (NIC France) – Immeuble International (www.nic.fr)	Registrations are made on a 'first come first served' basis and NIC France will not act as arbitrator or mediator in disputes. Parties can choose the rules they wish to apply or have the matter determined by the court.
.gg	Guernsey	Island Networks Ltd. (www.nic.gg)	The Registry's own policy applies whereby the registry will assist parties to resolve disputes. If this does not work, the Registry can decide to suspend a name and the parties can thereafter pursue litigation in the local Island Courts.

TLD	Country	Registry and URL for Registration Services	Applicable Dispute Resolution Policy and Additional Useful Notes
.gr	Greece	ICS-FORTH GR (www.hostmaster.gr)	Own policy applies whereby disputes are first referred to an ICS manager and thereafter to a panel to resolve. ICS can decide who should sit on this panel and failing resolution thereafter the parties can pursue their case in the local national courts.
.gt	Guatemala	Universidad del Valle de Guatemala (www.gt)	UDRP applies.
.hk	Hong Kong	University of Hong Kong (www.cuhk.hk)	'First come, first served' policy applies. Parties in dispute must refer their case to the Hong Kong Arbitration Centre or through litigation in court.
.ie	Ireland	IE Domain Registry Limited (www.domainregistry.ie)	At the time of publication, it is intended that UDRP (or a policy very similar to this) will be adopted and the Irish Registry is in consultation with WIPO regarding this.

TLD	Country	Registry and URL for Registration Services	Applicable Dispute Resolution Policy and Additional Useful Notes
.il	Israel	Internet Society of Israel www.isoc.org.il	Domain Allocation Rules apply. Under these, a 'first come first served' policy is used but in the case of a dispute an 'Advisory Committee' is constituted to rule on the dispute.
.im	Isle of Man	Isle of Man Government (www.nic.im)	No policy currently in place.
.in	India	National Centre for Software Technology (domain.ncst.ernet.in)	Indian Internet Domain Name Dispute Resolution Policy applies. Under this the Registrar hears complaints and determines the case. If a party is unhappy with the outcome it can file court proceedings in Mumbai.
.is	Iceland	ISNIC – Internet Iceland Ltd (www.isnic.is)	'First come first served' policy is used, but under registration rules, a Board of Appeals handles disputes regarding the delegation of domains. If legal proceedings are instigated during the time when a Board is deciding on a matter, it will suspend its decision pending the outcome of the court case.

TLD	Country	Registry and URL for Registration Services	Applicable Dispute Resolution Policy and Additional Useful Notes
.it	Italy	IAT – CNR (www.NIC.it)	There is no current policy for resolving disputes. Parties to a dispute have common law rights and remedies which should be pursued.
.je	Jersey	Island Networks Jersey Ltd. (www.nic.je)	The Registry's own policy applies whereby the registry will assist parties to resolve disputes. If this does not work, the Registry can decide to suspend a name and the parties can thereafter pursue litigation in the local Island Courts.
.jp	Japan	Japan Registry Service Co., Ltd (www.jprs.jp)	JPNIC is developing a new dispute resolution policy. This policy will endorse the Japanese Intellectual Property Arbitration Center as a dispute resolution organisation and will encourage parties to refer disputes to this centre.
.kr	Republic of Korea	Korea Network Information Center (www.nic.or.kr.)	The Registry will effect transfers on the basis of 'due process' and the Korean courts will order transfer of domain names in the event of breach of a claimant's intellectual property rights (such as a registered trade mark) in a name registered by a Registrant.

TLD	Country	Registry and URL for Registration Services	Applicable Dispute Resolution Policy and Additional Useful Notes
.la	People's Democratic Republic of Laos	Science, Technology and Environment Organization (STENO)	UDRP applies.
.lu	Luxembourg	RESTENA (www.dns.lu)	The Registry does not determine disputes between parties, who may pursue matters themselves via court proceedings. Pending the outcome of the court or dispute resolution procedure entered into by the parties, the Registry can decide to suspend a name.
.mx	Mexico	NIC-Mexico (www.nic.mx)	A policy closely based on UDRP applies.
.my	Malaysia	MIMOS Berhad (www.mynic.net)	Registrations are undertaken on a first come, first served basis. Disputes between the parties are to be settled by the contending parties and MYNIC does not act as an arbiter of such disputes.
.na	Namibia	Namibian Network Information Center (www.na-nic.com.na)	UDRP applies.

TLD	Country	Registry and URL for Registration Services	Applicable Dispute Resolution Policy and Additional Useful Notes
.nl	Netherlands	Stichting Internet Domeinregistratie Nederland (www.domain-registry.nl)	Registrations are undertaken on a 'first come, first served basis' and Norid does not arbitrate disputes. Parties must determine matters themselves or refer to the courts. At the time of writing, new rules are planned.
.no	Norway	UNINETT FAS A/S (www.norid.no)	The parties must determine a dispute between themselves using arbitration or court. Norid will only transfer or suspend a domain name upon written confirmation to do so from a domain name owner.
.nu	Niue	Internet Users Society – Niue (www.nunames.nu)	UDRP applies.
.nz	New Zealand	ISOC of New Zealand (www.domainz.net.nz)	Registration is undertaken on a 'first come, first served' basis. Domainz will not arbitrate or mediate disputes and the parties to a dispute must resolve matters themselves or refer to the courts.
.pa	Panama	Panamanian Academic National Network (www.nic.pa)	UDRP applies.

TLD	Country	Registry and URL for Registration Services	Applicable Dispute Resolution Policy and Additional Useful Notes
.pe	Peru	Red Cientifica Peruana (www.nic.pe)	The Registry takes no part in dispute resolution. It is for the parties then to determine the dispute in the manner they feel most appropriate.
.ph	Philipines	PH Domain Foundation (www.domreg.org.ph)	UDRP applies.
.pk	Pakistan	PKNIC (www.pknic.net.pk)	Registration is undertaken on a 'first come first served' basis. In the event of dispute, PKNIC may transfer the domain to the claimant provided it has a registered trade name, trademarks or registered company name at least one year before the registration date of the domain name in question. Additionally PKNIC will abide by decisions of the courts of Pakistan.
.pn	Pitcairn Island	Pitcairn Island Administration (www.nic.pn)	UDRP applies.

TLD	Country	Registry and URL for Registration Services	Applicable Dispute Resolution Policy and Additional Useful Notes
.pt	Portugal	Fundacao para a Computacao Cientifica Nacional (www.dns/pt)	Disputes are resolved using arbitration. Each party nominates one arbitrator and both arbitrators nominate a chairperson. Either party may refer the matter to court in the event that the determination by the arbitrators is unsatisfactory.
.py	Paraguay	NIC-PY (www.nic.py)	No details regarding dispute resolution currently available.
.ro	Romania	National Institute for R&D in Informatics (www.rnc.ro)	UDRP applies.
.ru	Russian Federation	Russian Institute for Public Networks (www.ripn.net/nic)	No policy currently exists although discussions with ICANN for a policy similar to UDRP applies have been undertaken. In the absence of a policy, the parties should refer the matter to the court for determination.
.sa	Saudi Arabia	King Abdulaziz City for Science and Technology (www.saudinic.net.sa)	Saudinic does not involve itself in disputes and the parties should refer disputes the matter to the court for determination.
.se	Sweden	II-Stiftelsen (www.iis.se)	UDRP applies.

TLD	Country	Registry and URL for Registration Services	Applicable Dispute Resolution Policy and Additional Useful Notes
.sg	Singapore	Singapore Network Information Centre (SGNIC) Pte Ltd (www.nic.net.sg)	The Singapore Domain Name Dispute Resolution Policy applies, which is substantially similar to UDRP. Alternatively, the parties may opt for mediation.
.st	Sao Tome and Principe	Tecnisys (www.sg-registry.technisys.net)	The Policy of the Domain Council of Sao Tome and Principe applies – no details of what this consists of are available, but the Registry indicates that it will comply with the principles set by ICANN. The Registry will also cancel or transfer a registration in accordance with an order from a 'competent' court.
.sv	El Salvador	SVNet (www.svnet.org.sv)	In the case of dispute the parties are encouraged to negotiate a settlement between themselves.
.tc	Turks and Caicos Islands	Melrex TC (www.tc.)	The Registry will at the claimant's request refer disputes to an arbitrator chosen at random from among the list of independent experts kept by the Registry, who shall determine the matter.

TLD	Country	Registry and URL for Registration Services	Applicable Dispute Resolution Policy and Additional Useful Notes
.th	Thailand	Asian Institute of Technology (www.thnic.net)	THNIC will not act as an arbitrator. Parties should refer the matter to the court for determination.
.tm	Turkmenistan	TM Domain Registry (www.nic.tm)	No details currently available.
.to	Tonga	Government of the Kingdom of Tonga (www.tonic.to)	No details currently available – although TONIC makes its policy on registrations for the purposes of spamming very clear!
.tr	Turkey	Middle East Technical University Department of Computer Engineering (www.dns.metu.edu.tr)	Disputes should be referred to the courts for determination.
.tt	Trinidad and Tobago	University of the West Indies, Faculty of Engineering (www. ns1.tstt.net.tt/nic)	UDRP applies.
.tv	Tuvalu	Ministry of Finance and Tourism (www.tv)	UDRP applies.
.tw	Taiwan	Taiwan Network Information Center (www.twnic.net.tw)	TWNIC does not involve itself in disputes and the parties should refer the matter to the court for determination.
.uk	United Kingdom	Nominet UK (www.nic.uk)	Nominet's DRP applies (see D5 THE NOMINET DISPUTE RESOLUTION POLICY).
.us	United States of America	United States Domain Registry (www.nic.us)	UDRP applies.

TLD	Country	Registry and URL for Registration Services	Applicable Dispute Resolution Policy and Additional Useful Notes
.ve	Venezuela	REACCIUN – Red Academica de Centros de Investigacion y Universidades Nacionales (www.nic.ve)	UDRP applies.
.vn	Vietnam	General Department of Posts and Telecommunications of Vietnam (www.vnnic.net.vn)	VNNIC does not determine disputes and parties must resolve these by recourse to the courts or commercial arbitration.
.ws	Western Samoa	Government of Western Samoa	UDRP applies.
.yu	Yugoslavia	YUNET Association Telecommunications Society (www.nic.yu)	Individuals may not apply for registration of domain names in Yugoslavia. In the event of dispute, the parties must resolve these by recourse to the courts or commercial arbitration.
.za	South Africa	UNINET Project (www2.frd.ac.za/uninet/zadomain)	At the time of publication, the functions of this Registry were being transferred to a new entity. New dispute resolution policies may be applied and the reader should check the .za Registry website for more information.

Table of Country Code Top Level Domains

.ac	Ascension Island	.ba	Bosnia Herzegovina	.by	Belarus
.ad	Andorra	.bb	Barbados	.bz	Belize
.ae	United Arab Emirates	.bd	Bangladesh	.ca	Canada
.af	Afghanistan	.be	Belgium	.cc	Cocos Islands
.ag	Antigua and Barbuda	.bf	Burkina Faso	.cd	Democratic Republic of the Congo
.ai	Anguilla	.bg	Bulgaria		
.al	Albania	.bh	Bahrain	.cf	Central African Republic
.am	Armenia	.bi	Burundi	.cg	Republic of Congo
.an	Netherland Antilles	.bj	Benin	.ch	Switzerland
.ao	Angola	.bm	Bermuda	.ci	Cote d'Ivoire
.aq	Antarctica	.bn	Brunei	.ck	Cook Islands
.ar	Argentina	.bo	Bolivia	.cl	Chile
.as	American Samoa	.br	Brazil	.cm	Cameroon
.at	Austria	.bs	Bahamas	.cn	China
.au	Australia	.bt	Bhutan	.co	Colombia
.aw	Aruba	.bv	Bouvet Islands	.cr	Costa Rica
.az	Azerbaijan	.bw	Botswana	.cu	Cuba

Code	Country	Code	Country	Code	Country
.cv	Cap Verde	.fj	Fiji	.gs	South Georgia and South Sandwich Islands
.cx	Christmas Islands	.fk	Falkland Islands	.gt	Guatemala
.cy	Cyprus	.fm	Micronesia	.gu	Guam
.cz	Czech Republic	.fo	Faroe Islands	.gw	Guinea – Bissau
.de	Germany	.fr	France	.gy	Guyana
.dj	Dijibouti	.ga	Gabon	.hk	Hong Kong
.dk	Denmark	.gd	Grenada	.hm	Heard and McDonald Islands
.dm	Dominica	.ge	Georgia	.hn.	Honduras
.do	Dominican Republic	.gf	French Guiana	.hr	Croatia
.dz	Algeria	.gg	Guernsey	.ht	Haiti
.ec	Ecuador	.gh	Ghana	.hu	Hungary
.ee	Estonia	.gi	Gibraltar	.id	Indonesia
.eg	Egypt	.gl	Greenland	.ie	Ireland
.eh	Western Sahara	.gm	Gambia	.il	Israel
.er	Eritrea	.gn	Guinea	.im	Isle of Man
.es	Spain	.gp	Guadeloupe	.in	India
.et	Ethiopia	.gq	Equatorial Guinea	.io	British Ocean Territory
.fi	Finland	.gr	Greece		

Code	Country	Code	Country	Code	Country
.iq	Iraq	.ky	Cayman Islands	.mh	Marshall Islands
.ir	Iran	.kz	Kazakhstan	.mk	Macedonia
.is	Iceland	.la	People's Democratic Republic of Lao	.ml	Mali
.it	Italy	.lb	Lebanon	.mm	Myanmar
.je	Jersey	.lc	St. Lucia	.mn	Mongolia
.jm	Jamaica	.li	Liechtenstein	.mo	Macau
.jo	Jordan	.lk	Sri Lanka	.mp	Northern Mariana Islands
.jp	Japan	.lr	Liberia	.mq	Martinique
.ke	Kenya	.ls	Lesotho	.mr	Mauritania
.kg	Kyrgyzstan	.lt	Lithuania	.ms	Montserrat
.kh	Cambodia	.lu	Luxembourg	.mt	Malta
.ki	Kiribati	.lv	Latvia	.mu	Mauritius
.km	Comoros	.ly	Libya	.mv	Maldives
.kn	St. Kitts and Nevis	.ma	Morroco	.mw	Malawi
.kp	Peoples Democratic Republic of Korea	.mc	Monaco	.mx	Mexico
.kr	Republic of Korea	.md	Republic of Maldovia	.my	Malaysia
.kw	Kuwait	.mg	Madagasgar	.mz	Mozambique
				.na	Namibia

.nc	New Caledonia	.pl	Poland	.sj	Svalbard and Jan Mayen Islands
.ne	Niger	.pm	St Pierre and Miquelon	.sk	Slovak Republic
.nf	Norfolk Island	.pn	Pitcairn Island	.sl	Sierra Leone
.ng	Nigeria	.pr	Puerto Rico	.sm	San Marino
.ni	Nicaragua	.ps	Palestinian Territories	.sn	Senegal
.nl	Netherlands	.pt	Portugal	.so	Somalia
.no	Norway	.pw	Palau	.sr	Suriname
.np	Nepal	.ru	Russian Federation	.st	Sao Tome and Principe
.nr	Nauru	.rw	Rwanda	.sv	El Salvador
.nu	Niue	.sa	South Africa	.sy	Syrian Arab Republic
.nz	New Zealand	.sb	Solomon Islands	.sz	Swaziland
.om	Oman	.sc	Seychelles	.tc	Turks and Caicos Islands
.pa	Panama	.sd	Sudan	.td	Chad
.pe	Peru	.se	Sweden	.tf	French Southern Territories
.pf	French Polynesia	.sg	Singapore	.tg	Togo
.pg	Papua New Guinea	.sh	St Helena	.th	Thailand
.ph	Philipines	.si	Slovenia	.tj	Tajikistan
.pk	Pakistan				

.tk	Tokelau	.uk	United Kingdom	.vn	Vietnam
.tm	Turkmenistan	.um	United States of America Outlying Islands	.vu	Vanuatu
.tn	Tunisia			.wf	Wallis and Futuna Islands
.to	Tonga	.us	United States of America	.ws	Western Samoa
.tp	East Timor	.uy	Uruguay	.ye	Yemen
.tr	Turkey	.uz	Uzbekistan	.yt	Mayotte
.tt	Trinidad and Tobago	.va	Vatican State	.yu	Yugoslavia
.tv	Tuvalu	.vc	Saint Vincent and The Grenadines	.za	South Africa
.tw	Taiwan			.zm	Zambia
.tz	Tanzania	.ve	Venezuela	.zw	Zimbabwe
.ua	Ukraine	.vg	British Virgin Islands		
.ug	Uganda	.vi	US Virgin Islands		

Table of Cases A

Table of Cases B

Table of Statutes

Table of Statutory Instruments

Table of European Legislation

Index

287

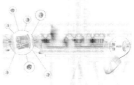